The Best of FRENCH Cooking

The Best of
FRENCH
Cooking

Hamlyn
London · New York · Sydney · Toronto

English edition published by
The Hamlyn Publishing Group Limited
London · New York · Sydney · Toronto
Astronaut House, Feltham, Middlesex, England

ISBN 0 600 33676 X

ACKNOWLEDGEMENT
The publisher would like to thank Daniel Fauchon
for supplying the photograph which appears opposite
the title page and on the back jacket of this book.

Front jacket photography by Eric Carter

Phototypeset by Tradespools Ltd, Frome, Somerset
Printed in Italy

Contents

Useful facts and figures

Notes on metrication

In this book quantities are given in metric, Imperial and American measures. Exact conversion from Imperial to metric measures does not usually give very convenient working quantities and so the metric measures have normally been rounded off into units of 25 grams. The table below shows the recommended equivalents. Over 16 oz the approximate kg conversions are given.

Ounces	Approx g to nearest whole figure	Recommended conversion to nearest unit of 25
1	28	25
2	57	50
3	85	75
4	113	100
5	142	150
6	170	175
7	198	200
8	227	225
9	255	250
10	283	275
11	312	300
12	340	350
13	368	375
14	396	400
15	425	425
16 (1 lb)	454	450
1 lb } 1¼ lb }		0·5 kg
1½ lb } 1¾ lb }		0·75 kg
2 lb } 2¼ lb }		1 kg

Note When converting quantities over 16 oz first add the appropriate figures in the centre column, then adjust to the nearest unit of 25. As a general guide, 1 kg (1000 g) equals 2·2 lb or about 2 lb 3 oz. This method of conversion gives good results in nearly all cases, although in certain pastry and cake recipes a more accurate conversion is necessary to produce a balanced recipe. On the other hand, quantities of such ingredients as vegetables, fruit, meat and fish which are not critical, are rounded off to the nearest quarter of a kg as this is how they are likely to be purchased.

Liquid measures The millilitre has been used in this book and the following table gives a few examples.

Imperial	Approx ml to nearest whole figure	Recommended ml
¼ pint	142	150 ml
½ pint	283	300 ml
¾ pint	425	450 ml
1 pint	567	600 ml
1½ pints	851	900 ml
1¾ pints	992	1000 ml (1 litre)

Spoon measures All spoon measures given in this book are level unless otherwise stated.

Can sizes At present, cans are marked with the exact (usually to the nearest whole number) metric equivalent of the Imperial weight of the contents, so we have followed this practice when giving can sizes.

Herbs Unless stated otherwise, herbs used in the recipes are fresh. If substituting dried, use half the quantity suggested for fresh.

Flour If not specified, either plain or self-raising flour can be used in the recipes.

Potato flour This is widely used in France as a thickening agent for sauces, etc. It is usually obtainable in good grocery shops, otherwise you can satisfactorily substitute half the amount of cornflour.

Oven temperatures
The table below gives recommended equivalents.

	°C	°F	Gas Mark
Very cool	110	225	$\frac{1}{4}$
	120	250	$\frac{1}{2}$
Cool	140	275	1
	150	300	2
Moderate	160	325	3
	180	350	4
Moderately hot	190	375	5
	200	400	6
Hot	220	425	7
	230	450	8
Very hot	240	475	9

Notes for American and Australian users
In America the 8-oz measuring cup is used. In Australia metric measures are now used in conjunction with the standard 250-ml measuring cup. The Imperial pint, used in Britain and Australia, is 20 fl oz, while the American pint is 16 fl oz. It is important to remember that the Australian tablespoon differs from both the British and American tablespoons; the table below gives a comparison. The British standard tablespoon, which has been used throughout this book, holds 17·7 ml, the American 14·2 ml, and the Australian 20 ml. A teaspoon holds approximately 5 ml in all three countries.

British	American	Australian
1 teaspoon	1 teaspoon	1 teaspoon
1 tablespoon	1 tablespoon	1 tablespoon
2 tablespoons	3 tablespoons	2 tablespoons
$3\frac{1}{2}$ tablespoons	4 tablespoons	3 tablespoons
4 tablespoons	5 tablespoons	$3\frac{1}{2}$ tablespoons

Note: WHEN MAKING ANY OF THE RECIPES IN THIS BOOK, ONLY FOLLOW ONE SET OF MEASURES AS THEY ARE NOT INTERCHANGEABLE.

American terms
Although the recipes in this book give American measures and ingredients, the list below gives some equivalents or substitutes for terms and equipment which may be unfamiliar to American readers.

BRITISH/AMERICAN
cake or loaf tin/cake or loaf pan
cake mixture/cake batter
cling film/saran wrap
cocktail stick/toothpick
double saucepan/double boiler
flan tin/pie pan
foil/aluminum foil
frying pan/skillet
greaseproof paper/wax paper
grill/broil(er)
gut fish/clean fish
hard-boil eggs/hard-cook eggs
knock back dough/punch down dough
liquidise(r)/blend(er)
mince/grind
muslin/cheesecloth
packet/package
piping bag/pastry bag
polythene/plastic
prove dough/rise dough
pudding basin/ovenproof bowl
stoned/pitted
whisk eggs/beat eggs

Symbols
Each recipe is coded to give the reader an indication of how much skill and effort is required to make that particular recipe:

🎃 very easy

🎃🎃 easy

🎃🎃🎃 more complicated

🍇 At the end of many of the recipes, a suggestion is made for a suitable wine to accompany that dish.

Introduction

Can you cook steak with green pepper butter, or spiced chicken with saffron? The very mention of them is enough to make the mouth water.

Well, nothing could be easier! All you need do is to follow the clear and simple instructions in the recipes contained in this book, with the colour photographs above each to guide you.

Leaf through the book and look over it. On each page is a full-colour illustration with the recipe written out beneath it. As well as the English title, the original French name is given, so you can call your dish whichever you prefer. First of all comes an indication of the time required for preparation and the cooking time. This will prove invaluable for those days when you find yourself rushed off your feet, and need to know how long things will take. There follows a full list of ingredients, with metric, Imperial and American measures, listed in the order they are used in the recipe, so you will be in no doubt as to what is needed next. Then comes the method itself, clear and precise with no complications or confusing terms. It is divided into simple short paragraphs that are easy to follow. And last of all a wine is specially recommended for some of the recipes, to form a worthy accompaniment to your masterpiece.

If you are not very confident, or consider yourself a novice cook, then start with the recipes that are marked with the symbol showing one small black casserole. This indicates that they are very easy, both to prepare and cook. Then have a try at the recipes with two and then three casseroles. You will progressively reach the level of the great classical dishes. But even the simplest recipes here include a hidden something; an unexpected spice, cream to thicken, that gastronomic finishing touch that transforms everything. It is no more difficult than cooking something completely basic and it is so much more satisfying.

Furthermore you have a choice of 306 superb recipes in this book. You will find in it country dishes with a taste of the soil, exotically flavoured ones using unusual and exciting ingredients, other new easy-to-cook recipes and finally those marvellous traditional dishes in which game, fish and shellfish become food for the gods.

Whether you are choosing a recipe for a special occasion or for everyday, whether you decide on a sumptuous terrine of foie gras or a simple chicken liver pâté, a turkey with all the trimmings or a modest fresh country soup, everything is delicious, original and full of creativity.

You will find this cookery book indispensable and packed full of new ideas; a book in which the recipes are grouped together so that you can immediately turn to the section you want. Fish, meat and poultry dishes follow soups and starters, and are followed on by vegetables, salads and desserts. A full alphabetical index helps you find your recipe at a glance, and the print throughout is legible even from a distance, so you need not pore over the book too much when cooking. And . . . but that is enough of the joys of using such a practical and precious book. Better to leave you the pleasure of discovering it for yourself.

Here's to your success. And . . . *bon appétit.*

Green summer soup

(Potage Angevin)

Preparation time 25 minutes
Cooking time 1 hour 20 minutes

Serves 6

METRIC/IMPERIAL
0.5kg/1lb fresh peas
1kg/2lb fresh broad beans
4 spring onions
1 small lettuce
50g/2oz butter
2–3 sprigs of savory
1.5 litres/2¾ pints boiling water
or stock
1 egg yolk
2 tablespoons double cream
salt and pepper
Garnish
chopped parsley

Shell the peas and broad beans. Finely chop the spring onions. Wash and dry the lettuce, shred finely.

Soften the spring onions in the hot butter. When they begin to turn golden, add the peas, beans, lettuce and savory. Cover and cook for 10 minutes over a very gentle heat. Then pour in the boiling water, season and cook for 1 hour over a gentle heat.

When the soup is cooked, use a skimming ladle to remove a spoonful of the peas and beans. Keep them hot.

Pass the soup through a vegetable mill, or liquidise in a blender. Return to the heat and add the reserved peas and beans. Season.

Thin the egg yolk with the cream and a little of the hot soup. Pour this into the rest of the soup and thicken over a gentle heat, stirring all the time and without boiling. Sprinkle with chopped parsley and serve very hot.

Preparation time 25 minutes
Cooking time 1 hour 20 minutes

Serves 6

AMERICAN
1lb fresh peas
2lb fresh fava or lima beans
4 scallions
1 small head lettuce
¼ cup butter
2–3 sprigs of savory
3½ pints boiling water or stock
1 egg yolk
3 tablespoons heavy cream
salt and pepper
Garnish
chopped parsley

Mushroom soup

(Potage aux champignons)

Preparation time 15 minutes
Cooking time 35 minutes

Serves 6

METRIC/IMPERIAL
225g/8oz button mushrooms
2 shallots
50g/2oz butter
1.75 litres/3 pints chicken stock
6 slices stale bread
3 tablespoons double cream
salt and pepper
Garnish
chopped parsley

Cut off the tips of the mushroom stalks, wash and wipe the mushrooms. Chop about 175g/6oz (US 1½ cups) of them and finely slice the rest. Peel and finely chop the shallots.

Melt 40g/1½oz (US 3 tablespoons) butter in a saucepan. Toss in the shallots and soften, stirring with a wooden spoon. They must scarcely turn golden.

Add the chopped mushrooms to the shallots and cook for 3 minutes. Pour in the chicken stock and cook over a gentle heat for 30 minutes.

During this time, sauté the finely sliced mushrooms in the remaining butter.

Remove the crusts from the bread slices and crumble the bread finely. Toss these breadcrumbs into the soup 7–8 minutes before the end of cooking.

Just before serving add the cream and the sliced mushrooms and heat through. Adjust seasoning if necessary.

Pour the soup into individual bowls or into a soup tureen, sprinkle with chopped parsley and serve immediately.

Preparation time 15 minutes
Cooking time 35 minutes

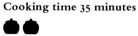

Serves 6

AMERICAN
½lb button mushrooms
2 shallots
¼ cup butter
3¾ pints chicken stock
6 slices stale bread
¼ cup heavy cream
salt and pepper
Garnish
chopped parsley

Sorrel soup

(Potage à l'oseille)

Preparation time 15 minutes
Cooking time 45 minutes

Serves 6

METRIC/IMPERIAL
350g/12oz sorrel
3 large potatoes
50g/2oz butter
1.15 litres/2 pints chicken stock
or water
salt and pepper
450ml/¾ pint milk
2 egg yolks
4 tablespoons double cream

Cut the stalks off the sorrel, wash and wipe it. Peel the potatoes, cut into large dice.

Soften the sorrel over a very gentle heat in half the warmed butter, stirring from time to time so it does not catch. When it is very soft, pour on the boiling chicken stock or water. Add the potatoes, season and cook for 35 minutes. Liquidise the soup in a blender or pass through a vegetable mill. Stir in the milk and reheat.

Thin the egg yolks with cream and a little of the hot soup, pour into the rest of the soup. Return to the lowest possible heat and thicken for a few moments without boiling, stirring continuously.

Just before serving, stir in the remaining butter.

Note Never boil a mixture thickened with egg yolk.

Preparation time 15 minutes
Cooking time 1¾ hours

Serves 6

AMERICAN
¾ lb sorrel
3 large potatoes
¼ cup butter
5 cups chicken stock or water
salt and pepper
2 cups milk
2 egg yolks
⅓ cup heavy cream

Pistou soup

(Soupe au pistou)

**Preparation time 30 minutes
plus overnight soaking
Cooking time 1¾ hours**

Serves 6

METRIC/IMPERIAL
**2 potatoes
2 small carrots
2 small leeks
2 courgettes
0.5kg/1lb French beans
4 tomatoes
100g/4oz dried haricot beans,
soaked overnight
175g/6oz dried kidney beans,
soaked overnight
sea salt
40g/1½oz large vermicelli
100g/4oz Parmesan cheese, grated
2 cloves garlic
3 sprigs of basil
4 tablespoons olive oil**

Peel the potatoes and carrots, wash then cut them into small dice. Wash, trim and finely slice the leeks. Wash the courgettes without peeling them, cut into dice. Slice the French beans into short lengths. Peel the tomatoes, remove seeds and crush the flesh.

Bring to the boil 3 litres/5 pints (US 6½ pints) stock or water (it will reduce during cooking), and toss in all the vegetables, including the drained beans. Cover and cook for 1½ hours, seasoning with salt halfway through cooking.

When the soup is cooked, add the vermicelli and cook for a further 10 minutes. Stir in half the grated cheese and simmer for 5 minutes, stirring all the time.

Crush the garlic in a mortar with a small pinch of sea salt, then add the basil leaves. Pound this pistou, gradually blending into it the oil, until a smooth paste is obtained. Thin with a ladle of hot stock, then pour it into the boiling soup.

Serve the soup in a soup tureen, and hand the rest of the grated cheese separately.

**Preparation time 30 minutes
plus overnight soaking
Cooking time 1¾ hours**

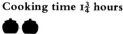

Serves 6

AMERICAN
**2 potatoes
2 small carrots
2 small leeks
2 zuchinni
1lb green beans
4 tomatoes
½ cup dried navy beans,
soaked overnight
1 cup dried kidney beans,
soaked overnight
coarse salt
1½oz large vermicelli
1 cup grated Parmesan cheese
2 cloves garlic
3 sprigs of basil
⅓ cup olive oil**

Winter vegetable soup

(Soupe d'hiver)

Preparation time 20 minutes
Cooking time 1½ hours

Serves 6

METRIC/IMPERIAL
3 medium leeks
2 carrots
2 turnips
2 potatoes
2 small sticks celery
¼ white cabbage
350g/12oz pumpkin
50g/2oz butter
salt and pepper

Clean the leeks, discard the green parts and shred the white. Peel and wash the carrots, turnips and potatoes, cut into small dice. Chop the celery. Clean the cabbage, shred finely. Peel and dice the pumpkin.

Soften the leeks, celery, carrots and turnips in half the butter over a gentle heat.

When the vegetables are soft but not coloured, pour on 2 litres/3½ pints (US 4½ pints) stock or boiling water, season and cook for 1 hour over a gentle heat.

Then add the cabbage, pumpkin and potatoes and cook for a further 30 minutes.

Pour into a soup tureen, add the rest of the butter and serve very hot.

Preparation time 20 minutes
Cooking time 1½ hours

Serves 6

AMERICAN
3 medium leeks
2 carrots
2 turnips
2 potatoes
2 small stalks celery
¼ head white cabbage
¾lb pumpkin
¼ cup butter
salt and pepper

French cheese soup

(Gratinée de fête)

Preparation time 20 minutes
Cooking time 20 minutes

Serves 6

METRIC/IMPERIAL
3 large onions
50g/2oz butter
½ bottle champagne (if unavailable,
150ml/¼ pint dry white wine)
1.25 litres/2¼ pints beef stock
50g/2oz Roquefort or other good
blue cheese
½ very ripe Camembert
3 tablespoons brandy
salt and pepper
pinch of cayenne
½ French loaf
100g/4oz Cheddar cheese, grated

Soften the finely sliced onions in the heated butter. Stir often, until a golden colour. Add the white wine and stock and cook for 10 minutes. If using champagne add only 3 minutes before the end of the cooking time.

Meanwhile, work together with a fork the Roquefort, Camembert (rind removed) and the brandy. Do not salt but add pepper to taste.

Melt the creamed cheeses in the hot stock and cook for 2 minutes over a very low heat, stirring. Taste to adjust seasoning, add a pinch of cayenne and pour into heated soup bowls.

Cut the bread into thin slices and toast. Put a few slices in each bowl, sprinkle with grated Cheddar, brown under the grill and serve very hot.

Preparation time 20 minutes
Cooking time 20 minutes

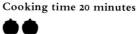

Serves 6

AMERICAN
3 large onions
¼ cup butter
½ bottle champagne (if unavailable,
⅔ cup dry white wine)
5¾ cups beef stock
2oz Roquefort or other good blue
cheese
½ very ripe Camembert
¼ cup brandy
salt and pepper
dash of cayenne pepper
½ French loaf
1 cup grated Cheddar cheese

Cream of vegetable soup   (Julienne en velouté)

Preparation time 20 minutes
Cooking time 1¼ hours

Serves 6

METRIC/IMPERIAL
giblets of 2–3 chickens
1 small veal bone
salt and pepper
2 new carrots
2 new turnips
2 leeks
1 stick celery
175g/6oz shelled peas
1 bouquet garni
1 cucumber
225g/8oz sorrel or spinach
3 tablespoons double cream
2 egg yolks
Garnish
chopped chervil

Put the chicken giblets and veal bone in a large saucepan. Cover with 3 litres/5 pints (US 6½ pints) cold salted water. Bring very slowly to the boil, skim and simmer, uncovered.

Peel, wash and wipe the carrots, turnips and leeks. Finely dice the carrots and turnips. Finely slice the leeks and celery. Add these vegetables to the pan with the peas and bouquet garni. Cook over a low heat for 1 hour. When cooking is completed the stock should have reduced by one-third.

Peel the cucumber and cut in two lengthwise. Remove the seeds and finely dice the flesh. Wash the sorrel, remove the stalks and chop the leaves. Ten minutes before serving remove the bouquet garni, giblets and bone from the soup. Add the sorrel and diced cucumber and continue cooking.

Mix the cream with the egg yolks and a little hot soup. Pour into the rest of the soup; reheat to thicken soup but do not allow to boil. Adjust seasoning, sprinkle with chopped chervil and serve immediately.

Preparation time 20 minutes
Cooking time 1¼ hours

Serves 6

AMERICAN
giblets of 2–3 chickens
1 small veal bone
salt and pepper
2 new carrots
2 new turnips
2 leeks
1 stalk celery
1¼ cups shelled peas
1 bouquet garni
1 cucumber
½lb sorrel or spinach
¼ cup heavy cream
2 egg yolks
Garnish
chopped chervil

Savoy vegetable soup (Potage des Allobroges)

Preparation time 20 minutes
Cooking time 1 hour 10 minutes

Serves 4

METRIC/IMPERIAL
2 onions
2 leeks
1 turnip
½ celeriac
2 large potatoes
50g/2oz butter
salt and pepper
900ml/1½ pints boiling water or stock
450ml/¾ pint milk
12–16 small pieces bread
100g/4oz Tome de Savoie or strong Cheddar cheese

Peel and wash all the vegetables. Chop the onions, thinly slice the leeks, turnip and celeriac. Dice the potatoes.

Melt 20g/¾oz (US 1½ tablespoons) butter in a flameproof casserole. Toss into it the chopped onions and let them brown slightly. Then add the leeks, turnip and celeriac and stir well together. Cover the casserole and leave to soften over a gentle heat for 15 minutes.

At the end of this time, add the diced potatoes, season with salt and pepper and pour on the boiling water. Cover and cook for 35–40 minutes.

Heat the milk and pour it into the casserole. Continue cooking for a further 15 minutes.

Meanwhile, fry the bread in the remaining butter. Remove and drain on absorbent paper. Cut the cheese into small pieces and place on the bread croûtons.

To serve, pour the soup into a heated tureen. Place the cheese-topped croûtons on top and serve immediately.

Preparation time 20 minutes
Cooking time 1 hour 10 minutes

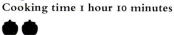

Serves 4

AMERICAN
2 onions
2 leeks
1 turnip
½ celeriac
2 large potatoes
¼ cup butter
salt and pepper
3¾ cups boiling water or stock
2 cups milk
12–16 small pieces bread
¼lb Tome de Savoie or strong Cheddar cheese

Split pea soup

(Potage aux pois cassés)

**Preparation time 20 minutes
plus overnight soaking
Cooking time 1½ hours**

Serves 6

METRIC/IMPERIAL
**275g/10oz split peas
2 onions
1 carrot
2 cloves
2 small leeks
1 bouquet garni
1 small clove garlic
100g/4oz smoked bacon
50g/2oz butter
salt and pepper**
To serve
fried bread croûtons

Soak the split peas overnight in cold water.

Peel the onions and the carrot, thinly slice the latter. Chop one of the onions and stick the other with the cloves. Clean the leeks, trim and shred.

Drain and rinse the split peas. Place in a large saucepan with 2 litres/3½ pints (US 4½ pints) cold water and add the whole onion, bouquet garni and crushed garlic. Bring gently to the boil and simmer for about 1 hour. Skim as necessary.

Lightly brown the diced bacon in half the butter then remove. In the same butter, soften and slightly brown the carrot, the chopped onion and the shredded leeks. Moisten with a little stock from the split peas, leave to boil for a moment then add to the split peas. Season and cook for a further 20 minutes.

At the end of cooking, remove the whole onion and the bouquet garni and liquidise the soup in a blender, or pass through a vegetable mill. Return to the pan with the bacon pieces and bring to the boil. Add the rest of the butter just before serving, and accompany with fried bread croûtons.

**Preparation time 20 minutes
plus overnight soaking
Cooking time 1½ hours**

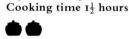

Serves 6

AMERICAN
**1¼ cups dried peas
2 onions
1 carrot
2 cloves
2 small leeks
1 bouquet garni
1 small clove garlic
¼lb smoked picnic shoulder
¼ cup butter
salt and pepper**
To serve
fried bread croûtons

Cream of haricot soup

(Crème aux haricots frais)

Preparation time 20 minutes
plus overnight soaking
Cooking time 1¼ hours

Serves 6

METRIC/IMPERIAL
0.5 kg/1 lb unshelled haricot beans
or 225 g/8 oz dried haricot beans,
soaked overnight
3 onions
3 tomatoes
50 g/2 oz butter
1 clove garlic
2 sprigs of parsley
1 sprig of thyme
½ bay leaf
salt and pepper
3 tablespoons single cream

Shell the haricot beans or drain the dried beans. Peel and finely slice the onions. Peel the tomatoes, remove seeds and cut the flesh into small dice.

Cook the onions in hot butter without allowing them to brown. When they begin to colour add the haricots. Cover at once and cook over a very low heat for 10–15 minutes.

Now stir in the diced tomatoes. Turn up the heat slightly and add 1.75 litres/3 pints (US 7½ cups) boiling water. Add the crushed garlic, parsley, thyme and bay leaf and simmer for 1 hour.

When the beans are cooked remove the herbs. Liquidise the soup in a blender or press through a vegetable mill. Season to taste, add the cream and heat through without boiling.

Pour into a soup tureen and serve very hot. Accompany with small croûtons of toasted or fried bread.

Preparation time 20 minutes
plus overnight soaking
Cooking time 1¼ hours

Serves 6

AMERICAN
1 lb unshelled navy beans or
½ lb dried navy beans, soaked
overnight
3 onions
3 tomatoes
¼ cup butter
1 clove garlic
2 sprigs of parsley
1 sprig of thyme
½ bay leaf
salt and pepper
¼ cup light cream

Parisian soup pot

(Petite marmite Parisienne)

Preparation time 25 minutes
Cooking time 3½ hours

Serves 6

METRIC/IMPERIAL
1 marrow bone
1 veal bone
0.5 kg/1 lb top rib of beef
0.75 kg/1½ lb knuckle of veal
giblets of 4 chickens
2 onions
3 leeks
3 carrots
2 turnips
2 cloves
2 sticks celery
1 bouquet garni
sea salt
pepper
pinch of allspice
To serve
French bread

Place the marrow bone in a large saucepan with the veal bone and all the meats. Cover with 4 litres/7 pints (US 9 pints) cold water and bring to the boil.

Peel and brown one of the onions in a moderately hot oven (200°C, 400°F, Gas Mark 6) for 20 minutes. This will add colour to the stock.

When the stock is foaming steadily add 1 tablespoon cold water and skim thoroughly. Bring to the boil again. Add the prepared vegetables to the saucepan: the trimmed leeks tied in a bunch, carrots, turnips, the onion browned in the oven and the second onion stuck with the cloves, the celery and bouquet garni. Once again, bring to the boil then reduce the heat and simmer over a gentle and even heat for 3 hours. Season with sea salt, pepper and allspice halfway through cooking. Skim from time to time, if necessary.

Serve the soup with all its ingredients and accompany with slices of French bread, toasted in the oven.

Preparation time 25 minutes
Cooking time 3½ hours

Serves 6

AMERICAN
1 marrow bone
1 veal bone
1 lb chuck steak
1½ lb veal knuckle
giblets of 4 chickens
2 onions
3 leeks
3 carrots
2 turnips
2 cloves
2 stalks celery
1 bouquet garni
coarse salt
pepper
dash of allspice
To serve
French bread

Fish soup

(Soupe de poissons)

Preparation time 25 minutes
Cooking time 35 minutes

Serves 6

METRIC/IMPERIAL
0.5 kg/1 lb assorted small fish
e.g. mullet, herrings, sprats
3 onions
4 tablespoons olive oil
2 cloves garlic
1 teaspoon dried fennel
1 bouquet garni
3 tablespoons tomato purée
pinch of saffron
salt and pepper
To serve
few slices French bread, dried out
in the oven and rubbed with
garlic
100 g/4 oz Parmesan cheese, grated

Prepare, wash and wipe the fish. Lightly brown the chopped onions in the hot olive oil. When golden, add the crushed cloves of garlic, the fennel, bouquet garni and tomato purée. Cook for 2–3 minutes, stirring with a wooden spoon. Pour on 2 litres/3½ pints (US 4½ pints) stock or boiling water, add the saffron and bring to the boil. Add the fish to this boiling liquid and simmer for 20 minutes. Season.

Remove the bouquet garni. Discard the heads and large bones from the fish and pass the stock and fish through a vegetable mill or liquidise in a blender. Sieve to remove any small bones, return to the heat then pour into a soup tureen.

Serve very hot, accompanied by the French bread and grated Parmesan.

Preparation time 25 minutes
Cooking time 35 minutes

Serves 6

AMERICAN
1 lb assorted small fish
e.g. red snapper, herrings
3 onions
⅓ cup olive oil
2 cloves garlic
1 teaspoon dried fennel
1 bouquet garni
¼ cup tomato paste
dash of saffron
salt and pepper
To serve
few slices French bread, dried out
in the oven and rubbed with
garlic
1 cup grated Parmesan cheese

Shrimp bisque

(Bisque de crevettes)

Preparation time 30 minutes
Cooking time 35 minutes

Serves 6

METRIC/IMPERIAL
2 medium onions
1 stick celery
2 small carrots
1 sprig of thyme
¼ bay leaf
100 g/4 oz butter
225 g/8 oz shelled shrimps
4 tablespoons brandy
100 ml/4 fl oz dry white wine
1.25 litres/2¼ pints fish stock
50 g/2 oz long-grain rice
1 tablespoon tomato purée
150 ml/¼ pint single cream
salt and pepper
pinch of cayenne

Soften the finely chopped onions and celery, diced carrots, thyme and bay leaf in half the butter. Do not brown. Add the shelled shrimps and cook over a high heat for 5 minutes. Pour on half the brandy and flame.

Add the white wine and then the fish stock. Bring to the boil, add the rice and continue cooking for 20 minutes.

Pass the bisque through a vegetable mill or liquidise in a blender. Return to the heat and stir in the tomato purée and cream. Reheat gently, whisking continuously, but do not allow to boil.

Add the remaining butter and the rest of the brandy. Continue whisking until the butter melts, being careful not to boil. Season with salt, pepper and a little cayenne. Serve very hot.

Preparation time 30 minutes
Cooking time 35 minutes

Serves 6

AMERICAN
2 medium onions
1 stalk celery
2 small carrots
1 sprig of thyme
¼ bay leaf
½ cup butter
½ lb shelled shrimp
⅓ cup brandy
½ cup dry white wine
5¾ cups fish stock
¼ cup long-grain rice
1 tablespoon tomato paste
⅔ cup light cream
salt and pepper
dash of cayenne pepper

Nantes cream soup

(Velouté Nantais)

Preparation time 20 minutes
Cooking time 45 minutes

Serves 4-6

METRIC/IMPERIAL
225g/8oz carrots
225g/8oz potatoes
50g/2oz butter
225g/8oz shelled shrimps
1 tablespoon brandy
450ml/¾ pint dry white wine
50g/2oz flour
1 litre/1¾ pints hot milk
salt and pepper
Garnish
50g/2oz peeled prawns

Peel, wash and dice the carrots and potatoes. Soften for 15 minutes in a pan with half the hot butter. Add the shelled shrimps. Sprinkle with the brandy and flame. Pour in the white wine and cook over a gentle heat for 5–6 minutes.

Meanwhile, make a roux with the rest of the butter and the flour. Moisten gradually with the hot milk, stirring continuously. Season and pour into the shrimp and wine mixture. Stir together and cook gently for 25 minutes.

Pour into a heated soup tureen, garnish with the prawns and serve immediately.

Preparation time 20 minutes
Cooking time 45 minutes

Serves 4-6

AMERICAN
½ lb carrots
½ lb potatoes
¼ cup butter
½ lb shelled shrimp
1 tablespoon brandy
2 cups dry white wine
½ cup all-purpose flour
4¼ cups hot milk
salt and pepper
Garnish
⅓ cup shelled shrimp

Bouillabaisse

(La bouillabaisse)

**Preparation time 40 minutes
plus 3–4 hours marinating time
Cooking time 40 minutes**

Serves 6

METRIC/IMPERIAL
**1 kg/2 lb assorted fish e.g. mullet,
cod, bream, whiting
2 cloves garlic
4 onions
4 potatoes
thyme, bay leaves, parsley and
dried fennel
2 leeks, finely chopped
salt, pepper, saffron
150 ml/¼ pint olive oil
3 tablespoons tomato purée
6 thin slices French bread
25 g/1 oz garlic butter**
Red sauce
**1 clove garlic
1 small red pepper
5 tablespoons olive oil
50 g/2 oz fresh breadcrumbs,
moistened with bouillabaisse
stock
1 tablespoon tomato purée**

Clean and gut the fish without cutting off the heads. Wash them and dry on absorbent paper. Cut into pieces if too large for the saucepan.

Peel and crush the garlic. Peel the onions and potatoes and cut into thick slices.

Put the fish, potatoes and herbs in alternating layers in a large saucepan; between each layer put the garlic, leeks and onions. Add saffron, salt and pepper. Pour over the olive oil and leave to marinate for 3–4 hours.

Bring 3 litres/5 pints (US 6½ pints) water to the boil. Stir in the tomato purée and pour over the fish mixture. Return to the boil and cook for 30 minutes.

Make the red sauce. Crush the garlic in a mortar with the chopped pepper, moistening with a little oil. Add the well squeezed breadcrumbs. Gradually work in the rest of the oil and the tomato purée. Thin this sauce with a little bouillabaisse stock.

Strain the fish stock and serve in a soup tureen with the slices of bread, toasted and spread with garlic butter. Serve the fish and potatoes very hot with the red sauce.

**Preparation time 40 minutes
plus 3–4 hours marinating time
Cooking time 40 minutes**

Serves 6

AMERICAN
**2 lb assorted fish e.g. red snapper,
cod or other white fish
2 cloves garlic
4 onions
4 potatoes
thyme, bay leaves, parsley and
dried fennel
2 leeks, finely chopped
salt, pepper, saffron
⅔ cup olive oil
¼ cup tomato paste
6 thin slices French bread
2 tablespoons garlic butter**
Red sauce
**1 clove garlic
1 small red pepper
6 tablespoons olive oil
1 cup fresh soft bread crumbs,
moistened with bouillabaisse
stock
1 tablespoon tomato paste**

Bourride

(La bourride)

Preparation time 25 minutes
Cooking time 15-20 minutes

Serves 8

METRIC/IMPERIAL
2kg/4½lb fish (bream, herring,
red mullet or whiting)
sea salt
rosemary, sage, thyme, bay leaves,
parsley, fennel and basil
4 cloves garlic
2 onions
strip of orange peel
250ml/8fl oz olive oil
6 egg yolks
thin slices French bread

Clean and gut the fish, cut off the heads and put to one side. Cut the fish into pieces. Put 3.5 litres/6 pints (US 7½ pints) water into a large saucepan. Add the salt, herbs, 2 crushed garlic cloves, the sliced onions, orange peel and 4 tablespoons (US ⅓ cup) olive oil. Bring to the boil before adding the fish and fish heads. Leave to cook for 10–15 minutes, then skim.

Meanwhile prepare the aïoli. In a kitchen mortar crush the 2 remaining garlic cloves with a pinch of sea salt, moistening with a little oil to obtain a smooth paste.

Incorporate into it 1 egg yolk then gradually add the rest of the oil, as for a mayonnaise, which the aïoli resembles in appearance and consistency.

Strain the fish stock and discard the orange rind, bay leaves and fish heads. Reserve the fish and keep hot, and reheat the fish stock slowly.

Mix the remaining egg yolks into the aïoli and thin with a little hot stock. Just before serving the soup, stir in the aïoli.

Serve this soup in a soup tureen, accompanied by the pieces of fish and toasted French bread.

Preparation time 25 minutes
Cooking time 15-20 minutes

Serves 8

AMERICAN
4½lb fish (bream, herring or other
white fish)
coarse salt
rosemary, sage, thyme, bay leaves,
parsley, fennel and basil
4 cloves garlic
2 onions
strip of orange peel
1 cup olive oil
6 egg yolks
thin slices French bread

Consommé Alice

(Consommé Alice)

(Consommé Alice)

Preparation time 20 minutes
Cooking time 45 minutes

Serves 6

METRIC/IMPERIAL
2 large globe artichokes
juice of 1 lemon
50g/2oz butter
salt and pepper
2 litres/3½ pints hot chicken stock
1 small lettuce
50g/2oz vermicelli
2 egg yolks
3 tablespoons double cream
Garnish
chopped chervil

Trim the artichokes, leaving only the bottoms. Discard the hairy choke and slice the hearts thinly. Sprinkle with the lemon juice and cook over a gentle heat in the hot butter. Add salt and pepper and cover the pan to avoid browning.

After 10 minutes moisten the artichoke hearts with chicken stock and bring to the boil.

Wash the lettuce and shred as finely as possible. Add to the pan while still boiling and continue cooking.

Ten minutes before serving sprinkle the vermicelli into the soup. Simmer for a few minutes. Mix the egg yolks with the cream and a little of the hot stock, add to the rest of the soup and heat through carefully without boiling.

Adjust seasoning and pour into a heated soup tureen. Sprinkle with chervil and serve at once.

Preparation time 20 minutes
Cooking time 45 minutes

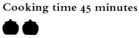

Serves 6

AMERICAN
2 large globe artichokes
juice of 1 lemon
¼ cup butter
salt and pepper
4½ pints hot chicken stock
1 small head lettuce
½ cup vermicelli
2 egg yolks
¼ cup heavy cream
Garnish
chopped chervil

Madeira consommé

(Consommé Madeira)

Preparation time 20 minutes
Cooking time 20 minutes

Serves 6

METRIC/IMPERIAL
4 onions
40 g/1½ oz butter
225 g/8 oz mushrooms
1.5 litres/2¾ pints beef stock
2 tablespoons tomato purée
100 ml/4 fl oz Madeira
salt and pepper
pinch of cayenne
Garnish
1 tablespoon chopped chives
1 tablespoon chopped chervil

Peel and finely chop the onions. Soften with the butter in a saucepan. Cover to avoid browning.

Cut the tips off the mushroom stalks. Wash the mushrooms quickly and wipe. Slice thinly and add to the softened onions. Cook for 5 minutes.

Meanwhile heat the beef stock. Mix the tomato purée into this hot stock and pour over the onions and mushrooms. Simmer for 6–7 minutes then add the Madeira.

Remove the consommé from the heat. Taste and adjust for seasoning, heightening with a pinch of cayenne.

Pour into heated soup bowls and sprinkle with the chopped chives and chervil. Serve very hot.

Preparation time 20 minutes
Cooking time 20 minutes

Serves 6

AMERICAN
4 onions
3 tablespoons butter
½ lb mushrooms
7 cups beef stock
3 tablespoons tomato paste
½ cup Madeira
salt and pepper
dash of cayenne pepper
Garnish
1 tablespoon chopped chives
1 tablespoon chopped chervil

Chinese-style soup

(Soupe Chinoise)

Preparation time 20 minutes
Cooking time 20 minutes

Serves 6

METRIC/IMPERIAL
3 chicken stock cubes
2 litres/3½ pints water
150 g/5 oz unsmoked streaky bacon
100 g/4 oz egg noodles
3 spring onions
½ cucumber, thinly sliced
few sprigs of chervil
few shelled shrimps (optional)
few sprigs of watercress
To serve
2 small chilli peppers
soy sauce

Make up the chicken stock with the cubes and water. Bring to the boil, toss in the diced bacon and cook for 10 minutes.

Add the noodles to the stock and cook for a further 10 minutes.

Divide between six soup bowls the chopped spring onions, cucumber slices and some of the chervil. Pour the boiling soup into each bowl, sharing out the noodles and bacon equally. You can also add a few shrimps, if liked. Sprinkle each bowl with watercress and the rest of the chervil.

Accompany the soup with rings of chilli pepper and a bowl of soy sauce.

Preparation time 20 minutes
Cooking time 20 minutes

Serves 6

AMERICAN
3 chicken bouillon cubes
4½ pints water
8 bacon slices
¼ lb egg noodles
3 scallions
½ cucumber, thinly sliced
few sprigs of chervil
few shelled shrimp (optional)
few sprigs of watercress
To serve
2 small chili peppers
soy sauce

Iced consommé

(Consommé glacé)

Preparation time 8 minutes
Cooking time 5 minutes

Serves 6

METRIC/IMPERIAL
1 lemon
2 spring onions
1 celery heart
1.5 litres/2¾ pints clear soup or chicken stock made from stock cubes
300 ml/½ pint tomato juice
salt and pepper
pinch of cayenne
Garnish
chopped parsley or chervil

Wash the lemon and dry. Cut 6 thin slices from the lemon and squeeze the rest to give 2 teaspoons of juice.

Peel and finely chop the spring onions, slice the celery as thinly as possible.

Bring the clear soup or stock to the boil. Remove from the heat. Add the celery and spring onions and allow to cool.

Stir the tomato juice and lemon juice into the cold consommé. Adjust seasoning and add a pinch of cayenne. Chill in the refrigerator.

Just before serving pour the soup into consommé bowls. Add the lemon slices and sprinkle with chopped parsley or chervil. You can also add ice cubes.

Preparation time 8 minutes
Cooking time 5 minutes

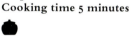

Serves 6

AMERICAN
1 lemon
2 scallions
1 celery heart
7 cups clear soup or chicken stock made from bouillon cubes
1¼ cups tomato juice
salt and pepper
dash of cayenne pepper
Garnish
chopped parsley or chervil

Chilled cucumber soup
(Potage glacé au concombre)

Preparation time 25 minutes

Serves 4

METRIC/IMPERIAL
1 cucumber
salt
1 small bunch chives
1 small bunch chervil
900 ml/1½ pints natural yogurt
juice of ½ lemon
½ teaspoon freshly ground pepper
½ teaspoon cumin seeds, crushed,
or a pinch of ground cumin

Wash and dry the cucumber but do not peel. Split in two lengthwise and scoop out the seeds with a teaspoon. Cut into small dice, sprinkle lightly with salt and leave for 20 minutes.

Wash and chop the chives and chervil.

Tip the cucumber with its liquid into a soup tureen. Add the yogurt and lemon juice. Season with pepper and cumin seeds. Mix all well together and stir in the chopped herbs, reserving some for garnish.

Place the soup in the refrigerator. If necessary, add a few ice cubes before serving well chilled.

Preparation time 25 minutes

Serves 4

AMERICAN
1 cucumber
salt
1 small bunch chives
1 small bunch chervil
3¾ cups plain yogurt
juice of ½ lemon
½ teaspoon freshly ground pepper
½ teaspoon cumin seeds, crushed,
or a dash of ground cumin

Gazpacho

(Le Gaspacho)

Preparation time 20 minutes plus 1 hour chilling time

Serves 4

METRIC/IMPERIAL
3 large tomatoes
3 green peppers
1 cucumber
2 onions
1 clove garlic
juice of 1 lemon
4 tablespoons olive oil
75 g/3 oz fresh breadcrumbs
2 tablespoons vinegar
1 litre/1¾ pints iced water
salt and pepper
Garnish
chopped chervil, parsley and chives

Peel and deseed the tomatoes. Wash and dry the peppers, remove core and seeds. Peel the cucumber. Cut all these vegetables into dice. Finely chop the onions and crush the garlic.

Keep half the diced vegetables and pass the rest with the crushed garlic through a vegetable mill, or blend in a liquidiser. Pour the obtained purée into a bowl and stir in the lemon juice and half the oil. Add the breadcrumbs and chopped onions. Work the mixture with a wooden spoon, adding the vinegar, the rest of the oil and the iced water. Season to taste and refrigerate.

Just before serving divide the rest of the diced vegetables between four soup bowls. Pour in the chilled soup. Sprinkle with the chopped herbs and serve.

Preparation time 20 minutes plus 1 hour chilling time

Serves 4

AMERICAN
3 large tomatoes
3 green peppers
1 cucumber
2 onions
1 clove garlic
juice of 1 lemon
⅓ cup olive oil
1½ cups fresh soft bread crumbs
3 tablespoons vinegar
4¼ cups iced water
salt and pepper
Garnish
chopped chervil, parsley and chives

Scallops with parsley and wine (Saint-Jacques à la persillade)

Preparation time 20 minutes
Cooking time 35 minutes

Serves 4

METRIC/IMPERIAL
8 scallops
175 ml/6 fl oz dry white wine
4 tablespoons water
2 sprigs of parsley
1 small sprig of thyme
½ teaspoon freshly ground pepper
salt
2 shallots
2 cloves garlic
2 tablespoons finely chopped parsley
100 g/4 oz slightly salted butter

Remove the black intestine from each scallop and carefully wash the flesh in cold running water. Wipe on absorbent paper.

Chop the flesh coarsely, keeping the corals whole. Place in a small saucepan, add the white wine and water, the parsley, thyme and freshly ground pepper. Salt lightly. Warm over a gentle heat, cover and cook for 15 minutes.

Remove the scallops, strain the stock and reduce it by one-third, by open boiling over a brisk heat.

During this time, peel and finely chop the shallots and garlic and mix with the chopped parsley. Melt the butter in the top of a double saucepan.

Carefully wash the four largest empty scallop shells and dry them. Divide the diced scallop flesh and the coral between these shells, sprinkle each with 2–3 tablespoons (US ¼ cup) white wine stock. Scatter over the chopped parsley mixture and coat generously with all of the melted butter.

Arrange the four filled shells in a large ovenproof dish. Cover and place in a moderately hot oven (200°C, 400°F, Gas Mark 6) for 20 minutes.

 a Sauvignon (white)

Preparation time 20 minutes
Cooking time 35 minutes

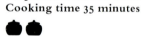

Serves 4

AMERICAN
8 scallops
¾ cup dry white wine
⅓ cup water
2 sprigs of parsley
1 small sprig of thyme
½ teaspoon freshly ground pepper
salt
2 shallots
2 cloves garlic
3 tablespoons finely chopped parsley
½ cup slightly salted butter

Breton scallops

(Saint-Jacques Bretonnes)

Preparation time 25 minutes
Cooking time 15-20 minutes

Serves 4

METRIC/IMPERIAL
12 scallops
200 ml/7 fl oz dry white wine
½ teaspoon freshly ground pepper
1 small sprig of thyme
1 small bay leaf
4 small onions
90 g/3½ oz butter
100 g/4 oz dried breadcrumbs
2 cloves garlic
2 tablespoons chopped parsley
25 g/1 oz flour
salt
breadcrumbs to sprinkle
Garnish
sprigs of parsley

Remove and discard the small black intestines from the scallops. Carefully wash the flesh, wipe and place in a small saucepan with the wine, freshly ground pepper, thyme and bay leaf. Cover and simmer for 8–10 minutes.

Drain the scallops, strain the cooking liquor and set it aside.

Chop the onions, lightly brown over a gentle heat in a shallow frying pan with 40 g/1½ oz (US 3 tablespoons) butter. Cut the scallop flesh and corals into dice, keeping 4 corals whole for garnish. Add the diced flesh, breadcrumbs, crushed garlic and parsley to the onions. Brown all the ingredients, stirring with a wooden spoon.

Make a white roux over a very gentle heat with 25 g/1 oz (US 2 tablespoons) butter and the flour. Add the reserved scallop cooking liquor, making it up to 300 ml/½ pint (US 1¼ cups) with milk. Cook for 2–3 minutes, stirring. Pour this sauce over the scallop mixture and season to taste.

Divide the mixture between four large scallop shells, then sprinkle with a few breadcrumbs and the rest of the melted butter.

Brown under a preheated grill and serve very hot, topped with the reserved corals. Garnish the serving dish with parsley sprigs.

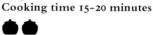 a Gros Plant (dry white)

Preparation time 25 minutes
Cooking time 15-20 minutes

Serves 4

AMERICAN
12 scallops
¾ cup dry white wine
½ teaspoon freshly ground pepper
1 small sprig of thyme
1 small bay leaf
4 small onions
7 tablespoons butter
1 cup dry bread crumbs
2 cloves garlic
3 tablespoons chopped parsley
¼ cup all-purpose flour
salt
bread crumbs to sprinkle
Garnish
sprigs of parsley

Stuffed mussels

(Moules farcies)

Preparation time 25 minutes
Cooking time 15 minutes

Serves 3-4

METRIC/IMPERIAL
1.4 litres/2 pints large mussels
3 shallots
2 cloves garlic
1 bunch parsley
175g/6oz slightly salted butter
75g/3oz dried breadcrumbs
1 teaspoon freshly ground pepper
Garnish
sprigs of parsley

Sort, scrape and wash the mussels, discarding any which do not close when given a sharp tap.

Open them by boiling over a brisk heat in a little water, then drain. Remove the empty half shell from each one and discard, leaving the mussel attached to the other half shell.

Peel and finely chop the shallots and garlic, chop the parsley.

Cut the butter into small pieces and work with a wooden spoon, mixing in the breadcrumbs, freshly ground pepper, garlic, shallots and parsley.

Fill each mussel with this stuffing. Arrange in a flame-proof dish and brown under the grill. Serve at once, garnished with parsley.

 a Muscadet (dry white)

Preparation time 25 minutes
Cooking time 15 minutes

Serves 3-4

AMERICAN
2½ pints large mussels
3 shallots
2 cloves garlic
1 bunch parsley
¾ cup slightly salted butter
¾ cup dry bread crumbs
1 teaspoon freshly ground pepper
Garnish
sprigs of parsley

Spanish mussels

(Moules Pilar)

**Preparation time 30 minutes
Cooking time 20 minutes**

Serves 4-6

METRIC/IMPERIAL
**3 litres/4 pints large mussels
50g/2oz ground almonds
50g/2oz pine nuts
2 cloves garlic
2 tablespoons chopped parsley
1 teaspoon paprika
12 peppercorns
5 tablespoons olive oil
2 large onions
2 tablespoons tomato purée
salt and pepper
pinch of cayenne**

Sort, scrape and wash the mussels, discarding any which do not close when given a sharp tap. Open them by boiling over a brisk heat with a little water, shaking the pan frequently. Drain the mussels and strain their cooking liquor. Reserve.

Blend in a liquidiser the ground almonds, pine nuts, crushed garlic, parsley, paprika, peppercorns and half the oil. Mix for a few seconds in order to obtain a smooth thick paste. If you have no liquidiser, you can pound all the ingredients together in a kitchen mortar.

Brown the finely chopped onions in the remaining oil. Stir in the almond paste and mix over a brisk heat, stirring with a wooden spoon. Add the tomato purée and thin with the mussel liquor to obtain a thick and well blended sauce. Adjust the seasoning and add a pinch of cayenne.

Remove the empty half shell from each mussel. Arrange the mussels in their shells on a serving dish and carefully fill each one with the sauce. Serve at once.

 a white Rioja (Spanish)

**Preparation time 30 minutes
Cooking time 20 minutes**

Serves 4-6

AMERICAN
**5 pints large mussels
½ cup ground almonds
¼ cup pine nuts
2 cloves garlic
3 tablespoons chopped parsley
1 teaspoon paprika pepper
12 peppercorns
6 tablespoons olive oil
2 large onions
3 tablespoons tomato paste
salt and pepper
dash of cayenne pepper**

Scalloped mussels

(Coquilles de moules)

Preparation time 20 minutes
Cooking time 30 minutes

Serves 4

METRIC/IMPERIAL
1 onion
450 ml/¾ pint dry white wine
1 teaspoon crushed peppercorns
2 litres/3½ pints mussels
40 g/1½ oz butter
40 g/1½ oz flour
1 tablespoon double cream
salt and pepper
Garnish
chopped parsley

Peel and finely chop the onion. Place in a large pan with the white wine and crushed peppercorns. Reduce to 300 ml/ ½ pint (US 1¼ cups) by open boiling over a low heat.

Meanwhile carefully sort out the mussels, discarding any which do not close when given a sharp tap. Scrape, wash and drain them. Toss into the reduced boiling wine and allow the mussels to open, shaking the pan often.

When the mussels have opened, drain and strain the cooking liquor through muslin. Take the mussels out of their shells.

Melt the butter in a small saucepan, add the flour and stir over a low heat. When the mixture begins to bubble, add the mussel liquor. Cook the sauce for 7–8 minutes, stirring, until it has the consistency of a béchamel sauce. Add the mussels and cream and mix. Taste and adjust for seasoning.

Transfer the mixture to four scallop shells. Sprinkle with chopped parsley and serve immediately.

 a Gros Plant (dry white)

Preparation time 20 minutes
Cooking time 30 minutes

Serves 4

AMERICAN
1 onion
2 cups dry white wine
1 teaspoon crushed peppercorns
4½ pints mussels
3 tablespoons butter
6 tablespoons all-purpose flour
1 tablespoon heavy cream
salt and pepper
Garnish
chopped parsley

Seafood moulds (Couronnes marinières)

Preparation time 30 minutes
Cooking time 25 minutes

Serves 5-6

METRIC/IMPERIAL
2 litres/3½ pints mussels
100 ml/4 fl oz dry white wine
4 crushed peppercorns
1 onion
1 sprig of parsley
225 g/8 oz long-grain rice
4 sticks celery
2 spring onions
250 ml/8 fl oz thick mayonnaise
(see page 314)
2 tablespoons tomato ketchup
pinch of cayenne
150 g/5 oz peeled prawns
175 g/6 oz cold cooked peas
Garnish
lettuce leaves
chopped parsley, chervil and chives
few unpeeled prawns

Sort, scrape and wash the mussels, discarding any which do not close when given a sharp tap. Steam open in the white wine with the crushed peppercorns, chopped onion and parsley. Cover the pan, place over a high heat and shake from time to time. When the mussels open, strain the cooking liquor through muslin.

Measure the rice, add enough water to the mussel liquor to give liquid equal to one and a half times the volume of rice. Wash the rice well and add to the boiling liquid. Cook gently for 15 minutes. Cool under running water and drain well.

Take the mussels out of their shells. Chop the celery and spring onions.

Mix two-thirds of the mayonnaise with the tomato ketchup and season with a little cayenne. Mix this sauce with half the prawns, the mussels, spring onions and celery.

Mix the remaining mayonnaise with the rice and peas. Press this mixture into five or six small oiled ring moulds, compress well and tip out on to a plate lined with lettuce leaves.

Fill the centres with the seafood mixture. Sprinkle with the chopped herbs and garnish with the remaining prawns.

 a Muscadet (dry white)

Preparation time 30 minutes
Cooking time 25 minutes

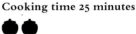

Serves 5-6

AMERICAN
4½ pints mussels
½ cup dry white wine
4 crushed peppercorns
1 onion
1 sprig of parsley
1 cup long-grain rice
4 stalks celery
2 scallions
1 cup thick mayonnaise (see page 314)
3 tablespoons tomato ketchup
dash of cayenne pepper
5 oz shelled shrimp
1¼ cups cold cooked peas
Garnish
lettuce leaves
chopped parsley, chervil and chives
few unshelled shrimp

Cockles with vodka

(Coques à la vodka)

Preparation time 30 minutes
Cooking time 25 minutes

Serves 4

METRIC/IMPERIAL
2 litres/3½ pints cockles
3 onions
1 bunch parsley
6 ripe tomatoes
40g/1½oz butter
50g/2oz ground almonds
1 teaspoon paprika
100ml/4fl oz vodka
pinch of cayenne
salt and pepper
Garnish
chopped parsley

Wash the cockles carefully and place in a saucepan with a little water. Cover the pan and open the cockles over a high heat, shaking the pan often. When open, drain and strain the cooking juices through muslin or a double thickness of absorbent paper. Then discard the empty shell from each cockle.

Chop the onions as finely as possible. Chop the parsley. Peel the tomatoes, remove the seeds and dice the flesh.

Cook the onions in the hot butter until golden. Add the tomatoes and cook until reduced to a purée.

Stir in half the chopped parsley, the ground almonds and paprika. Mix for a few minutes over a gentle heat to give a very thick mixture, then dilute with a little of the cockle juice. Cook for a further 5 minutes, stirring with a wooden spoon.

Add the vodka, cayenne and seasoning to taste.

Put the cockles back in the sauce to reheat, then pour into a shallow dish and sprinkle with chopped parsley. This dish can be served either hot or very cold.

🍇 a dry white

Preparation time 30 minutes
Cooking time 25 minutes

Serves 4

AMERICAN
4½ pints cockles
3 onions
1 bunch parsley
6 ripe tomatoes
3 tablespoons butter
½ cup ground almonds
1 teaspoon paprika pepper
½ cup vodka
dash of cayenne pepper
salt and pepper
Garnish
chopped parsley

Marinated kipper fillets

(Filets de harengs marinés)

**Preparation time 20 minutes
plus 24 hours marinating time**

Serves 6

METRIC/IMPERIAL
**3 kippers or 1 packet kipper fillets
2 onions
2 bay leaves
2 teaspoons black peppercorns
200 ml/7 fl oz oil**

Prepare the dish one day in advance.

If using packeted kipper fillets it is sufficient to separate them. If using whole kippers (which will give a better flavour) then remove the skin, and bone them by slipping a knife blade along either side of the back bone.

Peel the onions and cut into rounds. Separate into rings.

Place a layer of kipper fillets in the base of a shallow dish over a bay leaf. Cover with onion rings, dot with peppercorns and sprinkle with oil. Continue in this way until the ingredients are used up. Finish with a layer of onions, peppercorns, a bay leaf and the rest of the oil.

Marinate for 24 hours, not in the refrigerator. The longer the fillets marinate the better they will taste. The oil can be used again for the same purpose.

 a dry white

**Preparation time 20 minutes
plus 24 hours marinating time**

Serves 6

AMERICAN
**3 kippers or 1 package kipper fillets
2 onions
2 bay leaves
2 teaspoons black peppercorns
¾ cup oil**

Shrimp cocktail

(Cocktail de crevettes)

Preparation time 15 minutes

Serves 6

METRIC/IMPERIAL
1 small lettuce
100 g/4 oz shelled shrimps
1 small can palm hearts
3 small tomatoes
½ celery heart
½ cucumber
juice of ½ lemon
300 ml/½ pint mayonnaise
(see page 314)
pinch of cayenne
Garnish
12 unshelled shrimps
mayonnaise
chopped chervil

Wash the lettuce and put 6 small leaves to one side. Tear the rest into thin strips and use to line the bottom of six individual dishes.

In a bowl mix together half the shrimps, almost all the palm hearts cut into rounds, the diced tomatoes and the sliced celery. Reserve 6 slices of cucumber, dice the remainder and add to the mixture.

Sprinkle over the lemon juice and stir in the mayonnaise. Toss to coat the ingredients and season with a little cayenne. Add the reserved lettuce leaf to each dish and pile in the shrimp cocktail mixture. Arrange the remaining shrimps on top.

Garnish each dish with 2 unshelled shrimps and a cucumber slice. Top with a round of palm heart and a dollop of mayonnaise. Finally sprinkle with chopped chervil and serve cold.

 a dry Vouvray (white)

Preparation time 15 minutes

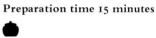

Serves 6

AMERICAN
1 small head lettuce
¼ lb shelled shrimp
1 small can palm hearts
3 small tomatoes
½ celery heart
½ cucumber
juice of ½ lemon
1 cup mayonnaise (see page 314)
dash of cayenne pepper
Garnish
12 unshelled shrimp
mayonnaise
chopped chervil

Avocado and cucumber vinaigrette (Concombre à l'avocat)

**Preparation time 10 minutes
plus 1 hour standing time**

Serves 4-5

METRIC/IMPERIAL
**1 cucumber
salt and pepper
2 avocado pears
2 tablespoons vinegar
5 tablespoons olive oil
1 clove garlic
chopped parsley or chives
(optional)**

Peel the cucumber and slice thinly. Sprinkle lightly with salt and leave to drain for 1 hour.

Cut the avocados in half, remove the stones and flesh. Dice the flesh.

Put the vinegar in a bowl with a pinch of salt. Add the oil and the finely crushed garlic. Blend well together.

Rinse and drain the cucumber and place in a salad bowl with the diced avocado. Pour over the vinaigrette dressing, add pepper and mix gently. Sprinkle with parsley or chives, if liked, and serve cold.

Small portions of this salad could also be used to fill avocado halves.

 a Gros Plant (dry white)

**Preparation time 10 minutes
plus 1 hour standing time**

Serves 4-5

AMERICAN
**1 cucumber
salt and pepper
2 avocados
3 tablespoons vinegar
½ cup olive oil
1 clove garlic
chopped parsley or chives
(optional)**

Californian avocados

(Avocats Californienne)

Preparation time 20 minutes

Serves 4

METRIC/IMPERIAL
2 avocado pears
100 g/4 oz green grapes
¼ cucumber
1 (198-g/7-oz) can sweetcorn
2 slices pineapple
juice of 1 lemon
Sauce
150 ml/¼ pint mayonnaise
(see page 314)
1 tablespoon tomato ketchup
1 tablespoon brandy
salt
pinch of cayenne
Garnish
paprika
1 tablespoon chopped parsley

Cut the avocados in half and remove the stones. Take out the flesh with a small spoon, being careful not to damage the shells.

Put the avocado flesh in a bowl with the grapes, peeled and pips removed, the diced cucumber, the drained sweetcorn and the pineapple, cut into small pieces. Reserve 4 pieces of pineapple for garnish. Sprinkle the whole with the lemon juice and stir.

Prepare the sauce by mixing together the mayonnaise, tomato ketchup and brandy. Season with salt and cayenne.

Spoon this sauce over the avocado mixture. Combine gently and fill the avocado halves. Place a piece of pineapple in the centre of each and sprinkle with paprika and a little chopped parsley. Serve very cold.

 a Tavel (rosé)

Preparation time 20 minutes

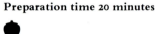

Serves 4

AMERICAN
2 avocados
¼ lb white grapes
¼ cucumber
1 (7-oz) can corn
2 slices pineapple
juice of 1 lemon
Sauce
⅔ cup mayonnaise (see page 314)
1 tablespoon tomato ketchup
1 tablespoon brandy
salt
dash of cayenne pepper
Garnish
paprika pepper
1 tablespoon chopped parsley

Crab-stuffed avocados

(Avocats au crabe)

Preparation time 20 minutes

Serves 4

METRIC/IMPERIAL
2 avocado pears
1 tablespoon lemon juice
1 (92-g/3¼-oz) can crabmeat
salt and pepper
Mayonnaise
1 teaspoon French mustard
2 egg yolks
200 ml/7 fl oz oil
Garnish
lettuce leaves
paprika
chopped parsley

Cut the avocado pears in half and remove the stones. Sprinkle the cut surfaces with half the lemon juice. Drain and flake the crabmeat.

Prepare the mayonnaise by blending together the mustard and egg yolks, adding the oil a little at a time. When firm blend in the remaining lemon juice and season to taste.

Season the avocado halves and fill each with a little crabmeat. Top with the mayonnaise and then the rest of the crabmeat. Arrange on a bed of lettuce leaves and sprinkle with paprika and chopped parsley. Serve well chilled.

 a Provence rosé

Preparation time 20 minutes

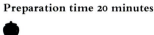

Serves 4

AMERICAN
2 avocados
1 tablespoon lemon juice
1 (3¼-oz) can crab meat
salt and pepper
Mayonnaise
1 teaspoon French mustard
2 egg yolks
¾ cup oil
Garnish
lettuce leaves
paprika pepper
chopped parsley

Asparagus hors-d'oeuvre

(Hors-d'oeuvre Angevin)

Preparation time 30 minutes
Cooking time 20-25 minutes

Serves 6

METRIC/IMPERIAL
1 bunch small asparagus
0.5 kg/1 lb small shelled peas or frozen peas
1 lettuce
1 (275-g/10-oz) can artichoke hearts
salt and pepper
Chantilly mayonnaise
1 teaspoon French mustard
2 egg yolks
250 ml/8 fl oz oil
1 teaspoon lemon juice
100 ml/4 fl oz double cream
Garnish
1 tomato
1 lemon
chopped parsley

Cook the asparagus and peas separately in boiling salted water until tender. Drain and leave to cool.

Wash the lettuce and shred. Drain the artichoke hearts. Reserve 6 and dice the remainder finely. Cut about 7.5 cm/ 3 inches from the tips of 12 asparagus spears and reserve for garnish. Finely dice the rest of the stalks and the remaining asparagus spears.

Prepare the mayonnaise by blending together the mustard and egg yolks, adding the oil a little at a time. Flavour with lemon juice and fold in the lightly whipped cream.

Mix the lettuce, diced artichoke hearts and asparagus and three-quarters of the peas into half the mayonnaise. Stir gently, season to taste and spoon into a round serving dish.

Garnish with the asparagus tips arranged in pairs and joined by a strip of tomato flesh. In between each pair place an artichoke heart filled with peas. In the centre place a lemon slice and sprinkle all over with chopped parsley.

Serve very cold, with the rest of the Chantilly mayonnaise separately. If liked, serve all of the mayonnaise separately and simply arrange the salad ingredients in the serving dish, as illustrated.

 a Tavel (rosé)

Preparation time 30 minutes
Cooking time 20-25 minutes

Serves 6

AMERICAN
1 bunch small asparagus
1 lb small shelled peas or frozen peas
1 head lettuce
1 (10-oz) can artichoke hearts
salt and pepper
Chantilly mayonnaise
1 teaspoon French mustard
2 egg yolks
1 cup oil
1 teaspoon lemon juice
$\frac{1}{2}$ cup heavy cream
Garnish
1 tomato
1 lemon
chopped parsley

Asparagus mimosa

(Asperges à la Flamande)

Preparation time 25–30 minutes
Cooking time 25 minutes

Serves 4–6

METRIC/IMPERIAL
1.25 kg/2½ lb asparagus
6 eggs
125 g/4½ oz butter
salt and pepper
1 tablespoon chopped parsley

Cut away the tough ends of the asparagus stem and peel (scraping is not enough). Tie the asparagus into four small bundles, and put into a fairly large pan of boiling salted water, tips uppermost. Leave to cook for 20–25 minutes, depending upon the age of the asparagus.

Hard-boil the eggs, run under cold water, shell them and keep warm in a saucepan of hot water.

Melt the butter in a pan over a gentle heat. Add the yolks of 4 hard-boiled eggs, and beat with a wooden spoon until a soft, cream-like mixture. Season well, generously with pepper, and keep warm in a sauceboat placed in a pan of hot water.

Drain the asparagus and arrange on a dish lined with a folded napkin. Sprinkle the tips of the asparagus with the chopped parsley and the finely chopped yolks and whites of the remaining hard-boiled eggs.

Serve immediately with the sauce.

 a white Burgundy

Preparation time 25–30 minutes
Cooking time 25 minutes

Serves 4–6

AMERICAN
2½ lb asparagus
6 eggs
½ cup plus 1 tablespoon butter
salt and pepper
1 tablespoon chopped parsley

Asparagus with ham

(Asperges au jambon)

Preparation time 30 minutes
Cooking time 30 minutes

Serves 4

METRIC/IMPERIAL
16 tender asparagus spears
4 large thin slices Parma ham
Chantilly mayonnaise
2 egg yolks
1 teaspoon French mustard
200 ml/7 fl oz oil
100 ml/4 fl oz double cream
Garnish
lettuce leaves
1 tomato
salt
sprigs of parsley

Peel and trim the asparagus and cook for 20 minutes in boiling salted water, keeping the tips uppermost. Drain carefully and allow to cool.

Wash and pat dry the lettuce leaves for garnish. Cut the tomato into slices and sprinkle with a little salt. Chop half the parsley.

Prepare a thick mayonnaise by blending together the egg yolks and mustard, adding the oil a little at a time. Whip the cream until thick and fold into the mayonnaise.

Line a serving dish with the lettuce leaves. Divide the asparagus into four small bundles. Wrap a slice of ham around each bundle, and arrange on the serving dish with the sliced tomato. Scatter over chopped parsley and garnish with the remaining parsley sprigs.

Serve at once, accompanied by the Chantilly mayonnaise.

 a Sancerre (dry white)

Preparation time 30 minutes
Cooking time 30 minutes

Serves 4

AMERICAN
16 tender asparagus spears
4 large thin slices Parma ham
Chantilly mayonnaise
2 egg yolks
1 teaspoon French mustard
¾ cup oil
½ cup heavy cream
Garnish
lettuce leaves
1 tomato
salt
sprigs of parsley

Tomato hors-d'oeuvre

(Tomates Ninette)

Preparation time 20 minutes

Serves 6

METRIC/IMPERIAL
6 tomatoes
salt and pepper
2 eggs, hard-boiled
1 (99-g/3½-oz) can tuna
3 tablespoons finely chopped
parsley
1 tablespoon lemon juice
1 (397-g/14-oz) can mixed
vegetables
Mayonnaise
1 teaspoon French mustard
2 egg yolks
250 ml/8 fl oz oil
Garnish
lettuce leaves
7 anchovy fillets
7 black olives
½ lemon
chopped parsley

Cut the tops off the tomatoes. Scoop out the pulp with a teaspoon, sprinkle lightly with salt and leave upside down to drain.

Prepare a thick mayonnaise by blending together the mustard and egg yolks, adding the oil a little at a time.

In a bowl, mix together the chopped hard-boiled eggs, the flaked tuna, chopped parsley and 3 tablespoons mayonnaise. Add the lemon juice and season to taste. Fill the drained tomatoes with this mixture.

Carefully drain the mixed vegetables and mix into the rest of the mayonnaise.

Line a serving dish with lettuce leaves. Arrange on top the tomatoes, alternating with mounds of the vegetable mayonnaise, piling the rest into the centre of the dish. Garnish with anchovy fillets and black olives, halved lemon slices and chopped parsley, as illustrated.

Serve chilled.

 a Provence rosé

Preparation time 20 minutes

Serves 6

AMERICAN
6 tomatoes
salt and pepper
2 eggs, hard-cooked
1 (3½-oz) can tuna
¼ cup finely chopped parsley
1 tablespoon lemon juice
1 (14-oz) can mixed vegetables
Mayonnaise
1 teaspoon French mustard
2 egg yolks
1 cup oil
Garnish
lettuce leaves
7 anchovy fillets
7 ripe olives
½ lemon
chopped parsley

Aïoli with crudités

(L'ailloli)

Preparation time 1 hour
plus overnight soaking
Cooking time 45 minutes

Serves 6

METRIC/IMPERIAL
1 kg/2 lb dried salt cod
3 small courgettes
3 large carrots
6 medium potatoes
3 bulbs fennel
1 small cauliflower
0.5 kg/1 lb French beans
2 bay leaves
6 eggs
Aïoli
5 cloves garlic
pinch of sea salt
250 ml/8 fl oz olive oil
2 egg yolks
salt and pepper
1 tablespoon lemon juice

To remove the salt from the cod, cut into pieces and place in a colander skin-side up. Place the colander in a large pan of cold water and leave overnight under a slowly running tap.

The following day wash the courgettes but do not peel. Cut lengthwise into quarters or halves. Peel the carrots and potatoes and trim the fennel. Cut into sections. Clean the cauliflower and divide into florets. String the beans.

Cook the vegetables separately in boiling salted water, until cooked but still crisp. Drain and cool.

Drain the cod and put into a pan of cold water with the bay leaves. Bring almost to the boil and simmer gently for 15–20 minutes. Do not allow to boil. Drain and cool.

Hard-boil the eggs, dip into cold water, shell and halve them.

Prepare the aïoli. Peel the garlic, place in a kitchen mortar and crush with a little sea salt, adding sufficient oil to produce a fine purée. Add the egg yolks and continue beating in the oil as for a mayonnaise. This sauce should resemble mayonnaise in appearance and consistency. Season to taste and finally add the lemon juice. Mix well.

Cut up the cod and arrange it with the eggs and vegetables on a large plate. Serve the aïoli in a sauceboat to accompany the crudités.

a Côtes-de-Provence (light red or rosé)

Preparation time 1 hour
plus overnight soaking
Cooking time 45 minutes

Serves 6

AMERICAN
2 lb dried salt cod
3 small zucchini
3 large carrots
6 medium potatoes
3 bulbs fennel
1 small cauliflower
1 lb green beans
2 bay leaves
6 eggs
Aïoli
5 cloves garlic
dash of coarse salt
1 cup olive oil
2 egg yolks
salt and pepper
1 tablespoon lemon juice

Spring hors-d'oeuvre

(Aspics printaniers)

**Preparation time 40 minutes
plus 3 hours setting time
Cooking time 30 minutes**

Serves 6

METRIC/IMPERIAL
**225 g/8 oz new carrots
225 g/8 oz French beans
225 g/8 oz new turnips
225 g/8 oz shelled peas
salt
few spring onions
2 sprigs of tarragon
1 slice ham
1 bunch radishes
100 ml/4 fl oz aspic jelly (made up
according to instructions on
packet)**
Mayonnaise
**1 teaspoon French mustard
2 egg yolks
250 ml/8 fl oz oil**
Garnish
**lettuce leaves
chopped chives
few cucumber slices
tomato half**

This dish must be prepared the day before or at least 3 hours in advance. Dice the carrots, beans and turnips. Cook these and the peas in boiling salted water, until tender. Drain well and cool.

Chop the spring onions, tarragon and ham. Slice some of the radishes, keeping the rest for garnish.

Prepare the mayonnaise by blending together the mustard and egg yolks, adding the oil a little at a time. Whisk the prepared aspic jelly into it (it must be cold but still liquid). Add the chopped spring onions and tarragon. Pour this sauce over the vegetables, ham and radish slices. Stir well together.

Pour into oiled individual moulds and allow to set in a cool place.

Turn out on to a dish lined with lettuce leaves. Sprinkle chives over each and garnish the dish with halved cucumber slices and radishes. Place the tomato half in the centre and top with radish roses.

 a dry white Loire

**Preparation time 40 minutes
plus 3 hours setting time
Cooking time 30 minutes**

Serves 6

AMERICAN
**½ lb new carrots
½ lb green beans
½ lb new turnips
1½ cups shelled peas
salt
few scallions
2 sprigs of tarragon
1 slice cooked ham
1 bunch radishes
½ cup aspic jelly (made up
according to instructions on
package)**
Mayonnaise
**1 teaspoon French mustard
2 egg yolks
1 cup oil**
Garnish
**lettuce leaves
chopped chives
few cucumber slices
tomato half**

Mayonnaise-filled vegetables
(Mayonnaise de crudités)

Preparation time 30 minutes

Serves 5

METRIC/IMPERIAL
1 bunch watercress
5–6 new carrots
few radishes
100 g/4 oz button mushrooms
1 tablespoon lemon juice
1 cucumber
5 small round tomatoes
salt and pepper
**250 ml/8 fl oz mayonnaise
(see page 314)**

Separate the watercress into small sprigs, reserving the stalks; wash carefully then drain and wipe.

Peel and grate the carrots, cut the radishes into roses.

Wash and wipe the mushrooms. Slice very thinly and sprinkle with the lemon juice to prevent discoloration.

Wash and dry the cucumber, do not peel but cut off both ends. Slice into 6 equal sections and scoop out the centres. Sprinkle inside with a little salt and leave to drain.

Wash and dry the tomatoes, cut off the tops, partly scoop out the seeds and flesh, sprinkle with salt and leave upside down to drain.

Mix half the mayonnaise with the grated carrots and half with the sliced mushrooms.

Line a serving dish with watercress sprigs. Place a cucumber wedge in the centre and fill with the radish roses and a few watercress leaves.

Fill the remaining cucumber wedges with the grated carrot, and the tomatoes with the mushroom mayonnaise. Place these alternately round the edge of the dish and finally garnish with watercress stalks. Serve chilled.

 a Montlouis (dry white)

Preparation time 30 minutes

Serves 5

AMERICAN
1 bunch watercress
5–6 new carrots
few radishes
¼ lb button mushrooms
1 tablespoon lemon juice
1 cucumber
5 small round tomatoes
salt and pepper
1 cup mayonnaise (see page 314)

Cucumber boats

(Barquettes au concombre)

Preparation time 35 minutes
Cooking time 10 minutes

Serves 4

METRIC/IMPERIAL
1 cucumber
salt and pepper
4 eggs
1 lettuce
chervil, parsley and chives
1 lemon
1 (99-g/3½-oz) can tuna
2 tomatoes
Mayonnaise
1 teaspoon French mustard
2 egg yolks
250 ml/8 fl oz oil

Wash the cucumber but do not peel. Cut in half lengthwise. Remove the seeds with a small spoon. Sprinkle lightly with salt and leave upside down to drain.

Hard-boil the eggs, then dip into cold water and shell. Wash the lettuce. Keep the outer leaves for garnish and chop the heart. Finely chop the herbs.

Cut the lemon in half. Squeeze the juice from one half and reserve the other half for garnish.

Prepare a mayonnaise by blending together the mustard and egg yolks, adding the oil a little at a time. Drain and flake the tuna. Chop 3 of the eggs and mix with the tuna. Add most of the chopped herbs, the lettuce heart, half the mayonnaise and the lemon juice. Combine well together. Rinse the cucumber halves and fill with this mixture.

Line a serving dish with lettuce leaves and place the cucumber boats on it. Garnish with the halved tomatoes (topped with mayonnaise), the remaining hard-boiled egg and the lemon half. Sprinkle over the herbs and hand the remaining mayonnaise separately.

a Gros Plant (dry white)

Preparation time 35 minutes
Cooking time 10 minutes

Serves 4

AMERICAN
1 cucumber
salt and pepper
4 eggs
1 head lettuce
chervil, parsley and chives
1 lemon
1 (3½-oz) can tuna
2 tomatoes
Mayonnaise
1 teaspoon French mustard
2 egg yolks
1 cup oil

Egg and tomato starter

(Hors-d'oeuvre petit poucet)

Preparation time 20 minutes
Cooking time 10 minutes

Serves 6

METRIC/IMPERIAL
6 eggs
salt and pepper
6 round tomatoes
1 small bunch watercress
1 bunch parsley
Mayonnaise
1 teaspoon French mustard
2 egg yolks
250 ml/8 fl oz oil
Garnish
1 bunch radishes

Hard-boil the eggs in a pan of cold, slightly salted water. Simmer for 10 minutes.

Prepare a thick mayonnaise by blending together the mustard and egg yolks, adding the oil a little at a time.

Wash and wipe the tomatoes, watercress and parsley. Cut a thick slice from the stem side of the tomatoes. Finely chop the parsley.

When the eggs are cooked, immediately place in cold water and shell. Cut off both ends so they will stand upright. From one end gently take out the yolks, being careful not to damage the whites. Leave to cool.

Mix the sieved egg yolks with 3 tablespoons (US $\frac{1}{4}$ cup) mayonnaise, the chopped parsley and seasoning. When smooth and uniform, spoon back into the egg whites.

Line a serving dish with watercress sprigs. Place on it the eggs, standing them upright. Place a tomato on each egg to look like mushrooms. Dot the top with mayonnaise. Garnish the dish with small radish roses.

Serve very cold and hand the rest of the mayonnaise separately.

 a Gros Plant (dry white)

Preparation time 20 minutes
Cooking time 10 minutes

Serves 6

AMERICAN
6 eggs
salt and pepper
6 round tomatoes
1 small bunch watercress
1 bunch parsley
Mayonnaise
1 teaspoon French mustard
2 egg yolks
1 cup oil
Garnish
1 bunch radishes

Egg and pepper hors-d'oeuvre (Hors-d'oeuvre Oriental)

Preparation time 20 minutes
Cooking time 15 minutes

Serves 6

METRIC/IMPERIAL
3 eggs
350g/12oz red peppers or 1 (184-g/6½-oz) can pimientos
2 lemons
salt and pepper
4 tablespoons olive oil
6 thin slices smoked meat (pork, ham or beef)
1 tablespoon chopped parsley
25g/1oz black olives
1 large onion

Hard-boil the eggs, cool under running water, shell and quarter.

Sear the peppers under the grill, allowing the skin to turn black. Cool in cold water, peel and cut into strips. If using canned pimientos, drain and cut into strips.

Squeeze the juice of 1 lemon, season and mix with the oil. Slice the second lemon and halve each slice.

Arrange the pepper strips in the centre of a serving dish and sprinkle with the lemon juice and oil. Surround with the egg quarters, lemon slices and rolled slices of smoked meat. Cover the peppers with chopped parsley, black olives and onion rings. Serve cold.

 a light red

Preparation time 20 minutes
Cooking time 15 minutes

Serves 6

AMERICAN
3 eggs
¾ lb red peppers or 1 (6½-oz) can pimientos
2 lemons
salt and pepper
⅓ cup olive oil
6 thin slices smoked meat (pork, ham or beef)
1 tablespoon chopped parsley
1 oz ripe olives
1 large onion

Grapefruit cocktail

(Pamplemousses cocktail)

Preparation time 20 minutes

Serves 6

METRIC/IMPERIAL
3 large grapefruit
1 (198-g/7-oz) can crabmeat
salt
pinch of cayenne
1 tablespoon brandy, gin or whisky
100g/4oz drained sweetcorn
Mayonnaise
2 egg yolks
½ teaspoon French mustard
200ml/7fl oz oil
Garnish
1 tablespoon chopped parsley
6 lettuce leaves

Prepare the mayonnaise by blending together the egg yolks and mustard, adding the oil a little at a time, until thick and firm.

Wash and dry the grapefruit. Cut in half then carefully remove the segments with a grapefruit knife. Discard pith and pips and collect the juice and set it aside.

Open the can of crabmeat, drain and mix the crab juice with the grapefruit juice. Season with salt and a pinch of cayenne. Add the chosen spirit.

Flake the crabmeat, removing any gristly parts. Mix with the grapefruit segments and sweetcorn and sprinkle with the crab juice mixture. Fill the grapefruit halves.

Surround each with a border of mayonnaise, pipe a little on top, sprinkle with chopped parsley and arrange on a lettuce leaf. Serve cold.

 a Chablis (dry white)

Preparation time 20 minutes

Serves 6

AMERICAN
3 large grapefruit
1 (7-oz) can crab meat
salt
dash of cayenne pepper
1 tablespoon brandy, gin or whiskey
¾ cup drained corn kernels
Mayonnaise
2 egg yolks
½ teaspoon French mustard
¾ cup oil
Garnish
1 tablespoon chopped parsley
6 lettuce leaves

Chicken liver pâté

(Terrine de foies)

Preparation time 50 minutes
Cooking time 1½–2 hours

Serves 8–10

METRIC/IMPERIAL
0.5 kg/1 lb chicken livers
350 g/12 oz streaky bacon
225 g/8 oz pie veal
2 onions
3 shallots
little crumbled thyme
2 tablespoons finely chopped parsley
1 egg
1 tablespoon double cream
3 tablespoons brandy
1 teaspoon coarsely ground pepper
salt and allspice
4 rashers streaky bacon
2 bay leaves
7 g/¼ oz gelatine

Trim and wipe the livers. Cut the bacon and the veal into dice. Peel the onions and shallots, cut into pieces then pass through a mincer.

Pass the livers, bacon and veal separately through the fine blade of the mincer. Repeat if necessary to obtain a fine mixture. Blend in the minced onions and shallots, the crumbled thyme, parsley and the egg beaten with the cream and brandy. Season with the pepper, salt and all-spice and mix all these ingredients well together.

Line the bottom of an ovenproof terrine with the bacon rashers and place over them a bay leaf. Then pile in the pâté mixture. Smooth over and top with the second bay leaf.

Stand the terrine in a pan of hot water, cover and cook in a moderate oven (180°C, 350°F, Gas Mark 4) for 1½–2 hours. Remove from the oven, cool and cover with a weighted plate (this is vital for the success of the pâté). Chill in the refrigerator for 24 hours.

Dissolve the gelatine in 150 ml/¼ pint (US ⅔ cup) water and leave to cool slightly. Remove the weighted plate from the pâté and pour over the liquid gelatine.

Serve from the terrine when the gelatine has set.

 a Beaujolais Villages (light red)

Preparation time 50 minutes
Cooking time 1½–2 hours

Serves 8–10

AMERICAN
1 lb chicken livers
¾-lb bacon piece
½-lb pie veal
2 onions
3 shallots
little crumbled thyme
3 tablespoons finely chopped parsley
1 egg
1 tablespoon heavy cream
¼ cup brandy
1 teaspoon coarsely ground pepper
salt and allspice
4 bacon slices
2 bay leaves
1 envelope gelatin

Terrine of foie gras

(Terrine de foie gras)

Preparation time 40 minutes plus overnight soaking
Cooking time 1-1¼ hours

Serves 6

METRIC/IMPERIAL
1 goose liver (about 800-900g/
1¾-2lb)
salt and pepper
1 truffle
450g/1lb sausagemeat
3 shallots
pinch of allspice
100ml/4fl oz brandy
1 rasher streaky bacon
75g/3oz lard or goose fat

Soak the liver overnight in lightly salted cold water. The following day, wipe carefully with absorbent paper. Trim it, removing the small blood vessels. Cut the truffle into small dice, keeping the trimmings. Slip the diced truffle into the centre of the goose liver and season with salt and pepper.

Mix the sausagemeat with the finely chopped shallots and the truffle trimmings. Season with salt, pepper and allspice and moisten with half the brandy. Mix together well to obtain an even stuffing.

Line the bottom of an ovenproof terrine with the rasher of bacon and cover with a thin layer of the sausagemeat stuffing. Also spread the stuffing around the sides of the terrine. Place the liver in the centre of the terrine and sprinkle with the rest of the brandy. Fill the empty spaces around the liver and cover it with the remaining stuffing.

Cover the dish and stand in a pan of hot water. Cook in a moderate oven (180°C, 350°F, Gas Mark 4), for 1-1¼ hours.

When cool, melt the lard and pour over the top of the terrine. Keep in the refrigerator for several days before eating.

 a Graves (dry white)

Preparation time 40 minutes plus overnight soaking
Cooking time 1-1¼ hours

Serves 6

AMERICAN
1 goose liver (about 1¾-2lb)
salt and pepper
1 truffle
2 cups sausage meat
3 shallots
dash of allspice
½ cup brandy
1 bacon slice
6 tablespoons shortening or goose
fat

Terrine of pork

(Rillettes de porc)

Preparation time 1 hour
Cooking time 4 hours

Serves 6–8

METRIC/IMPERIAL
1 kg/2 lb belly of pork
225 g/8 oz pig's liver
salt and pepper
3 sprigs of parsley
1 small bunch dried thyme
1 bay leaf
about 300 ml/½ pint water
about 100 g/4 oz pork fat or lard

Cut the pork into pieces and place in an earthenware dish. Chop the liver and mix with the pork. Season with salt and pepper and sprinkle with the chopped parsley and crumbled thyme. Add the bay leaf and pour in the water.

Cover and cook in a cool oven (140°C, 275°F, Gas Mark 1) for 4 hours, stirring from time to time.

When the meat has cooled, blend it in the liquidiser or mince it. Pack the mixture into earthenware pots.

Melt the fat and pour a layer over the surface of each pot. Cool in the refrigerator and serve with French bread.

 a Beaujolais Villages (light red)

Preparation time 1 hour
Cooking time 4 hours

Serves 6–8

AMERICAN
2 lb salt pork
½ lb pork liver
salt and pepper
3 sprigs of parsley
1 small bunch dried thyme
1 bay leaf
about 1¼ cups water
½ cup pork fat or shortening

Aubergine caviar

(Caviar d'aubergines)

Preparation time 30 minutes
Cooking time 20–30 minutes

Serves 6-8

METRIC/IMPERIAL
4 large aubergines
3 cloves garlic
salt and pepper
150 ml/¼ pint olive oil
juice of 2 lemons
Garnish
lettuce leaves
lemon slices
tomato quarters
small black olives
chopped parsley

Place the unpeeled aubergines on a baking sheet in a hot oven (220°C, 425°F, Gas Mark 7) and cook for 20–30 minutes or until soft, turning frequently. Remove from the oven, cut in half and scoop out the pulp with a small spoon.

Reduce this pulp, by mashing or liquidising in the blender, to a fine, oily purée. Leave to cool.

Peel the garlic, place in a kitchen mortar and pound with a pinch of salt and a little oil, to make a thick paste.

Mix this into the aubergine purée and gradually add the rest of the oil. Beat continuously as for a mayonnaise. Add lemon juice to taste and adjust for seasoning.

Arrange the aubergine caviar on a serving dish lined with lettuce leaves. Surround with lemon slices and tomato quarters and garnish the dish with olives and chopped parsley. Serve very cold.

 a Côtes-de-Provence rosé

Preparation time 30 minutes
Cooking time 20–30 minutes

Serves 6-8

AMERICAN
4 large eggplant
3 cloves garlic
salt and pepper
⅔ cup olive oil
juice of 2 lemons
Garnish
lettuce leaves
lemon slices
tomato quarters
small ripe olives
chopped parsley

Blinis

(Les blinis)

Preparation time 20 minutes
plus 3 hours rising time
Cooking time 2 minutes per blini

Serves 6

METRIC/IMPERIAL
15g/½oz fresh yeast
or 7g/¼oz dried yeast
250ml/8fl oz milk
300g/11oz plain flour
3 eggs, separated
salt
100ml/4fl oz single cream
50g/2oz butter
To serve
75g/3oz butter
12 thin slices smoked salmon
1 small jar salmon roes (optional)
150ml/¼ pint clotted or double
cream

Dissolve the yeast in the warmed milk. Place the flour in a large bowl and make a well in the centre. Pour in the milk mixture and egg yolks and add a little salt. Mix well together and leave to rise for 3 hours.

Just before using add the cream and then fold in the stiffly whisked egg whites.

Heat a knob of butter in an 18-cm/7-inch frying pan. Pour in just enough batter to form a small, thick pancake. Brown on one side before turning to cook the other side.

Keep the blinis hot under foil in a warm oven while the remainder are being cooked. This quantity makes about 12 blinis.

Serve with butter, smoked salmon, salmon roes and clotted cream, according to taste.

 a Graves (dry white)

Preparation time 20 minutes
plus 3 hours rising time
Cooking time 2 minutes per blini

Serves 6

AMERICAN
½ cake compressed yeast or
½ package active dry yeast
1 cup milk
2¾ cups all-purpose flour
3 eggs, separated
salt
½ cup light cream
¼ cup butter
To serve
6 tablespoons butter
12 thin slices smoked salmon
1 small jar salmon roes (optional)
⅔ cup heavy cream

Chicken and mushroom vol-au-vents (Bouchées à la reine)

Preparation time 30 minutes
plus 2 hours steeping time
Cooking time 30 minutes

Serves 6

METRIC/IMPERIAL
100 g/4 oz calf's sweetbreads
2 tablespoons vinegar
juice of ½ lemon
1 bouquet garni
50 g/2 oz butter
100 g/4 oz button mushrooms
100 g/4 oz breast of chicken, cooked
6 cooked vol-au-vent cases
Sauce
50 g/2 oz butter
50 g/2 oz flour
300 ml/½ pint chicken stock
4 tablespoons single cream
salt and pepper

Steep the veal sweetbreads in cold water and vinegar for 2 hours. Drain, rinse and place in a small saucepan of cold salted water with the lemon juice and bouquet garni. Simmer for 10 minutes. Drain and wipe the sweetbread and allow to cool pressed between two plates. When cold dice and brown in half the heated butter.

Clean the mushrooms and sauté whole in the remaining butter.

Dice the chicken breast, add to the veal sweetbreads together with the mushrooms. Keep warm over a gentle heat.

Heat the vol-au-vent cases in a moderate oven (180°C, 350°F, Gas Mark 4) for 5–10 minutes.

Prepare the sauce. Make a white roux with the butter and flour. When it begins to bubble stir in the hot chicken stock. Cook for 3–5 minutes, stirring continuously. Add the cream and season to taste. Do not boil.

Stir the chicken mushroom mixture into this sauce; it should be quite thick.

Fill the vol-au-vent cases just before serving and serve very hot.

a white Mâcon (dry)

Preparation time 30 minutes
plus 2 hours steeping time
Cooking time 30 minutes

Serves 6

AMERICAN
¼ lb veal sweetbread
3 tablespoons vinegar
juice of ½ lemon
1 bouquet garni
¼ cup butter
¼ lb button mushrooms
¼ lb chicken breast, cooked
6 cooked vol-au-vent cases
Sauce
¼ cup butter
½ cup all-purpose flour
1¼ cups chicken stock
⅓ cup light cream
salt and pepper

Little forest pies

(Petits pâtés forestiers)

Preparation time 30 minutes
Cooking time 35 minutes

Serves 6

METRIC/IMPERIAL
450g/1lb puff pastry
1 egg yolk
Filling
3 shallots
100g/4oz mushrooms
1 teaspoon lemon juice
15g/½oz butter
1 veal escalope (about 100g/4oz)
50g/2oz packaged stuffing mix
1 egg yolk
2 teaspoons double cream
1 tablespoon finely chopped parsley
salt and pepper

Prepare the filling. Finely chop the shallots and mushrooms, sprinkle the latter with lemon juice.

Soften the shallots in the hot butter until transparent, add the chopped mushrooms. Dry out this mixture over a gentle heat, stirring with a wooden spoon. Remove from the heat and leave to cool.

Mince the veal escalope. Combine this with the stuffing mix, the shallots and mushrooms, the egg yolk beaten with the cream and the chopped parsley. Add salt and pepper and mix well together.

Set the oven to hot (220°C, 425°F, Gas Mark 7).

Roll out the pastry and cut twelve rounds of the same size, round or oval. Spread the stuffing over six of these rounds, leaving a border of 2.5cm/1 inch around the edge. Moisten this with water. Cover with the remaining rounds and pinch the edges together to seal. Garnish each with a pastry leaf. Brush these pies with the egg yolk thinned with 2 tablespoons (US 3 tablespoons) water.

Place on a baking sheet lightly moistened with water and cook in the oven for 20–25 minutes.

Serve the pies well browned, hot or warm.

 a Bourgueil (light fruity red)

Preparation time 30 minutes
Cooking time 35 minutes

Serves 6

AMERICAN
1lb puff paste
1 egg yolk
Filling
3 shallots
¼lb mushrooms
1 teaspoon lemon juice
1 tablespoon butter
1 veal scallop (about ¼lb)
2oz packaged stuffing mix
1 egg yolk
2 teaspoons heavy cream
1 tablespoon finely chopped parsley
salt and pepper

Spiced cod steaks

(Cabillaud aux épices)

Preparation time 20 minutes
plus 1-2 hours marinating time
Cooking time 20-25 minutes

Serves 4

METRIC/IMPERIAL
4 individual cod steaks
flour to coat
3 tablespoons oil
2 onions
2 cloves garlic
salt and pepper
Marinade
2 cloves
pinch of sea salt
8-10 peppercorns
½ teaspoon cumin seeds
½ teaspoon dried fennel
1 tablespoon curry powder
juice of 1 lemon
3 tablespoons oil
Garnish
sprig of parsley

Prepare the marinade. In a kitchen mortar pound the cloves, sea salt, peppercorns, cumin seeds and fennel. Mix in the curry powder and spoon over the cod steaks.

Sprinkle the lemon juice over the fish and brush with oil. Spread the ground spices evenly and leave for at least 1–2 hours to marinate.

Just before cooking drain the cod if necessary and coat with flour. Fry in the very hot oil until golden all over, about 5–10 minutes. Peel and slice the onions, crush the garlic. Add to the hot oil and brown with the fish. Season with a little salt and pepper and cook for a further 10 minutes.

Serve just as it is with lemon wedges, or with pilaf rice and a highly seasoned tomato sauce. Garnish with a sprig of parsley.

 a white Cassis (very dry)

Preparation time 20 minutes
plus 1-2 hours marinating time
Cooking time 20-25 minutes

Serves 4

AMERICAN
4 individual cod steaks
flour to coat
¼ cup oil
2 onions
2 cloves garlic
salt and pepper
Marinade
2 cloves
dash of coarse salt
8-10 peppercorns
½ teaspoon cumin seeds
½ teaspoon dried fennel
1 tablespoon curry powder
juice of 1 lemon
¼ cup oil
Garnish
sprig of parsley

Baked cod fillet

(Filet de cabillaud au four)

Preparation time 15 minutes
Cooking time 25 minutes

Serves 4

METRIC/IMPERIAL
1kg/2lb cod fillet
salt and freshly ground pepper
4 shallots
225g/8oz mushrooms
juice of 1 lemon
25g/1oz butter
150ml/¼ pint double cream
250ml/8fl oz dry white wine
½ teaspoon crushed peppercorns

Wash and wipe the fish and salt slightly.

Set the oven to hot (220°C, 425°F, Gas Mark 7).

Peel the shallots. Wash the mushrooms, wipe then chop as finely as possible with the shallots. Sprinkle with lemon juice.

Generously butter an ovenproof dish, cover the base with the chopped shallots and mushrooms and place the fish on top of them.

Thin the cream with the white wine, season with a little salt and freshly ground pepper. Pour over the fish, place in the oven and cook for about 25 minutes (according to the thickness of the fish).

Serve hot sprinkled with crushed peppercorns.

 a Muscadet (dry white)

Preparation time 15 minutes
Cooking time 25 minutes

Serves 4

AMERICAN
2lb cod fillet
salt and freshly ground black pepper
4 shallots
½lb mushrooms
juice of 1 lemon
2 tablespoons butter
⅔ cup heavy cream
1 cup dry white wine
½ teaspoon crushed peppercorns

Cod Américaine

(Cabillaud à l'Américaine)

Preparation time 20 minutes
Cooking time 40 minutes

Serves 6

METRIC/IMPERIAL
6 medium onions
4 shallots
6 individual cod steaks
4 tablespoons olive oil
5 tablespoons brandy
3 tablespoons tomato purée
300 ml/½ pint tomato juice
250 ml/8 fl oz medium dry white wine
1 small clove garlic
1 small bouquet garni
salt and pepper
pinch of cayenne
Garnish
chopped parsley

Peel and slice the onions, peel and chop the shallots. Wash the cod steaks and dry on absorbent paper. Heat the oil in a frying pan and cook the onions and shallots until transparent. Add the cod and cook for a few moments over a high heat until firm. Pour over the brandy and flame.

Stir in the tomato purée, tomato juice and white wine. Add the crushed garlic and the bouquet garni. Season with salt, pepper and a pinch of cayenne. Cover and cook over a low heat for 30 minutes.

Just before serving remove the bouquet garni. Pour into a heated serving dish and sprinkle with chopped parsley. Serve very hot.

 a Chablis (dry white)

Preparation time 20 minutes
Cooking time 40 minutes

Serves 6

AMERICAN
6 medium onions
4 shallots
6 individual cod steaks
⅓ cup olive oil
6 tablespoons brandy
¼ cup tomato paste
1¼ cups tomato juice
1 cup medium dry white wine
1 small clove garlic
1 small bouquet garni
salt and pepper
dash of cayenne pepper
Garnish
chopped parsley

Cod in curried cream sauce (Cabillaud Mauresque)

Preparation time 15 minutes
Cooking time 20–25 minutes

Serves 4–6

METRIC/IMPERIAL
1 kg/2 lb cod
salt and freshly ground pepper
1 onion
4 shallots
40 g/1½ oz butter
3 tablespoons brandy
2 tomatoes or 1 tablespoon tomato purée
1 small clove garlic
1 teaspoon curry powder
300 ml/½ pint double cream
pinch of cayenne
Garnish
chopped parsley

Wash and wipe the fish and cut into even pieces. Season.

Fry the very finely chopped onion and shallots in a frying pan with the hot butter. When golden add the cod, and cook until firm over a high heat. Sprinkle with brandy and flame. Add the peeled and crushed tomatoes (or the purée diluted with a little water) and the crushed garlic. Season with salt, pepper and curry powder and cook for 10 minutes over a low heat, stirring from time to time.

Drain the fish and keep warm.

Strain the sauce through a conical sieve and place over a high heat. Add the cream and simmer for 2 minutes, beating with a wire whisk so that the cream thickens. Return the fish to the sauce, adjust seasoning and add a pinch of cayenne.

Pour into a serving dish and sprinkle with chopped parsley.

 a Sancerre (dry white)

Preparation time 15 minutes
Cooking time 20–25 minutes

Serves 4–6

AMERICAN
2 lb cod
salt and freshly ground pepper
1 onion
4 shallots
3 tablespoons butter
¼ cup brandy
2 tomatoes or 1 tablespoon tomato paste
1 small clove garlic
1 teaspoon curry powder
1¼ cups heavy cream
dash of cayenne pepper
Garnish
chopped parsley

Breton-style cod

(Morue à la Bretonne)

**Preparation time 25 minutes
plus 24 hours soaking time
Cooking time 30–40 minutes**

Serves 6

METRIC/IMPERIAL
1.25 kg/2½ lb dried salt cod
2 bay leaves
6 large potatoes
salt and pepper
50 g/2 oz butter
65 g/2½ oz flour
300 ml/½ pint milk
3 tablespoons double cream
Garnish
chopped parsley

Cut the cod into pieces and soak in cold water for 24 hours, changing the water twice. By the time of cooking, the cod must be completely desalted.

The following day, place the cod in a large saucepan, cover with cold water, add the bay leaves and poach gently without boiling for 30 minutes.

Wash the potatoes, peel and cook in boiling salted water for 15–20 minutes.

Prepare the sauce. Melt the butter over a gentle heat and stir in flour, using a wooden spoon. As soon as it begins to bubble, thin the roux with the warmed milk and 300 ml/½ pint (US 1¼ cups) of the fish cooking liquor. Stir until smooth and thickened. Add the cream and season to taste. Cook for 5 minutes, stirring continuously, but do not allow to boil.

Cut the potatoes into chunks or halves. Drain the cod, pile into a heated serving dish and surround with the potatoes. Pour over the sauce, sprinkle with chopped parsley and serve very hot.

 a Muscadet (dry white)

**Preparation time 25 minutes
plus 24 hours soaking time
Cooking time 30–40 minutes**

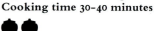

Serves 6

AMERICAN
2½ lb dried salt cod
2 bay leaves
6 large potatoes
salt and pepper
¼ cup butter
½ cup plus 2 tablespoons all-
 purpose flour
1¼ cups milk
¼ cup heavy cream
Garnish
chopped parsley

Soufflé-topped cod

(Morue à la mode de Porto)

**Preparation time 40 minutes
plus 24 hours soaking time
Cooking time 45 minutes**

Serves 6

METRIC/IMPERIAL
1 kg/2lb dried salt cod
1 kg/2lb potatoes
1 bay leaf
100 ml/4 fl oz olive oil
150 ml/¼ pint milk
salt and pepper
4 large onions
3 cloves garlic
pinch of saffron or turmeric
pinch of paprika
3 eggs

Put the cod to soak for 24 hours: cut into pieces, place in a sieve or colander, skin side uppermost. Put the sieve in a large saucepan and cover with cold water. Change the water at least twice.

The following day peel the potatoes and cook in boiling salted water.

Drain and rinse the cod, place in a saucepan with the bay leaf, cover with cold water. Heat without boiling and poach gently for 10 minutes.

Mash the potatoes and mix with 1 tablespoon olive oil and just enough warm milk to give a thick soft purée. Season lightly. Spread over the base of an ovenproof dish and keep hot in a warm oven.

Brown the finely sliced onions in the rest of the hot oil. When they are golden in colour, add the crushed garlic and then the cod, well drained and trimmed. Mix over a brisk heat, add the saffron and paprika. Adjust the seasoning and place on top of the potato.

Beat 2 whole eggs with the yolk of the third, then fold in the remaining white, stiffly whisked. Spoon over the top of the fish mixture and cook in a moderate oven (180°C, 350°F, Gas Mark 4) for 25–35 minutes, until the eggs are set and golden. Serve hot.

 a Portuguese green wine (Vinho verde)

**Preparation time 40 minutes
plus 24 hours soaking time
Cooking time 45 minutes**

Serves 6

AMERICAN
2lb dried salt cod
2lb potatoes
1 bay leaf
½ cup olive oil
⅔ cup milk
salt and pepper
4 large onions
3 cloves garlic
dash of saffron or turmeric
dash of paprika pepper
3 eggs

Fish goujons

(Poissons des isles)

**Preparation time 35 minutes
plus 1 hour marinating time
Cooking time 15–20 minutes**

Serves 6

METRIC/IMPERIAL
225 g/8 oz fillet of cod
juice of 1 lemon
1 teaspoon ground ginger
salt and pepper
1 litre/1¾ pints mussels
350 g/12 oz long-grain rice
flour to coat
oil for deep frying
Sauce
3 onions
0.75 kg/1½ lb ripe tomatoes
1 tablespoon lemon juice
½ teaspoon castor sugar
pinch of salt
pinch of cayenne
Garnish
lemon slices
chopped parsley

Wash and wipe the fish fillets, cut into thin strips and place in an earthenware dish. Sprinkle with the lemon juice, dust with ginger, add salt and pepper. Leave to marinate for about 1 hour.

Scrape and wash the mussels, discarding any that do not close when tapped. Place in a saucepan and cook over a brisk heat in a little water for 2–3 minutes. Strain their liquor, remove the mussels from their shells and keep hot.

Prepare the sauce. Peel and chop the onions, peel, deseed and crush the tomatoes. Blend these ingredients in the liquidiser. Pour the resulting purée into a saucepan with the mussel liquid, lemon juice, sugar, salt and cayenne. Reduce for 10 minutes over a gentle heat.

Wash the rice, cook for 10–15 minutes in plenty of boiling salted water, then drain.

Drain the strips of fish, toss in flour and deep fry in hot oil for about 10 minutes.

Place the hot rice in a wetted ring mould, pack it down well then turn out on to a serving dish. Place the fish and mussels in the centre. Garnish the rice with lemon slices and a few mussels. Sprinkle with parsley and serve at once with the sauce.

 a Riesling (fruity white)

**Preparation time 35 minutes
plus 1 hour marinating time
Cooking time 15–20 minutes**

Serves 6

AMERICAN
½ lb fillet of cod
juice of 1 lemon
1 teaspoon ground ginger
salt and pepper
2 pints mussels
1½ cups long-grain rice
flour to coat
oil for deep frying
Sauce
3 onions
1½ lb ripe tomatoes
1 tablespoon lemon juice
¼ teaspoon sugar
dash of salt
dash of cayenne pepper
Garnish
lemon slices
chopped parsley

Haddock Provençal

(Aiglefins à la Provençale)

Preparation time 35 minutes
Cooking time 30 minutes

Serves 4

METRIC/IMPERIAL
2 aubergines
salt and pepper
4 large fillets of haddock
4 onions
3 cloves garlic
0.75 kg/1½ lb tomatoes
175 ml/6 fl oz olive oil
100 ml/4 fl oz dry white wine
225 g/8 oz long-grain rice
pinch of saffron or turmeric
1 tablespoon flour
1 small bouquet garni
Garnish
1 lemon
chopped parsley

Peel the aubergines, dice, sprinkle with salt and leave to sweat. Wash and wipe the fish fillets and season. Peel and finely slice the onions. Chop 2 cloves garlic. Peel the tomatoes, leave 4 whole and finely dice the remainder.

Soften half the onions in 2 tablespoons (US 3 tablespoons) oil over a low heat. Use to line the base of a greased ovenproof dish.

Lay the fish fillets over these onions and sprinkle with the white wine. Cover and cook for 20 minutes in a moderately hot oven (200°C, 400°F, Gas Mark 6).

Wash the rice well and cook in 450 ml/¾ pint (US 2 cups) water for 15 minutes. Add the saffron or turmeric and season. Keep hot.

Cook the 4 whole tomatoes gently in a little oil then remove and keep hot. Brown the remaining sliced onions in 2 tablespoons (US 3 tablespoons) oil, then sprinkle with flour. Add the diced tomatoes, the whole clove garlic and the bouquet garni. Cook over a low heat.

Now wipe the diced aubergines and fry in the rest of the oil. When golden, sprinkle with the chopped garlic.

When the fish fillets are cooked, drain and keep hot. Add their cooking liquor to the tomato mixture. Cook for 5 minutes then strain this sauce through a conical sieve.

Arrange the fish fillets on a large serving dish; surround with the rice, diced aubergines and whole tomatoes. Spoon the sauce over the fish and garnish with halved lemon slices and chopped parsley.

a white Côtes-de-Provence (dry)

Preparation time 35 minutes
Cooking time 30 minutes

Serves 4

AMERICAN
2 eggplant
salt and pepper
4 large fillets of haddock
4 onions
3 cloves garlic
1½ lb tomatoes
¾ cup olive oil
½ cup dry white wine
1 cup long-grain rice
dash of saffron or turmeric
1 tablespoon all-purpose flour
1 small bouquet garni
Garnish
1 lemon
chopped parsley

Hake with seafood sauce

(Merlu des cailletots)

Preparation time 35 minutes
Cooking time 1–1¼ hours

Serves 6

METRIC/IMPERIAL
0.5 kg/1 lb white fish trimmings
(heads and bones)
2 onions
2 carrots
1 bouquet garni
juice of ½ lemon
1 litre/1¾ pints dry white wine
salt and freshly ground pepper
1 hake (about 1.5 kg/3 lb)
2 litres/3½ pints cockles
225 g/8 oz mushrooms
75 g/3 oz butter
4 shallots
225 g/8 oz peeled prawns
100 ml/4 fl oz calvados or brandy
1 tablespoon flour
300 ml/½ pint double cream
pinch of cayenne
Garnish
150 g/5 oz unpeeled prawns
lemon slices
parsley

Prepare the fish stock with the fish trimmings, the quartered onions, sliced carrots, bouquet garni, lemon juice and 750 ml/1¼ pints (US 3 cups) white wine. Season with a little salt and ground pepper. Simmer for 30 minutes while the liquid reduces, then strain and leave to cool.

Clean the fish and place whole in a fish kettle. Cover with the cold stock and the rest of the white wine. Poach by simmering gently for 30 minutes. Carefully lift the fish out of the liquor, drain and keep warm.

Meanwhile, open the cockles by boiling over a brisk heat in a little water; remove from their shells. Strain the juices through muslin.

Brown the sliced mushrooms in half the butter. Fry the chopped shallots in the remaining butter. As soon as they begin to colour, add the cockles and the peeled prawns. Pour over the calvados and flame. Sprinkle with the flour, mix for a few moments. Moisten with the cockle juice and the cream. Season with a pinch of cayenne, add the mushrooms and thicken over a gentle heat, stirring. Do not allow to boil.

Skin the cooked fish, leaving the head intact, and arrange on a long serving dish. Coat with the sauce. Garnish with prawns, lemon slices and parsley. Place on the fish's head a whole slice of lemon, sprinkled with chopped parsley. Serve immediately.

 a Chablis (dry white)

Preparation time 35 minutes
Cooking time 1–1¼ hours

Serves 6

AMERICAN
1 lb white fish trimmings (heads
and bones)
2 onions
2 carrots
1 bouquet garni
juice of ½ lemon
4¼ cups dry white wine
salt and freshly ground pepper
1 hake (about 3 lb)
4½ pints cockles
½ lb mushrooms
6 tablespoons butter
4 shallots
½ lb shelled shrimp
½ cup calvados or brandy
1 tablespoon all-purpose flour
1¼ cups heavy cream
dash of cayenne pepper
Garnish
5 oz unshelled shrimp
lemon slices
parsley

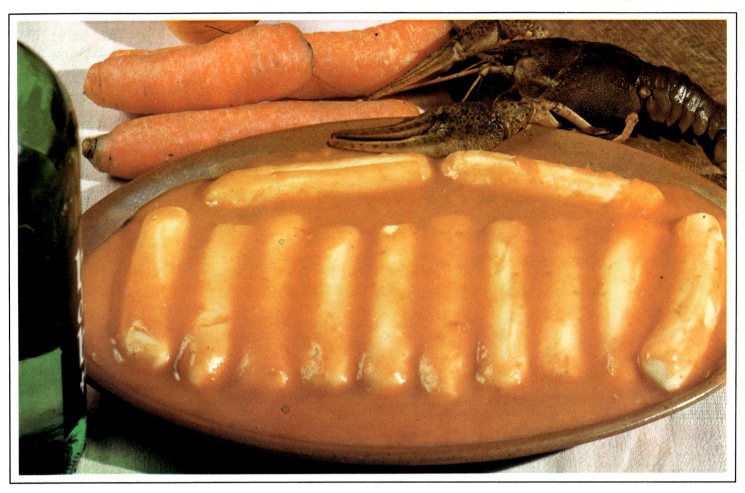

Fish quenelles

(Quenelles de brochet Nantua)

Preparation time 1 hour
Cooking time 25 minutes

Serves 6

METRIC/IMPERIAL
250 ml/8 fl oz milk
salt and freshly ground pepper
freshly grated nutmeg
50 g/2 oz butter
100 g/4 oz plain flour
3 egg yolks
0.5 kg/1 lb pike or cod flesh
(without skin or bones)
6 eggs
100 ml/4 fl oz double cream
600 ml/1 pint Nantua sauce, heated
(see page 311)

Heat the milk in a large saucepan with salt, pepper and nutmeg. Add the butter cut into small pieces.

Mix the flour and 3 egg yolks, combine with the hot milk. Thicken the mixture over a gentle heat, stirring with a wooden spoon until it forms a paste which leaves the bottom and sides of the pan clean. Spread out in a large oiled dish, leave to cool completely.

Pound the pike flesh, mince it finely in a liquidiser or pass it through a vegetable mill. Cut the cooled paste into small dice, add to the pike flesh. Beat all together well to obtain an even mixture. Pass once again through the vegetable mill. Add the 6 whole eggs, one by one, and finally the cream, beating well each time until a smooth even paste.

To form the quenelles, take a little of the mixture and roll into a sausage shape on a lightly floured working surface, or pipe through a large plain vegetable nozzle. Then toss a few at a time into simmering salted water. Poach them without boiling and remove as soon as they rise to the surface. Drain and place on a clean tea towel.

Arrange in a heated serving dish, pour over the sauce and serve immediately.

 an Apremont (dry white)

Preparation time 1 hour
Cooking time 25 minutes

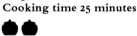

Serves 6

AMERICAN
1 cup milk
salt and freshly ground pepper
freshly grated nutmeg
¼ cup butter
1 cup all-purpose flour
3 egg yolks
2 cups pike or cod flesh (without skin or bones)
6 eggs
½ cup heavy cream
2½ cups Nantua sauce, heated
(see page 311)

Fillets of fish with sorrel

(Saint-Pierre à l'oseille)

**Preparation time 35 minutes
plus 30 minutes marinating time
Cooking time 25 minutes**

Serves 4

METRIC/IMPERIAL
**4 fillets of John Dory fish or sole
2 lemons
salt and pepper
0.75 kg/1½ lb sorrel or spinach
100 g/4 oz butter
flour to coat
1 egg yolk
100 ml/4 fl oz double cream**
Garnish
chopped parsley

Wash then wipe the fish fillets. Sprinkle with the juice of 1 lemon, season and leave to marinate for 30 minutes.

Trim, wash and shred the sorrel. Soften over a gentle heat in 25 g/1 oz (US 2 tablespoons) butter, taking care that it does not catch.

Wipe the fillets, toss in flour, then shake to remove any excess flour. Cook them until golden in the rest of the hot butter. Turn halfway through cooking.

When the sorrel is cooked, dry it out over a gentle heat, stirring with a wooden spoon, then bind with the egg yolk mixed into the cream. Do not allow to boil. Season to taste.

Arrange the fillets on a heated serving dish with the sorrel. Garnish with the remaining lemon and lightly sprinkle the whole with chopped parsley.

 a Muscadet (dry white)

**Preparation time 35 minutes
plus 30 minutes marinating time
Cooking time 25 minutes**

Serves 4

AMERICAN
**4 fillets of sole
2 lemons
salt and pepper
1½ lb sorrel or spinach
½ cup butter
flour to coat
1 egg yolk
½ cup heavy cream**
Garnish
chopped parsley

Fish Provençal

(Poisson Varoise)

Preparation time 25 minutes
Cooking time 40 minutes

Serves 6

METRIC/IMPERIAL
1.25 kg/2½ lb rock salmon or
haddock
2 cloves garlic
6 onions
4 green peppers
0.75 kg/1½ lb tomatoes
4 tablespoons olive oil
300 ml/½ pint dry white wine
300 ml/½ pint water
salt and pepper
1 bouquet garni
100 g/4 oz black olives
Garnish
chopped parsley

Wash and wipe the fish, cut into sections of equal size. Crush the cloves of garlic, finely slice the onions. Wash and wipe the peppers. Discard cores and seeds, cut the peppers into thin strips. Peel the tomatoes, remove seeds then cut the flesh into dice.

Heat the oil in a shallow frying pan. Cook the onions and garlic until light golden. Add the pepper strips and diced tomatoes. Mix over a brisk heat with a wooden spoon. Moisten with the white wine and water. Bring to the boil, season to taste, add the bouquet garni and olives. Add the pieces of fish to this sauce and leave to cook for 20 minutes, slightly reducing the heat. Remove the bouquet garni.

To serve, arrange the fish in a fairly deep dish. Pour over the sauce and sprinkle with chopped parsley. Serve immediately.

 a white Côtes-de-Provence

Preparation time 25 minutes
Cooking time 40 minutes

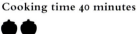

Serves 6

AMERICAN
2½ lb haddock
2 cloves garlic
6 onions
4 green peppers
1½ lb tomatoes
⅓ cup olive oil
1¼ cups dry white wine
1¼ cups water
salt and pepper
1 bouquet garni
¼ lb ripe olives
Garnish
chopped parsley

Fillets of sole in champagne (Filets de sole Remoise)

Preparation time 20 minutes
Cooking time 20 minutes

Serves 6

METRIC/IMPERIAL
12 fillets of sole
3 shallots, chopped
25 g/1 oz butter
½ bottle dry champagne
salt and pepper
150 ml/¼ pint double cream
1 tablespoon flour

Fold the sole fillets in half and flatten slightly so they do not curl up when cooking.

Soften the shallots in a saucepan with the melted butter. Do not allow to brown. Add the champagne, salt and pepper. Bring to the boil and poach the fillets of sole for 3–5 minutes over a gentle heat. Remove the fish and keep hot in a dish over a pan of boiling water.

Reduce the cooking liquor by half by open boiling. Mix the cream with the flour and pour into the saucepan, beating with a wire whisk. Thicken the sauce over a gentle heat for 3 minutes, continuing to beat lightly. Strain through a sieve.

Arrange the sole fillets on a warmed serving dish. Pour over the champagne sauce and serve immediately.

 a dry champagne or a Chablis (dry white)

Preparation time 20 minutes
Cooking time 20 minutes

Serves 6

AMERICAN
12 fillets of sole
3 shallots, chopped
2 tablespoons butter
½ bottle dry champagne
salt and pepper
⅔ cup heavy cream
1 tablespoon all-purpose flour

Paupiettes of sole

(Soles en paupiettes)

Preparation time 30 minutes
Cooking time 30-35 minutes

Serves 4

METRIC/IMPERIAL
fish heads and trimmings for stock
1 carrot
2 onions
1 lemon
1 bouquet garni
salt and pepper
750ml/1¼ pints dry white wine
8 fillets of sole
about 100g/4oz butter
1 bunch tarragon
225g/8oz button mushrooms
50g/2oz flour
150ml/¼ pint double cream
1 tablespoon tomato purée

Prepare the fish stock. Place the fish heads and trimmings in a saucepan. Add the finely sliced carrot and onions, the juice of half the lemon, bouquet garni, salt and pepper. Pour over 450ml/¾ pint (US 2 cups) wine and 450ml/¾ pint (US 2 cups) water. Bring to the boil, then reduce heat and simmer until the stock is reduced by half. Strain this stock through a sieve.

Place the sole fillets between two sheets of wet grease-proof paper and flatten slightly with a rolling pin. Butter and season them on one side. Roll up with the buttered side inside. Tie with cotton and place in a buttered ovenproof dish. Pour over the reduced fish stock. Cover and cook in a moderately hot oven (190°C, 375°F, Gas Mark 5) for 10–15 minutes.

Set aside 8 tarragon leaves and infuse the others in the rest of the white wine. Soften the mushrooms in 25g/1oz (US 2 tablespoons) butter.

Remove the sole paupiettes from the oven and arrange in a heated serving dish. Keep warm.

Prepare a white roux with 50g/2oz (US ¼ cup) butter and the flour. Stir in 150ml/¼ pint (US ⅔ cup) of the liquid in which the fish was cooked. Thicken over a gentle heat, stirring continuously, then add the strained tarragon wine, the cream, tomato purée and mushrooms. Bring slowly to the boil, stirring all the time. Correct the seasoning and cook gently for a further 5–10 minutes, stirring.

Pour this sauce over the paupiettes of sole. Garnish each with a tarragon leaf and lemon segment and serve immediately.

 a Chablis (dry white)

Preparation time 30 minutes
Cooking time 30-35 minutes

Serves 4

AMERICAN
fish heads and trimmings for stock
1 carrot
2 onions
1 lemon
1 bouquet garni
salt and pepper
3 cups dry white wine
8 fillets of sole
about ½ cup butter
1 bunch tarragon
½lb button mushrooms
¼ cup all-purpose flour
⅔ cup heavy cream
1 tablespoon tomato paste

Perch with herb mayonnaise

(Bar poché froid)

Preparation time 40 minutes
Cooking time 1½ hours

Serves 6

METRIC/IMPERIAL
1 perch (about 2kg/4½lb)
salt and pepper
3 carrots
3 onions
4 sprigs of parsley
40g/1½oz butter
1 litre/1¾ pints dry white wine
2 litres/3½ pints water
1 small bouquet garni
Herb mayonnaise
2 shallots
pinch of freshly ground pepper
4 tablespoons white wine vinegar
1 teaspoon French mustard
2 egg yolks
200ml/7fl oz oil
1 tablespoon chopped mixed herbs
(chervil, parsley and chives)
Garnish
lettuce leaves
6 small tomatoes
1 lemon
parsley
mayonnaise

Ask the fishmonger to clean and gut the perch. Wash and wipe it and season with salt and pepper.

Prepare a court-bouillon. Peel and finely slice the carrots and onions. Chop the parsley. Soften these ingredients in the hot butter, stirring with a wooden spoon. Do not allow to brown; they should scarcely change colour. Add the white wine, water, salt and bouquet garni and leave to simmer gently for 45 minutes. Season with pepper at the end of the cooking time. Strain and cool.

Place the perch in a fish kettle or a long, shallow pan. Pour over the court-bouillon and place over a very gentle heat. Simmer without boiling for 35 minutes, then leave the fish to cool in the court-bouillon.

Prepare the herb mayonnaise. Peel the shallots and chop as finely as possible. Place in a small saucepan with the freshly ground pepper and vinegar. Reduce slowly over a moderate heat until only 1 tablespoon of liquid remains.

Meanwhile, blend together the mustard and egg yolks, adding the oil a little at a time. When firm stir in the reduced shallots and vinegar, which should be still boiling, and the chopped herbs.

Cover a long serving dish with lettuce leaves and carefully slide the perch on to it. Surround with slices of tomato and lemon. Garnish with parsley and mayonnaise and serve cold, accompanied by the herb mayonnaise.

 a Pouilly Fuissé (dry white)

Preparation time 40 minutes
Cooking time 1½ hours

Serves 6

AMERICAN
1 carp (about 4½lb)
salt and pepper
3 carrots
3 onions
4 sprigs of parsley
3 tablespoons butter
4¼ cups dry white wine
4½ pints water
1 small bouquet garni
Herb mayonnaise
2 shallots
dash of freshly ground pepper
⅓ cup white wine vinegar
1 teaspoon French mustard
2 egg yolks
¾ cup oil
1 tablespoon chopped mixed herbs
(chervil, parsley and chives)
Garnish
lettuce leaves
6 small tomatoes
1 lemon
parsley
mayonnaise

Perch in green sauce

(Loup au vert)

Preparation time 25 minutes
Cooking time about 1 hour

Serves 6

METRIC/IMPERIAL
1 bunch watercress
0.5kg/1lb leaf beet or spinach
1 stick celery
1 small bunch parsley
1 small bunch chervil
50g/2oz butter
salt and pepper
1 perch (about 1.5kg/3lb)
3 egg yolks
Court-bouillon
½ bottle dry white wine
1 onion
1 bay leaf
juice of 1 lemon
6 peppercorns

First prepare the court-bouillon. Heat the wine, finely chopped onion, bay leaf, lemon juice and peppercorns with 1.15 litres/2 pints (US 5 cups) water. Simmer for 15 minutes then strain.

Select, wash and coarsely chop the watercress, leaf beet or spinach, celery, parsley and chervil.

Melt the butter in a frying pan, add the chopped vegetables and herbs and season with salt and pepper. Stir the ingredients well together and leave to soften for 10 minutes over a gentle heat. Place the mixture in a fish kettle or large saucepan.

Meanwhile, gut and wash the fish. Place it over the bed of greenery in the fish kettle, cover with the court-bouillon and cook for 40 minutes, simmering gently.

Take out the fish when it is cooked. Skin it immediately and remove the fins, but leave the head on. Arrange on an oval serving dish and keep warm in a low oven. Strain the cooking liquor from the vegetables.

Beat the egg yolks with a wire whisk. Pour into the reserved softened vegetables, whisking the mixture. Thicken over a gentle heat for 2 minutes, but do not allow to boil.

Pour this green sauce over the fish and serve immediately.

 a Muscadet (dry white)

Preparation time 25 minutes
Cooking time about 1 hour

Serves 6

AMERICAN
1 bunch watercress
1lb leaf beet or spinach
1 stalk celery
1 small bunch parsley
1 small bunch chervil
¼ cup butter
salt and pepper
1 carp (about 3lb)
3 egg yolks
Court-bouillon
½ bottle dry white wine
1 onion
1 bay leaf
juice of 1 lemon
6 peppercorns

Trout with almonds

(Truites aux amandes)

Preparation time 15 minutes
Cooking time 15 minutes

Serves 4

METRIC/IMPERIAL
4 trout
salt and pepper
50g/2oz flour
75g/3oz butter
100g/4oz flaked almonds
Garnish
1 lemon, peeled
finely chopped parsley

Gut the trout but leave their heads on. Wash them, dry carefully on absorbent paper, season and toss lightly in flour.

Heat 50g/2oz (US $\frac{1}{4}$ cup) butter in a frying pan; when it begins to turn golden, place the trout in it. Brown them well over a moderate heat; the butter must remain golden. Turn halfway through cooking.

Arrange the trout on a heated serving dish and keep hot.

Add the rest of the butter to the frying pan and use to sauté the flaked almonds. Cook until golden brown then sprinkle over the trout. Pour the juices from the pan over all.

Garnish each trout with two lemon slices and sprinkle one of these with chopped parsley.

Serve very hot.

 a Chablis (dry white)

Preparation time 15 minutes
Cooking time 15 minutes

Serves 4

AMERICAN
4 trout
salt and pepper
$\frac{1}{2}$ cup all-purpose flour
6 tablespoons butter
1 cup flaked almonds
Garnish
1 lemon, peeled
finely chopped parsley

Trout with walnut stuffing
(Truites farcies aux noix)

Preparation time 25 minutes
Cooking time 18 minutes

Serves 4

METRIC/IMPERIAL
4 trout
50g/2oz butter
salt and pepper
Stuffing
100g/4oz walnuts
2 shallots
1 small bunch parsley
100g/4oz dried breadcrumbs
1 teaspoon freshly ground pepper
125g/4½oz slightly salted butter
Garnish
4 walnut halves
1 lemon
chopped parsley

Gut the trout but keep their heads on. Wash and dry them carefully.

Prepare the stuffing. Grind or blend the walnuts to reduce them to fine crumbs. Chop the peeled shallots and the parsley. Mix these ingredients with the breadcrumbs, ground pepper and the butter cut into small pieces, to obtain an even mixture.

Fill the trout with this stuffing, reserving some for garnish.

Lightly brown the butter in a frying pan. Place the stuffed trout in this butter and cook them over a moderate heat. Season and leave to brown well before turning over.

Arrange the trout on a heated serving dish. Place a little of the reserved stuffing on each one. Place in a warm oven briefly to soften the stuffing. Finally garnish each trout with a walnut half and the dish with two lemon halves. Sprinkle with chopped parsley.

 a Saint Pourçain (dry white)

Preparation time 25 minutes
Cooking time 18 minutes

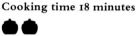

Serves 4

AMERICAN
4 trout
¼ cup butter
salt and pepper
Stuffing
1 cup walnuts
2 shallots
1 small bunch parsley
1 cup dry bread crumbs
1 teaspoon freshly ground pepper
½ cup plus 1 tablespoon slightly salted butter
Garnish
4 walnut halves
1 lemon
chopped parsley

Salmon trout with wine sauce (Truite saumonée à la Nordique)

Preparation time 30 minutes
Cooking time 45 minutes

Serves 4–5

METRIC/IMPERIAL
6 shallots
100 g/4 oz button mushrooms
1 tablespoon lemon juice
1 small salmon trout (about 1 kg/2 lb)
40 g/1½ oz butter
600 ml/1 pint dry white wine
300 ml/½ pint fish stock
salt and pepper
Sauce
100 g/4 oz butter
50 g/2 oz flour
150 ml/¼ pint double cream
50 g/2 oz smoked salmon
Garnish
2 lemons
3 thin strips smoked salmon
parsley

Peel and finely chop the shallots. Wash and wipe the mushrooms, chop them and sprinkle with the lemon juice.

Gut and wash the salmon trout. Generously butter a long ovenproof dish and cover the bottom with the chopped shallots and mushrooms. Place the salmon trout over these ingredients and cover with the white wine and fish stock. Season lightly, cover and cook in a moderately hot oven (190°C, 375°F, Gas Mark 5) for 30 minutes. Gently transfer the trout to a hot serving dish, and keep warm in the oven, which is switched off but still hot. Reduce the fish cooking liquor to 450 ml/¾ pint (US 2 cups), by open boiling over a moderate heat.

Prepare the sauce. Make a white roux with half the butter and the flour. Stir in the reduced fish liquor and cook for 10 minutes, stirring continuously. Add the cream and cook gently for a further 5 minutes. Prepare a salmon butter by mixing the rest of the butter with the finely minced smoked salmon. Draw the pan off the heat and stir this butter into the sauce. Taste and adjust for seasoning.

Skin the salmon trout, pour over the sauce and serve any remaining sauce separately. Garnish with lemon slices and halves, the strips of salmon and chopped parsley.

 a Sancerre (dry white)

Preparation time 30 minutes
Cooking time 45 minutes

Serves 4–5

AMERICAN
6 shallots
¼ lb button mushrooms
1 tablespoon lemon juice
1 small salmon trout (about 2 lb)
3 tablespoons butter
2½ cups dry white wine
1¼ cups fish stock
salt and pepper
Sauce
½ cup butter
½ cup all-purpose flour
⅔ cup heavy cream
2 oz smoked salmon
Garnish
2 lemons
3 thin strips smoked salmon
parsley

Salmon with cream sauce

(Saumon braisé au Quincy)

Preparation time 15 minutes
Cooking time 1 hour

Serves 6

METRIC/IMPERIAL
75 g/3 oz butter
5 shallots, chopped
1.5 kg/3 lb fresh salmon
1 bottle dry white wine
salt and pepper
1 bouquet garni
3 slices stale white bread
6 egg yolks
300 ml/½ pint double cream

Set the oven to moderate(160°C, 325°F, Gas Mark 3).

Heat 25 g/1 oz (US 2 tablespoons) butter in a flameproof casserole. Add the chopped shallots and cook until golden. Place the salmon on top of the shallots, pour in the white wine and add salt, pepper and the bouquet garni. Dot the fish with a few knobs of butter. Cover the casserole and cook in the oven for 35–45 minutes. Baste several times during cooking. At the end of this time, remove the fish from the casserole, skin it and arrange on a heated serving dish. Cover with a sheet of foil and keep warm in a low oven.

Remove the bouquet garni from the casserole and reduce the cooking liquor over a brisk heat on top of the oven for a few minutes. Then reduce the heat.

Cut the slices of bread into triangles, removing the crusts. Quickly fry them in the rest of the butter then set aside.

Beat the egg yolks with the cream. Pour this mixture into the reduced cooking liquor and continue to beat over a very gentle heat until the sauce is light and foamy.

Pour this sauce over the salmon. Garnish with the fried bread croûtons and serve immediately.

 a Quincy (very dry white)

Preparation time 15 minutes
Cooking time 1 hour

Serves 6

AMERICAN
6 tablespoons butter
5 shallots, chopped
3 lb fresh salmon
1 bottle dry white wine
salt and pepper
1 bouquet garni
3 slices stale white bread
6 egg yolks
1¼ cups heavy cream

Oven-baked bream

(Dorade Félicie)

Preparation time 20 minutes
Cooking time 30-40 minutes

Serves 4

METRIC/IMPERIAL
1 (1.25-kg/2½-lb) bream, gutted
4 onions
225g/8oz mushrooms
575g/1¼lb very small potatoes
50g/2oz butter
1 bay leaf
250ml/8fl oz dry white wine
350ml/12fl oz hot water or fish
stock
salt and pepper
breadcrumbs to sprinkle
Garnish
chopped parsley

Wash and wipe the bream. Peel and finely slice the onions. Clean and finely chop the mushrooms. Peel the potatoes.

Butter an ovenproof earthenware dish. Cover the base with the onions and bay leaf. Place the bream over these and surround with the potatoes and mushrooms. Pour over the wine and water or fish stock. Season. Sprinkle the fish with breadcrumbs and dot all over with the rest of the butter. Cook in a moderately hot oven (200°C, 400°F, Gas Mark 6) for 30–40 minutes.

Serve very hot sprinkled with parsley.

 a Gros Plant (dry white)

Preparation time 20 minutes
Cooking time 30-40 minutes

Serves 4

AMERICAN
1 (2½-lb) bream or other firm white
fish, gutted
4 onions
½lb mushrooms
1¼lb very small potatoes
¼ cup butter
1 bay leaf
1 cup dry white wine
1½ cups hot water or fish stock
salt and pepper
bread crumbs to sprinkle
Garnish
chopped parsley

Fish with saffron sauce

(Poisson au safran)

Preparation time 35 minutes
Cooking time 45 minutes

Serves 5

METRIC/IMPERIAL
10 red mullet (cut into pieces)
salt and pepper
flour to toss
0.75 kg/1½ lb onions
1 tomato
200 ml/7 fl oz olive oil
2 cloves garlic
1 bouquet garni
generous pinch of saffron
600 ml/1 pint boiling water
10 medium potatoes
Garnish
chopped parsley

Wash and dry the pieces of fish. Season with salt and pepper then toss in flour.

Peel and quarter the onions and tomato. Remove the tomato seeds. Heat 2 tablespoons (US 3 tablespoons) oil in a shallow frying pan, tip in the quartered onions and tomato. Add the crushed garlic and bouquet garni. Leave the vegetables to soften over a moderate heat, without browning.

Sprinkle the mixture with the saffron. Pour on the boiling water, season and bring to the boil. Add the peeled potatoes, cover and cook for 30 minutes.

Meanwhile, heat the rest of the oil in a frying pan and lightly brown the pieces of fish on all sides. Drain. 8 minutes before serving, add them to the saffron sauce. Do not allow to boil any more.

Drain and arrange the fish on a serving dish. Surround with the potatoes. Remove the bouquet garni from the sauce before pouring over the fish and potatoes. Sprinkle with chopped parsley and serve immediately.

 a white Cassis (dry)

Preparation time 35 minutes
Cooking time 45 minutes

Serves 5

AMERICAN
1 red snapper (cut into pieces)
salt and pepper
flour to toss
1½ lb onions
1 tomato
¾ cup olive oil
2 cloves garlic
1 bouquet garni
generous dash of saffron
2½ cups boiling water
10 medium potatoes
Garnish
chopped parsley

Fried red mullet

(Friture de rougets de roche)

**Preparation time 40 minutes
plus 1 hour marinating time
Cooking time 8 minutes**

Serves 6

METRIC/IMPERIAL
24 small red mullet
2 tablespoons lemon juice
salt and pepper
2 teaspoons dried fennel
5 tablespoons olive oil
2 eggs
flour to coat
dried breadcrumbs to coat
oil for frying
2 lemons

If the mullet are very small do not gut them. In any case do not remove the liver which is delicious. Do not wash either but simply wipe to remove scales. Sprinkle with lemon juice. Season with salt, pepper and dried fennel. Top with 3 tablespoons (US $\frac{1}{4}$ cup) olive oil and leave to marinate for 1 hour.

Beat the eggs with the rest of the olive oil in a shallow dish. Put the flour and breadcrumbs into two similar dishes.

Heat the oil in a frying pan. Dip the mullet in flour, then in beaten egg and finally into breadcrumbs. Leave to dry for a few moments before frying. Brown well for about 4 minutes on both sides and drain on absorbent paper. Serve very hot with lemon quarters.

 a white Cassis (dry)

**Preparation time 40 minutes
plus 1 hour marinating time
Cooking time 8 minutes**

Serves 6

AMERICAN
24 smelts
3 tablespoons lemon juice
salt and pepper
2 teaspoons dried fennel
6 tablespoons olive oil
2 eggs
flour to coat
dry bread crumbs to coat
oil for frying
2 lemons

Turbot fillets Trouville

(Filets de turbot Trouvillaise)

Preparation time 25 minutes
Cooking time 35 minutes

Serves 4-6

METRIC/IMPERIAL
2 turbots (each about 0.75 kg/1½ lb)
salt and freshly ground pepper
1 litre/1¾ pints cockles
1 litre/1¾ pints mussels
50 g/2 oz butter
250 ml/8 fl oz dry white wine
50 g/2 oz flour
100 ml/4 fl oz double cream
150 g/5 oz shelled shrimps
Garnish
chopped parsley

Ask the fishmonger to fillet the turbot. Wash and wipe the fish and season with salt and freshly ground pepper.

Carefully sort the cockles and mussels, discarding any which do not close when given a sharp tap; scrape the mussels. Wash them all and drain well.

Open in separate pans with a little added water. When open, drain. Strain the cooking juices through muslin. Remove the mussels and cockles from their shells.

Set the oven to hot (220°C, 425°F, Gas Mark 7).

Grease an ovenproof dish with a little butter and arrange the turbot fillets in it. Add the mussel and cockle juices and white wine. The liquid should cover the fish; if necessary top up with a little water. Season. Place in the oven and cook for 15–20 minutes.

When the fish is cooked, strain off 450 ml/¾ pint (US 2 cups) of the cooking liquor. Keep the fish hot.

Melt the rest of the butter, sprinkle with the flour and mix over a gentle heat. Thin this roux with the fish liquor and cook for 8–9 minutes, stirring continually. Then add the cream and cook for a further minute. Finally add the cockles, mussels and shelled shrimps.

Drain the turbot fillets and arrange on a heated serving dish. Pour over the sauce and sprinkle with chopped parsley. Serve immediately.

 a Graves (dry white)

Preparation time 25 minutes
Cooking time 35 minutes

Serves 4-6

AMERICAN
2 turbots (each about 1½ lb)
salt and freshly ground pepper
2 pints cockles
2 pints mussels
¼ cup butter
1 cup dry white wine
½ cup all-purpose flour
½ cup heavy cream
5 oz shelled shrimp
Garnish
chopped parsley

Skate in black butter

(Raie au beurre noir)

Preparation time 20 minutes
Cooking time 25 minutes

Serves 4

METRIC/IMPERIAL
about 1.25 kg/2½ lb wing of skate
250 ml/8 fl oz vinegar
1 bay leaf
1 bunch parsley
sea salt
Sauce
100 g/4 oz butter
1 tablespoon lemon juice
4 tablespoons capers
salt and pepper
Garnish
chopped parsley
1 lemon

Wash the skate in cold water to rid it of the slimy coating which covers it. Rinse in a mixture of water and half the vinegar. Drain and cut into 4 portions.

Poach the fish in a saucepan of cold water with the rest of the vinegar, bay leaf, parsley and sea salt. Simmer over a gentle heat for 20 minutes.

Meanwhile, make the sauce. Cut the butter into small pieces, tip into a saucepan and heat. As soon as it turns light brown in colour, add the lemon juice and then the capers. Season.

Drain the skate, trim and remove its skin. Arrange on a heated serving dish, pour over the butter sauce and sprinkle with chopped parsley. Garnish the dish with lemon wedges.

 a Gros Plant (dry white)

Preparation time 20 minutes
Cooking time 25 minutes

Serves 4

AMERICAN
about 2½ lb swordfish
1 cup vinegar
1 bay leaf
1 bunch parsley
coarse salt
Sauce
½ cup butter
1 tablespoon lemon juice
⅓ cup capers
salt and pepper
Garnish
chopped parsley
1 lemon

Fish en croûte

Preparation time 40 minutes
Cooking time 1 hour 10 minutes

Serves 6-8

METRIC/IMPERIAL
2 eggs
50g/2oz plain flour
150ml/¼ pint milk
50g/2oz butter
100g/4oz mushrooms
350g/12oz fillets of whiting
3 shallots
3 tablespoons dry white wine
3 tablespoons brandy
1 tablespoon chopped parsley
1 tablespoon chopped chives
salt and pepper
450g/1lb puff pastry

Break the eggs, separating the yolks from the whites. Mix the flour with the yolks and the hot milk. Add half the butter and thicken the sauce over a gentle heat, stirring continuously with a wooden spoon. Leave to cool.

Soften the finely sliced mushrooms in the rest of the hot butter.

Cut a third of the whiting fillets into small even dice. Chop the shallots. Drain the mushrooms and, in the same butter, brown the shallots and the diced whiting. Drain. Add the white wine to the pan juices and reduce by half over a brisk heat. Stir in the brandy.

Mince the rest of the fish to obtain a very fine purée. Mix this with the cooled sauce and the unbeaten egg whites. Beat the mixture well until very smooth, then add the mushrooms, shallots, diced whiting, reduced wine, parsley and chives. Season.

Roll out the puff pastry quite thinly and cut two pieces in the shape of a large fish. Spread the stuffing over one of these pieces and cover with the second. Mark in patterns with a knife, if liked. Moisten the edges and pinch together to seal. Brush the top with a little milk, or egg yolk thinned with water.

Cook for 20 minutes in a hot oven (220°C, 425°F, Gas Mark 7) then reduce to moderately hot (190°C, 375°F, Gas Mark 5) for a further 30 minutes. Serve at once.

 a Chablis (dry white)

Preparation time 40 minutes
Cooking time 1 hour 10 minutes

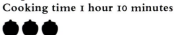

Serves 6-8

AMERICAN
2 eggs
½ cup all-purpose flour
⅔ cup milk
¼ cup butter
¼lb mushrooms
¾lb fillet of cod
3 shallots
¼ cup dry white wine
¼ cup brandy
1 tablespoon chopped parsley
1 tablespoon chopped chives
salt and pepper
1lb puff paste

Stuffed calamares

(Calmars farcis)

Preparation time 40 minutes
Cooking time 1 hour 40 minutes

Serves 6

METRIC/IMPERIAL
6 calamares
3 onions
4 tablespoons olive oil
0.5 kg/1 lb ripe tomatoes
1 small bouquet garni
1 clove garlic
100 ml/4 fl oz dry white wine
salt and pepper
Stuffing
100 g/4 oz long-grain rice
100 g/4 oz raisins
4 onions
3 tablespoons oil
150 g/5 oz smoked streaky bacon
3 cloves garlic
chopped parsley

Empty the calamares without tearing the pocket, clean, wash and dry them carefully. Cut off the tentacles and reserve for the stuffing.

Prepare the stuffing. Wash the rice and cook for 10 minutes in boiling salted water. Rinse under cold water and dry. Meanwhile, soak the raisins in water, rinse and dry well.

Brown the chopped onions in hot oil, add the finely chopped bacon and the calamares tentacles and cook for a few minutes. Add the chopped garlic, parsley, raisins and rice. Season and mix well together.

Fill the fish with this stuffing and secure with a wooden cocktail stick.

Finely chop the onions and brown in the hot oil. Add the peeled and deseeded tomatoes, breaking them up with a wooden spoon. Add the bouquet garni and crushed garlic and cook for 15 minutes. Strain.

Pour the sauce into a flameproof casserole, stir in the white wine and season to taste.

Add the calamares, coat with the sauce, cover the casserole and simmer over a gentle heat for 1 hour.

 a Graves (dry white)

Preparation time 40 minutes
Cooking time 1 hour 40 minutes

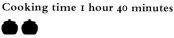

Serves 6

AMERICAN
6 squid
3 onions
⅓ cup olive oil
1 lb ripe tomatoes
1 small bouquet garni
1 clove garlic
½ cup dry white wine
salt and pepper
Stuffing
½ cup long-grain rice
¾ cup seeded raisins
4 onions
¼ cup oil
7–8 bacon slices
3 cloves garlic
chopped parsley

Paella

(La paella)

Preparation time 30 minutes
Cooking time 1 hour 10 minutes

Serves 8

METRIC/IMPERIAL
1 chicken
1.4 litres/2 pints large mussels
3 onions
2 cloves garlic
225 g/8 oz French beans
3 green peppers
4 tomatoes
175 ml/6 fl oz olive oil
8 Dublin Bay prawns
8 small crawfish (optional)
225 g/8 oz small shelled peas
generous pinch of saffron
350 g/12 oz long-grain rice
salt and pepper

Cut the chicken into small pieces and season. Clean the mussels, discarding any which do not close when tapped. Finely slice the onions, crush the garlic, cut the French beans into short sticks and the peppers into thin strips. Peel and deseed the tomatoes and crush the flesh.

Heat the oil over a moderate heat in a paella pan or large frying pan. Fry the pieces of chicken, turning until well browned, then drain and set aside. Keep warm.

In the same oil, cook the onions and garlic. Let them brown slightly, then take out and keep hot with the chicken.

Still in the same oil, brown the unpeeled prawns and crawfish, if used. Cook for 3–4 minutes only then remove.

Sauté the peppers then the tomatoes in the oil.

Place the following ingredients in the paella pan: chicken, onions, garlic, peppers and tomatoes. Moisten with 300 ml/½ pint (US 1¼ cups) boiling water, add the peas and French beans and leave to cook for 20 minutes.

Then add the saffron and rice, spreading it evenly in the pan. Pour on boiling water equal to twice the volume of the rice and season. Arrange on top of the dish the mussels, prawns and crawfish and continue cooking without moving the rice. As soon as the rice is cooked, serve in the paella pan.

 a Côtes-de-Provence rosé

Preparation time 30 minutes
Cooking time 1 hour 10 minutes

Serves 8

AMERICAN
1 chicken
2½ pints large mussels
3 onions
2 cloves garlic
½ lb green beans
3 green peppers
4 tomatoes
¾ cup olive oil
8 jumbo shrimp
8 small crayfish (optional)
1½ cups shelled peas
generous dash of saffron
1½ cups long-grain rice
salt and pepper

Deep-fried scampi

(Beignets de langoustines)

Preparation time 20 minutes
plus 2 hours marinating time
Cooking time 15 minutes

Serves 4

METRIC/IMPERIAL
1.5 kg/3 lb unpeeled Dublin Bay
prawns or scampi
salt and pepper
juice of 1 lemon
1 tablespoon chopped chives
3 tablespoons oil
oil for deep frying
Batter
250 g/9 oz plain flour
pinch of salt
2 tablespoons oil
350 ml/12 fl oz warm water
2 egg whites
Tartare sauce
250 ml/8 fl oz mayonnaise
(see page 314)
2 tablespoons capers
2 gherkins
2 tablespoons chopped tarragon
and chives
1 tablespoon chopped parsley

Peel the prawns or scampi. Place in a bowl, season and sprinkle with the lemon juice. Add the chopped chives and 3 tablespoons (US ¼ cup) oil and leave to marinate for 2 hours.

Prepare the batter which must also be left to stand for 2 hours. Sift the flour and salt into a large bowl and make a well in the centre. Pour in the oil and mix well with the warm water, until smooth. Leave to stand.

Before cooking prepare the sauce. Turn the mayonnaise into a bowl and add the capers, chopped gherkins, tarragon, chives and parsley.

Heat the oil for frying in a deep pan.

Whisk the egg whites until stiff and fold into the prepared batter. Use this batter immediately. Dip the scampi in the batter to form fritters. Add one by one to the hot oil. Allow to turn golden and puff up. Drain on absorbent paper and pile into a serving dish. Serve with the tartare sauce.

 a Bandol (light red)

Preparation time 20 minutes
plus 2 hours marinating time
Cooking time 15 minutes

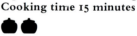

Serves 4

AMERICAN
3 lb jumbo shrimp
salt and pepper
juice of 1 lemon
1 tablespoon chopped chives
¼ cup oil
oil for deep frying
Batter
2¼ cups all-purpose flour
dash of salt
3 tablespoons oil
1½ cups warm water
2 egg whites
Tartare sauce
1 cup mayonnaise (see page 314)
3 tablespoons capers
2 sweet dill pickles
3 tablespoons chopped tarragon
and chives
1 tablespoon chopped parsley

Scampi kebabs

(Brochettes de langoustines)

**Preparation time 30 minutes
plus 2 hours marinating time
Cooking time 30 minutes**

Serves 6

METRIC/IMPERIAL
**60 unpeeled Dublin Bay prawns or
scampi
½ teaspoon dried fennel
½ teaspoon powdered thyme
pinch of powdered bay leaves
salt and freshly ground pepper
juice of 2 lemons
2 tablespoons oil
flour to coat
2 eggs, beaten
75g/3oz fresh breadcrumbs
melted butter**
Sauce
**3 onions
4 tablespoons olive oil
3 tablespoons brandy
1 small bouquet garni
1 sugar lump
3 tablespoons tomato purée
450ml/¾ pint dry white wine
pinch of cayenne**

Peel the scampi and place in a bowl. Reserve the claws and shells. Season the scampi with the fennel, thyme, bay leaves and salt and pepper. Sprinkle over the lemon juice and oil and marinate for 2 hours.

Prepare the sauce. Brown the chopped onions in hot olive oil. Add the scampi claws and shells. Cook until firm over a brisk heat then pour on the brandy and flame. Add the bouquet garni, sugar, tomato purée and white wine. Season with salt and pepper and a pinch of cayenne. Cook for 20 minutes and strain just before serving.

Meanwhile, drain the scampi and thread them lengthwise on skewers. Dip into flour, then into beaten egg and finally coat with breadcrumbs. Leave to dry.

Brush with melted butter and cook under the grill, or deep fry before threading on to skewers, until golden brown. Serve the kebabs immediately with the hot sauce.

 a Tavel (rosé)

**Preparation time 30 minutes
plus 2 hours marinating time
Cooking time 30 minutes**

Serves 6

AMERICAN
**60 unshelled jumbo shrimp
½ teaspoon dried fennel
½ teaspoon powdered thyme
dash of powdered bay leaves
salt and freshly ground pepper
juice of 2 lemons
3 tablespoons oil
flour to coat
2 eggs, beaten
1½ cups fresh soft bread crumbs
melted butter**
Sauce
**3 onions
⅓ cup olive oil
¼ cup brandy
1 small bouquet garni
1 sugar cube
¼ cup tomato paste
2 cups dry white wine
dash of cayenne pepper**

Skewered mussels

(Brochettes de moules)

Preparation time 20 minutes
Cooking time 15 minutes

Serves 6

METRIC/IMPERIAL
2 litres/3½ pints mussels
2 eggs
flour to coat
50 g/2 oz fresh breadcrumbs
oil for deep frying
Remoulade sauce
1 shallot
2 gherkins
1 small bunch mixed herbs
(chervil, parsley, chives,
tarragon)
1 tablespoon capers
250 ml/8 fl oz mayonnaise
(see page 314)

Scrape and wash the mussels, discarding any which do not close when given a sharp tap. Drain well. Place in a saucepan with a little water. Cover and set over a high heat, shaking the pan in order to make the mussels open. Discard any that remain closed. When open, drain and remove from shells.

Break the eggs into a shallow dish, beat well and add 2 tablespoons (US 3 tablespoons) water.

Place the flour and breadcrumbs in two shallow dishes.

Thread the mussels on to wooden cocktail sticks. Roll each small skewer in flour, then in beaten egg and finally in breadcrumbs. Leave to dry while the sauce is prepared.

Finely chop the shallot, gherkins and herbs. Add with the capers to the mayonnaise. Transfer to a sauceboat and sprinkle with chopped chives.

Heat the oil for frying. When very hot toss in the mussel skewers. Cook until golden brown, drain on absorbent paper, then quickly arrange on the serving dish. Stick a few of the skewers into a lemon.

Serve immediately accompanied by the remoulade sauce.

 a Sylvaner (fruity dry white)

Preparation time 20 minutes
Cooking time 15 minutes

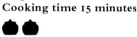

Serves 6

AMERICAN
4 pints mussels
2 eggs
flour to coat
1 cup fresh soft bread crumbs
oil for deep frying
Remoulade sauce
1 shallot
2 sweet dill pickles
1 small bunch mixed herbs
(chervil, parsley, chives,
tarragon)
1 tablespoon capers
1 cup mayonnaise (see page 314)

Crawfish croûtes

(Croûtes aux écrevisses)

Preparation time 1 hour
Cooking time 45 minutes

Serves 4

METRIC/IMPERIAL
1 carrot
2 onions
1 stick celery
90g/3½oz butter
1 small bouquet garni
24 cooked crawfish or large prawns
3 tablespoons brandy
½ bottle dry white wine
25g/1oz flour
150ml/¼ pint single cream
pinch of cayenne
salt and pepper
Croûtes
**1 small loaf stale white bread,
crusts removed**
oil for deep frying
Garnish
parsley

Dice the carrot, finely chop the onions and celery. Soften these ingredients in 50g/2oz (US ¼ cup) melted butter in a large frying pan. Add the bouquet garni for flavour and cook until golden, stirring continuously.

Wash the crawfish, reserve 8 for garnish, shell the remainder and discard the intestines. When the vegetables begin to brown remove the bouquet garni and add the crawfish. Cook over a high heat. Sprinkle with the brandy and flame. Add the white wine and cook gently for 15 minutes.

Prepare the croûtes. Cut 4 thick slices of bread from the loaf, each about 5cm/2 inches wide. Hollow them out, leaving at least 1cm/½ inch bread at the base and sides.

Remove the crawfish from the pan. Liquidise the sauce in a blender and then press through a sieve.

Melt the remaining butter over a low heat and stir in the flour to make a roux. Gradually stir in the blended wine sauce. Add the cream and crawfish and cook over a gentle heat for 10 minutes, stirring continuously; do not allow to boil. Add a pinch of cayenne and season to taste.

Heat the oil to 180°C/360°F, until a cube of bread turns golden in under 1 minute. Fry the croûtes, drain and fill with the crawfish mixture. Arrange on a heated serving dish and garnish with the whole crawfish and parsley.

 a Sauvignon (white)

Preparation time 1 hour
Cooking time 45 minutes

Serves 4

AMERICAN
1 carrot
2 onions
1 stalk celery
7 tablespoons butter
1 small bouquet garni
**24 cooked crayfish or jumbo
shrimp**
¼ cup brandy
½ bottle dry white wine
¼ cup all-purpose flour
⅔ cup light cream
dash of cayenne pepper
salt and pepper
Croûtes
**1 small loaf stale white bread,
crusts removed**
oil for deep frying
Garnish
parsley

Crawfish Américaine

(Langoustines à l'Américaine)

Preparation time 30 minutes
Cooking time 40 minutes

Serves 4

METRIC/IMPERIAL
1 kg/2lb crawfish or Dublin Bay
prawns
4 tablespoons olive oil
2 onions
6 shallots
3 tablespoons brandy
1 small clove garlic
2 sprigs of parsley
4 tablespoons fresh tomato sauce
(or 3 very ripe tomatoes, peeled,
seeded and crushed)
150 ml/¼ pint medium dry white
wine

Wash the crawfish and dry well on absorbent paper. Fry in the hot oil until firm. Drain.

In the same oil cook the chopped onions over a low heat, stirring with a wooden spoon. When they begin to turn golden add the chopped shallots and cook until soft.

Return the crawfish to the pan, warm through for a few minutes, sprinkle with the brandy and flame. Then add the crushed garlic, parsley, fresh tomato sauce, white wine, salt and plenty of freshly ground pepper. Heighten the seasoning with a little cayenne and cook for 10 minutes.

Drain the crawfish and arrange on a heated serving dish. Return the sauce to a high heat and add the butter cut into small pieces. Beat for 2 minutes with a wire whisk, pour over the crawfish and sprinkle with chopped parsley. Serve accompanied by pilaf rice.

 a Riesling (fruity white)

Preparation time 30 minutes
Cooking time 40 minutes

Serves 4

AMERICAN
2lb crayfish or jumbo shrimp
⅓ cup olive oil
2 onions
6 shallots
¼ cup brandy
1 small clove garlic
2 sprigs of parsley
⅓ cup fresh tomato sauce (or 3 very
ripe tomatoes, peeled, seeded
and crushed)
⅔ cup medium dry white wine
salt and freshly ground pepper
dash of cayenne pepper
¼ cup butter
Garnish
chopped parsley

Crawfish in port

(Langoustines au porto)

Preparation time 10 minutes
Cooking time 20 minutes

Serves 6

METRIC/IMPERIAL
30 unpeeled crawfish or Dublin Bay
prawns
75 g/3 oz butter
3 tablespoons brandy
1 tablespoon chopped shallots
100 ml/4 fl oz port
2 egg yolks
200 ml/7 fl oz double cream
½ teaspoon made English mustard
salt
pinch of cayenne

Wash the crawfish well and dry on absorbent paper. Heat the butter in a frying pan and brown the unpeeled crawfish. Stir well so they are completely sealed.

Warm the brandy in a small pan, pour over the crawfish and flame at once. Shake the pan well so that all the alcohol burns.

Add the chopped shallots and allow to colour slightly. Pour in the port and cook gently for 8–10 minutes.

Beat the egg yolks with the cream and mustard. Pour into a small saucepan and stir gently over a low heat, without boiling. Season with salt and a pinch of cayenne.

Arrange the crawfish on a heated dish, pour over the sauce and serve at once. Hand finger bowls separately.

 a Riesling (fruity white)

Preparation time 10 minutes
Cooking time 20 minutes

Serves 6

AMERICAN
30 unshelled crayfish or jumbo
shrimp
6 tablespoons butter
¼ cup brandy
1 tablespoon chopped shallots
½ cup port
2 egg yolks
¾ cup heavy cream
½ teaspoon prepared English
mustard
salt
dash of cayenne pepper

Créole stuffed crab

(Crabes farcis Créole)

Preparation time 40 minutes
Cooking time 25 minutes

Serves 4

METRIC/IMPERIAL
4 small crabs
6 shallots
4 onions
75 g/3 oz butter
225 g/8 oz mushrooms
2 cloves garlic
2 slices ham
1 tablespoon lemon juice
100 g/4 oz desiccated coconut
1 tablespoon chopped parsley
1 tablespoon vinegar
pinch of chilli powder
75 g/3 oz fresh breadcrumbs,
moistened with milk and
squeezed
1 egg
5 tablespoons rum
salt and pepper
4 tablespoons dried breadcrumbs
Garnish
sprigs of watercress

Wash the crabs and dry on absorbent paper. Remove the claws and legs from the crabs and take out all the white flesh. Using the point of a sharp knife, make an incision under the shell and pull until the body comes away from the shell. Discard the grey 'dead men's fingers' and the pouch, as these are poisonous. Take out the creamy brown meat and reserve.

Soften the chopped shallots and onions in 50 g/2 oz (US ¼ cup) melted butter. Add the finely chopped mushrooms and cook for several minutes, stirring. Then add the chopped garlic and ham, the crabmeat, lemon juice, coconut, parsley, vinegar mixed with the chilli powder, the moistened breadcrumbs, beaten egg and 2 tablespoons (US 3 tablespoons) rum. Add salt and pepper and heat through for a few minutes, stirring with a wooden spoon.

Rinse the empty crab shells and fill with this stuffing. Sprinkle with the dried breadcrumbs and the rest of the melted butter and brown in a moderately hot oven (190°C, 375°F, Gas Mark 5) for 10–15 minutes.

Arrange the crabs on a serving dish, garnish with watercress, sprinkle with the rest of the hot rum and flame at the table.

 a Riesling (fruity white)

Preparation time 40 minutes
Cooking time 25 minutes

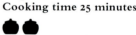

Serves 4

AMERICAN
4 small crabs
6 shallots
4 onions
6 tablespoons butter
½ lb mushrooms
2 cloves garlic
2 slices cooked ham
1 tablespoon lemon juice
1⅓ cups shredded coconut
1 tablespoon chopped parsley
1 tablespoon vinegar
dash of chili powder
1½ cups fresh soft bread crumbs,
moistened with milk and
squeezed
1 egg
6 tablespoons rum
salt and pepper
⅓ cup dry bread crumbs
Garnish
sprigs of watercress

Breton-style crab

(Tourteau à la Bretonne)

Preparation time 1 hour

Serves 5-6

METRIC/IMPERIAL
1 large crab
4 tablespoons oil
2 tablespoons vinegar
4 shallots
3 spring onions
1 clove garlic
3 tablespoons chopped parsley
Garnish
1 egg, hard-boiled
2-3 tablespoons mayonnaise
(see page 314)
lettuce leaves
2 tomatoes
chopped parsley

Wash the crab and dry on absorbent paper. Remove the claws and legs and take out all the white flesh and reserve. Using the point of a sharp knife, make an incision under the shell and pull until the body comes away from the shell. Discard the grey 'dead men's fingers' and the pouch, as these are poisonous. Take out the creamy brown meat from the body shell and combine it with the oil and vinegar. Add the chopped shallots, spring onions and garlic with the parsley and two-thirds of the white crab-meat.

Fill the shell with this mixture and cover with the rest of the white meat. Garnish the top with sliced hard-boiled egg topped with mayonnaise.

Arrange on a dish lined with lettuce leaves, surround with tomato quarters topped with mayonnaise and sprinkled with chopped parsley.

 a Muscadet (dry white)

Preparation time 1 hour

Serves 5-6

AMERICAN
1 large crab
⅓ cup oil
3 tablespoons vinegar
4 shallots
3 scallions
1 clove garlic
¼ cup chopped parsley
Garnish
1 egg, hard-cooked
about ¼ cup mayonnaise
(see page 314)
lettuce leaves
2 tomatoes
chopped parsley

Seafood fondue

(La fondue marine)

**Preparation time 30 minutes
plus 1 hour marinating time
Cooking time 40 minutes**

Serves 8–10

METRIC/IMPERIAL
8–10 small scallops
0.75 kg/1½ lb unpeeled Dublin Bay
prawns
1 kg/2 lb cod
salt and pepper
juice of 1 lemon
2 tablespoons oil
1.25 litres/2¼ pints mussels
450 ml/¾ pint mayonnaise
(see page 314)
2 tablespoons tomato ketchup
2 tablespoons chopped mixed herbs
Stock
1 kg/2 lb heads, bones and fish
trimmings
4 sprigs of parsley
1 onion stuck with 2 cloves
1 carrot, thinly sliced
1 lemon, quartered
1 bottle dry white wine

Discard the small black membrane attached to the scallops. Wash the flesh carefully and wipe. Peel the prawns. Wash and wipe the cod and dice. Place all these ingredients in a large deep dish and season with salt and pepper. Add the lemon juice and oil and leave to marinate for 1 hour. Meanwhile pick out and scrape the mussels, discarding any which do not close when tapped. Wash and open them over a high heat in a little water. Drain and remove from their shells. Strain the cooking juices.

Place all the ingredients for the stock in a pan. Add the mussel juices, season and cook gently for 40 minutes. The stock should reduce only by one-third.

Meanwhile thread the marinated fish, prawns, scallops and mussels on to small wooden skewers. Leave one-third of the mayonnaise as it is, season the second with tomato ketchup and the third with the freshly chopped mixed herbs.

Strain the stock and pour it still boiling into the fondue pot. Place over a table top burner. At the same time serve the skewers and sauces. Each guest plunges a skewer into the boiling stock and seasons with the sauce of his choice.

 a Gros Plant (dry white)

**Preparation time 30 minutes
plus 1 hour marinating time
Cooking time 40 minutes**

Serves 8–10

AMERICAN
8–10 small scallops
1½ lb unshelled jumbo shrimp
2 lb cod
salt and pepper
juice of 1 lemon
3 tablespoons oil
3 pints mussels
2 cups mayonnaise (see page 314)
3 tablespoons tomato ketchup
3 tablespoons chopped mixed herbs
Stock
2 lb heads, bones and fish
trimmings
4 sprigs of parsley
1 onion stuck with 2 cloves
1 carrot, thinly sliced
1 lemon, quartered
1 bottle dry white wine

Seafood pancakes

(Crêpes aux fruits de mer)

**Preparation time 1 hour
plus 2 hours standing time
Cooking time 45 minutes**

Serves 6

METRIC/IMPERIAL
**125 g/4 oz plain flour
pinch of salt
1 tablespoon oil
300 ml/½ pint milk or milk and
water
2 eggs
50 g/2 oz butter**
Filling
**4 shallots
50 g/2 oz butter
225 g/8 oz shelled shrimps or prawns
575 g/1¼ lb haddock
3 tablespoons calvados or brandy
2 litres/3½ pints mussels
1 tablespoon flour
150 ml/¼ pint double cream
1 tablespoon tomato purée
salt and pepper**
Garnish
**chopped parsley
few unshelled shrimps or prawns**

Prepare the pancake batter with the flour, salt, oil and milk (see page 268). Add the beaten eggs and leave to stand for 2 hours. Thin the batter if necessary with a little water and cook 10–12 pancakes, using the butter to fry. Keep hot in a low oven, covered with foil.

Prepare the filling. Cook the chopped shallots in the melted butter. When beginning to turn golden add the shrimps and diced haddock. Cook over a moderate heat and flame with the calvados.

Clean the mussels, place in a heavy-bottomed pan with a little water and open over a high heat. Drain and remove from their shells. Strain the cooking liquor.

Sprinkle the haddock and shrimps with flour. Allow to brown. Add the mussel liquor. Cook for 5 minutes then stir in the cream, tomato purée and mussels. Heat through without boiling and season to taste.

Spread the pancakes with this filling and roll up. Arrange closely on a heated serving dish. Garnish with parsley and shrimps and serve any remaining seafood mixture separately.

 a Pouilly Fuissé (dry white)

**Preparation time 1 hour
plus 2 hours standing time
Cooking time 45 minutes**

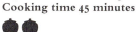

Serves 6

AMERICAN
**1 cup all-purpose flour
dash of salt
1 tablespoon oil
1¼ cups milk or milk and water
2 eggs
¼ cup butter**
Filling
**4 shallots
¼ cup butter
½ lb shelled shrimp
1¼ lb haddock
¼ cup calvados or brandy
4½ pints mussels
1 tablespoon all-purpose flour
⅔ cup heavy cream
1 tablespoon tomato paste
salt and pepper**
Garnish
**chopped parsley
few unshelled shrimp**

Seafood vol-au-vent

(Vol-au-vent marin)

Preparation time 25 minutes
Cooking time 25-30 minutes

Serves 4-5

METRIC/IMPERIAL
2 litres/3½ pints mussels
100 ml/4 fl oz dry white wine
0.5 kg/1 lb cod
225 g/8 oz unpeeled prawns
225 g/8 oz button mushrooms
75 g/3 oz butter
4 shallots
1 tablespoon flour
150 ml/¼ pint double cream
2 teaspoons tomato purée
pinch of cayenne
salt and pepper
1 large cooked vol-au-vent case
Garnish
chopped parsley

Scrape and wash the mussels, discarding any which do not close when given a sharp tap. Open them by boiling over a brisk heat with the white wine. Then remove from their shells and strain and reserve the cooking liquor.

Wash and wipe the cod, cut it into dice. Peel the prawns, keeping a few unpeeled for garnish.

Clean the mushrooms, wash and slice them finely, then cook until golden in 25 g/1 oz (US 2 tablespoons) butter.

Brown the chopped shallots in the rest of the hot butter. When they are scarcely beginning to turn golden, add the diced cod and seal over a brisk heat. Add the peeled prawns, sprinkle with the flour and mix carefully with a wooden spoon. Moisten this roux with the liquor from the mussels and cook for 5 minutes, stirring continuously. Then add the cream, mussels, tomato purée and cayenne and simmer for 2 minutes. Taste and adjust the seasoning.

Heat the vol-au-vent case in a moderate oven (180°C, 350°F, Gas Mark 4) for 10 minutes and fill it just before serving. Sprinkle with parsley and garnish the dish with the unpeeled prawns.

a Muscadet (dry white)

Preparation time 25 minutes
Cooking time 25-30 minutes

Serves 4-5

AMERICAN
4 pints mussels
½ cup dry white wine
1 lb cod
½ lb unshelled shrimp
½ lb button mushrooms
6 tablespoons butter
4 shallots
1 tablespoon all-purpose flour
⅔ cup heavy cream
2 teaspoons tomato paste
dash of cayenne pepper
salt and pepper
1 large cooked vol-au-vent case
Garnish
chopped parsley

Seafood brioche

(Brioche aux fruits de mer)

Preparation time 35 minutes
Cooking time 35 minutes

Serves 4

METRIC/IMPERIAL
1 large round brioche (see note)
Filling
6 scallops
1 sprig of thyme
2 sprigs of parsley
250 ml/8 fl oz dry white wine
100 ml/4 fl oz fish stock
salt and freshly ground pepper
0.5 kg/1 lb unpeeled Dublin Bay prawns or scampi
50 g/2 oz butter
4 shallots
150 g/5 oz shelled shrimps
3 tablespoons brandy or calvados
20 g/¾ oz flour
100 ml/4 fl oz double cream

First prepare the filling. Remove the edible portion of each scallop, discarding the black thread and membrane. Wash under cold running water. Place in a saucepan with the thyme, parsley, white wine and fish stock. Season. Bring slowly to the boil and simmer for 7–8 minutes, then strain and reserve the stock. Cut the scallops into large cubes.

Peel the prawns or scampi. Heat the butter in a small frying pan and add the finely chopped shallots. Cook until soft, stirring with a wooden spoon. Do not allow to brown. When ready add the prawns and shrimps. Cook until firm then pour on the brandy and flame. Sprinkle over the flour and mix with a wooden spoon. Moisten this roux with the reserved scallop stock. Cook gently for 2–3 minutes, stirring continually, then add the cream and scallops. Cook for a further 3–4 minutes. Do not allow to boil.

Cut a lid off the brioche and carefully scoop out the centre. Place the loaf in a cool oven (150°C, 300°F, Gas Mark 2) for 10–15 minutes to heat through.

Just before serving fill the brioche with the seafood mixture and replace the lid. Serve immediately very hot.

Note In France a brioche is an enriched bread made from a light yeast dough. For this recipe use a bought cottage loaf.

 a Muscadet (dry white)

Preparation time 35 minutes
Cooking time 35 minutes

Serves 4

AMERICAN
1 large round brioche (see note)
Filling
6 scallops
1 sprig of thyme
2 sprigs of parsley
1 cup dry white wine
½ cup fish stock
salt and freshly ground pepper
1 lb unshelled jumbo shrimp
¼ cup butter
4 shallots
5 oz shelled shrimp
¼ cup brandy or calvados
3 tablespoons all-purpose flour
½ cup heavy cream

Mustard steaks

(Steaks à la moutarde)

Preparation time 5 minutes
Cooking time 10 minutes

Serves 4

METRIC/IMPERIAL
2 rump steaks (each about 350g/12oz)
2 tablespoons strong mustard
1 tablespoon peppercorns
10 thin rashers smoked streaky bacon
75g/3oz butter
2 teaspoons chopped mixed herbs
few drops of tomato ketchup

Preheat the grill.

Brush the steaks on both sides with half the mustard, then sprinkle with the coarsely ground peppercorns.

Quickly seal the steaks under the grill then place them on a hot plate. Cover each with 5 bacon rashers and secure these with wooden cocktail sticks. Return the steaks to the grill and cook for about 3–5 minutes on each side, according to taste.

With a fork, mix the butter with the rest of the mustard and the herbs. Add the ketchup and combine all well together.

Arrange the steaks on a hot serving dish and accompany with the mustard butter.

 a Beaujolais (light fruity red)

Preparation time 5 minutes
Cooking time 10 minutes

Serves 4

AMERICAN
2 rump steaks (each about ¾ lb)
3 tablespoons strong mustard
1 tablespoon peppercorns
10 bacon slices
6 tablespoons butter
2 teaspoons chopped mixed herbs
few drops of tomato ketchup

Peppered steak

(Steak au poivre)

Preparation time 7 minutes
Cooking time 10 minutes

Serves 3-4

METRIC/IMPERIAL
salt
1 large sirloin steak (about
0.75kg/1½lb)
2 tablespoons crushed black
peppercorns
50g/2oz butter
5 tablespoons brandy
150ml/¼ pint double cream
Garnish
chopped parsley
sprigs of watercress

Salt the sirloin and sprinkle it on both sides with the crushed peppercorns; press lightly in with a rolling pin.

Melt the butter in a frying pan and when it is very hot, add the meat. Seal on both sides, turning when half-cooked. The cooking time varies according to taste.

When the meat is cooked, sprinkle with the brandy and flame. Drain the steak and place on a warmed serving dish. Keep hot.

Pour the cream into the frying pan and stir with a wooden spoon to incorporate all the meat juices. Cook for 2 minutes, stirring continuously.

Pour this sauce over the steak, sprinkle with chopped parsley and garnish with sprigs of watercress.

 a Châteauneuf-du-Pape (red)

Preparation time 7 minutes
Cooking time 10 minutes

Serves 3-4

AMERICAN
salt
1 large sirloin steak (about 1½lb)
3 tablespoons crushed black
peppercorns
¼ cup butter
6 tablespoons brandy
⅔ cup heavy cream
Garnish
chopped parsley
sprigs of watercress

Steak with green pepper butter

(Entrecôte Villette)

Preparation time 20 minutes
Cooking time 25 minutes

Serves 4

METRIC/IMPERIAL
4 shallots
2 tablespoons red wine
2 tablespoons wine vinegar
100g/4oz butter
2 teaspoons green peppercorns
salt and pepper
1 thick entrecôte steak (about 0.75kg/1½lb)
pinch of powdered thyme
Garnish
sprigs of watercress

Chop the shallots very finely and place in a small saucepan with the red wine and vinegar. Boil and reduce over a gentle heat until the liquid has completely evaporated.

Meanwhile cut the butter into small pieces and work with a wooden spoon until creamy.

Allow the reduced shallots to cool and add to the butter with the well-drained green peppercorns. Add a little salt and work the mixture together to give a uniform butter. Form into a roll, wrap in foil and place in the freezing compartment of the refrigerator to set.

Season the steak with salt, pepper and powdered thyme. Grill for 5–6 minutes each side, according to taste.

Place the entrecôte on a serving dish. Cut the roll of butter into rounds and place on the meat. Garnish with watercress and serve at once.

 a Beaujolais Villages (red)

Preparation time 20 minutes
Cooking time 25 minutes

Serves 4

AMERICAN
4 shallots
3 tablespoons red wine
3 tablespoons wine vinegar
½ cup butter
2 teaspoons green peppercorns
salt and pepper
1 thick sirloin steak (about 1½lb)
dash of powdered thyme
Garnish
sprigs of watercress

Steakburgers

(Hamburgers à cheval)

Preparation time 20 minutes
Cooking time 10–16 minutes

Serves 4

METRIC/IMPERIAL
2 shallots
575g/1¼lb good-quality minced steak
pinch of powdered thyme
1 tablespoon chopped parsley
75g/3oz butter
4 eggs
salt and pepper
To serve
potato chips
1 bunch watercress
2 tomatoes

Peel and finely chop the shallots. Knead the minced steak with the shallots, thyme and parsley. Season. Shape into 4 large hamburgers. Cook for 5–8 minutes each side in half the butter. Each can be cooked to the taste of the individual guest.

In the remaining butter fry the eggs. Trim all round to give a nice shape.

Arrange the hamburgers on a heated serving dish. Place an egg on each and surround with potato chips, watercress sprigs and tomato slices.

Serve immediately.

 a red Côtes-de-Provence

Preparation time 20 minutes
Cooking time 10–16 minutes

Serves 4

AMERICAN
2 shallots
1¼lb good-quality ground steak
dash of powdered thyme
1 tablespoon chopped parsley
6 tablespoons butter
4 eggs
salt and pepper
To serve
French fries
1 bunch watercress
2 tomatoes

Braised steak

(Boeuf braisé ménagère)

Preparation time 30 minutes
Cooking time 3 hours

Serves 4–6

METRIC/IMPERIAL
5 medium onions
3 cloves
1kg/2lb carrots
50g/2oz butter
2 tablespoons oil
1-kg/2¼-lb piece braising steak
100g/4oz smoked streaky bacon
25g/1oz flour
1 stock bone or 1 beef stock cube
1 bouquet garni
2 cloves garlic
small piece bacon rind
salt and pepper

Peel the onions and stick the cloves into one of them. Peel the carrots and slice, not too thinly.

Heat the butter and oil in a flameproof casserole, add the beef and the diced bacon. Brown well on all sides and remove the beef from the pan. Stir the flour into the pan juices with a wooden spoon.

Return the meat to this roux and add enough water to cover completely. Also add the stock bone or crumbled stock cube, carrots, onions, bouquet garni, crushed garlic and rolled bacon rind. Season, cover and simmer for 3 hours over a low heat.

Just before serving remove the bouquet garni, stock bone, cloves and bacon rind. Slice the meat and skim off any fat from the gravy. Arrange the carrots and onions in a shallow dish and place the slices of meat over them. Pour over the sauce and serve very hot.

 a red table wine

Preparation time 30 minutes
Cooking time 3 hours

Serves 4–6

AMERICAN
5 medium onions
3 cloves
2lb carrots
¼ cup butter
3 tablespoons oil
2-lb piece of chuck beef
6 slices smoked bacon
¼ cup all-purpose flour
1 stock bone or 1 bouillon cube
1 bouquet garni
2 cloves garlic
small piece bacon rind
salt and pepper

Daube of beef

(Boeuf en daube)

Preparation time 40 minutes
plus overnight marinating
Cooking time 2–4 hours

Serves 6–8

METRIC/IMPERIAL
2kg/4¼lb braising steak
salt and pepper
150g/5oz smoked streaky bacon
6 onions
3 cloves
1 calf's foot, boned (optional)
piece of bacon rind
75g/3oz lard
25g/1oz flour
2 cloves garlic
strip of orange peel
1 bouquet garni
1 sugar lump
Marinade
2 carrots
2 onions
1 clove garlic
1 bouquet garni
1.5 litres/2¾ pints red wine
2 tablespoons oil
4 tablespoons vinegar
Garnish
chopped parsley

Cut the meat into cubes and season.

Prepare the marinade. Peel and slice the carrots and onions. Crush the garlic. Put these ingredients in a bowl with the bouquet garni and the meat. Cover with the red wine, oil and vinegar and leave to marinate overnight.

Dice the bacon. Peel the onions. Cut 5 into quarters and stick the cloves into the remaining onion. Cut open the calf's foot, if used, and divide into pieces. Roll the bacon rind and tie it.

Drain and dry the meat on absorbent paper. Reduce the marinade by half, by boiling in an open pan.

In a flameproof casserole brown the diced bacon in the lard. Remove. In the same lard cook the quartered onions until soft, then remove. Increase the heat and brown the meat all over, to seal. Sprinkle in the flour and brown, stirring continuously.

Pour on the strained marinade to cover the meat, adding a little stock or hot water if necessary. Then add the bacon, quartered onions, the onion stuck with cloves, pieces of calf's foot, bacon rind, cloves of garlic, orange peel, bouquet garni and sugar lump.

Cover and simmer over a very low heat for at least 4 hours, or cook in a moderate oven (180°C, 350°F, Gas Mark 4) for 2 hours.

Remove the bouquet garni, bacon rind and cloves and serve very hot, sprinkled with parsley.

 a Corbières (full-bodied red)

Preparation time 40 minutes
plus overnight marinating
Cooking time 2–4 hours

Serves 6–8

AMERICAN
4¼lb chuck beef
salt and pepper
7–8 bacon slices
6 onions
3 cloves
1 calf's foot, boned (optional)
piece of bacon rind
6 tablespoons shortening
¼ cup all-purpose flour
2 cloves garlic
strip of orange peel
1 bouquet garni
1 sugar cube
Marinade
2 carrots
2 onions
1 clove garlic
1 bouquet garni
7 cups red wine
3 tablespoons oil
⅓ cup vinegar
Garnish
chopped parsley

Gipsy-style beef olives

(Paupiettes bohémienne)

Preparation time 25 minutes
Cooking time 1½–1¾ hours

Serves 5

METRIC/IMPERIAL
5 thin slices beef topside
5 small frankfurters
6 small onions
10 gherkins
3 tablespoons tarragon mustard
salt and pepper
25g/1oz lard
1 tablespoon flour
300ml/½ pint red wine or stock
1 small bouquet garni
Garnish
chopped parsley
sprigs of watercress

Flatten out the beef slices with a rolling pin or meat mallet. Cut the ends off each frankfurter. Peel then finely slice the onions. Split the gherkins in two lengthwise.

Spread each slice of meat with mustard. Scatter over half the sliced onions. Then arrange in turn two gherkin halves, one frankfurter and two more gherkin halves. Season lightly. Roll up each slice of beef into a parcel to enclose all the ingredients. Tie with string.

Heat the lard in a shallow frying pan and cook the beef olives with the remaining onions. Turn the olives to brown on all sides then place in an ovenproof casserole. Sprinkle the pan juices with the flour and stir in well. Pour in the red wine or stock, add the bouquet garni and a little seasoning and bring up to boiling point. Pour over the beef olives and cook in a moderate oven (180°C, 350°F, Gas Mark 4) for 1–1½ hours.

Arrange the beef olives on a heated serving dish and strain over the sauce from the casserole. Sprinkle with chopped parsley and garnish with sprigs of watercress. Serve very hot.

 a Chinon (light fruity red)

Preparation time 25 minutes
Cooking time 1½–1¾ hours

Serves 5

AMERICAN
5 thin slices beef round
5 small frankfurters
6 small onions
10 sweet dill pickles
¼ cup tarragon mustard
salt and pepper
2 tablespoons shortening
1 tablespoon all-purpose flour
1¼ cups red wine or stock
1 small bouquet garni
Garnish
chopped parsley
sprigs of watercress

Steak and pepper kebabs

(Brochettes de boeuf)

Preparation time 25 minutes
Cooking time 10 minutes

Serves 4

METRIC/IMPERIAL
1 red pepper
1 green pepper
1 clove garlic
pinch of sea salt
1 clove
½ teaspoon cumin seeds
12 peppercorns
1 tablespoon olive oil
½ teaspoon curry powder
0.75 kg/1½ lb rump steak
Sauce
2 onions
0.75 kg/1½ lb ripe tomatoes
1 clove garlic
juice of 1 lemon
4 tablespoons olive oil
salt and pepper

Wash the peppers, remove cores and seeds and cut into even-sized pieces.

Peel the garlic, crush with the blade of a knife and place in a kitchen mortar with a pinch of sea salt, the clove, cumin seeds and peppercorns. Grind these ingredients together, moistening gradually with the oil to obtain a smooth paste. Finally add the curry powder.

Cut the meat into cubes. Coat each piece thoroughly in the prepared mixture. Thread the cubes of meat on to skewers, alternating with the pieces of green and red pepper.

Now prepare the sauce. Peel and chop the onions, peel the tomatoes and remove seeds. Blend the onions, tomatoes, crushed garlic, lemon juice and oil for several seconds in the liquidiser, to make a purée. Season to taste, pour into a saucepan and simmer for 5 minutes.

Grill the kebabs, preferably over charcoal on a barbecue, otherwise under the grill, for about 10 minutes.

Serve the kebabs very hot accompanied by the sauce.

 a Gamay (red Beaujolais)

Preparation time 25 minutes
Cooking time 10 minutes

Serves 4

AMERICAN
1 red pepper
1 green pepper
1 clove garlic
dash of coarse salt
1 clove
½ teaspoon cumin seeds
12 peppercorns
1 tablespoon olive oil
½ teaspoon curry powder
1½ lb rump steak
Sauce
2 onions
1½ lb ripe tomatoes
1 clove garlic
juice of 1 lemon
⅓ cup olive oil
salt and pepper

Roast beef jardinière

(Rôti de boeuf jardinière)

Preparation time 30 minutes
Cooking time 1¼–1½ hours

Serves 6

METRIC/IMPERIAL
1 carrot
1 onion
1 stick celery
100 g/4 oz butter
1 bouquet garni
50 g/2 oz minced steak
1½ tablespoons flour
100 ml/4 fl oz dry white wine
300 ml/½ pint beef stock
100 ml/4 fl oz Madeira
salt and pepper
1.5-kg/3¼-lb piece silverside or rump steak, fat removed
To serve
0.5 kg/1 lb new carrots
0.5 kg/1 lb turnips
0.5 kg/1 lb French beans (fresh or frozen)
Garnish
chopped parsley

Prepare the sauce. Peel and finely chop the carrot, onion and celery. Soften them in half the butter with the bouquet garni, until golden. Add the minced steak and brown well. Next sprinkle with the flour, mix in and leave to colour. Pour in the wine and stock, add 1 tablespoon Madeira, stir well and bring up to boiling point. Season and simmer without boiling for 20 minutes.

Now prepare the vegetables. Peel and wash the carrots and turnips. Cut and trim them to required shape. Blanch for 10 minutes in boiling salted water then drain.

Meanwhile, heat the rest of the butter in a flameproof casserole. As soon as it is very hot, add the beef, tied into a neat oblong shape, and brown quickly all over. Add the carrots and turnips, cover and cook in a moderately hot oven (190°C, 375°F, Gas Mark 5) for 1–1¼ hours.

Strain the wine sauce through a conical sieve, pour around the meat and cook for a further 10 minutes. Meanwhile, slice and wash the French beans. Cook in boiling salted water for 5–8 minutes, then drain. Just before serving, add the rest of the Madeira to the sauce and heat through without boiling.

Arrange the beef on a heated serving dish, surround with the various vegetables, pour the sauce over all and finally sprinkle with chopped parsley. Serve very hot.

 a Chinon (light fruity red)

Preparation time 30 minutes
Cooking time 1¼–1½ hours

Serves 6

AMERICAN
1 carrot
1 onion
1 stalk celery
½ cup butter
1 bouquet garni
¼ cup ground steak
2 tablespoons all-purpose flour
½ cup dry white wine
1¼ cups beef stock
½ cup Madeira
salt and pepper
3¼-lb piece bottom round or rump steak, fat removed
To serve
1 lb new carrots
1 lb turnips
1 lb green beans (fresh or frozen)
Garnish
chopped parsley

Braised loin of veal

(Veau à la Poitevine)

Preparation time 30 minutes
Cooking time 2 hours 10 minutes

Serves 6

METRIC/IMPERIAL
1 boned loin of veal (about
1.5 kg/3 lb)
salt and pepper
50 g/2 oz butter
3 onions
2 carrots
1 small bouquet garni
100 ml/4 fl oz dry white wine
1 head celery
24 button onions
1 tablespoon castor sugar
1 tablespoon butter
2 teaspoons potato flour
or 1 teaspoon cornflour
150 ml/¼ pint stock

Tie the veal with string and season. Brown in a flameproof casserole in the hot butter with the finely sliced onions and carrots and the bouquet garni; leave to turn dark golden on all sides. Pour in the wine, and cook in a hot oven (230°C, 450°F, Gas Mark 8) for 40 minutes, then reduce to moderate (160°C, 325°F, Gas Mark 3) for 1½ hours. 30 minutes before serving, slice the celery into 2.5-cm/1-inch lengths and cook in boiling salted water for 10–15 minutes.

Clean the button onions without peeling them and tip into a saucepan. Add the sugar and butter and just enough water to cover. Cook until all the water evaporates and the liquid caramelises. Coat the onions thoroughly in this glaze.

Drain the celery and keep hot.

Remove the veal, arrange on a heated serving dish and surround with the celery and glazed onions.

Mix the potato flour with the stock, pour into the casserole and stir well to incorporate all the veal juices, having removed the bouquet garni. Cook, stirring, until thickened, then pour over the veal and vegetables.

Serve very hot.

 a Chinon (light fruity red)

Preparation time 30 minutes
Cooking time 2 hours 10 minutes

Serves 6

AMERICAN
1 boneless veal loin (about 3 lb)
salt and pepper
¼ cup butter
3 onions
2 carrots
1 small bouquet garni
½ cup dry white wine
1 head celery
24 button onions
1 tablespoon sugar
1 tablespoon butter
2 teaspoons potato flour or
1 teaspoon cornstarch
⅔ cup stock

Loin of veal with noodles

(Noix de veau Riviera)

Preparation time 25 minutes
Cooking time 1½–2 hours

Serves 6

METRIC/IMPERIAL
6 artichoke hearts
juice of ½ lemon
12 button onions
12 small carrots
75g/3oz butter
1 rolled and boned loin of
veal (about 1.5kg/3lb)
250ml/8fl oz dry white wine
salt and pepper
225g/8oz noodles
75g/3oz Parmesan cheese, grated
175g/6oz ham
1 sprig of tarragon
Garnish
chopped parsley

Finely slice the artichoke hearts and sprinkle with lemon juice. Clean the onions and remove the papery skin. Scrape and slice the carrots.

Melt 50g/2oz (US ¼ cup) butter in a flameproof casserole. As soon as it is really hot, add the veal. Turn several times so that it is well browned on all sides.

Add the onions and carrots to the pan. When golden moisten with the white wine. Season, then add the artichoke hearts. Cover the casserole and place in a moderately hot oven (200°C, 400°F, Gas Mark 6) for about 1–1½ hours.

Meanwhile, cook the noodles in plenty of boiling salted water. Drain carefully, toss in the rest of the butter and the grated Parmesan. Mould these noodles into small bowls or ramekin dishes.

Arrange the veal on a heated serving dish, surround with the turned-out noodle moulds, alternating with the cooked vegetables. Keep warm in a low oven.

Finely chop the ham and tarragon and add to the casserole. Mix well with the pan juices and pour over the meat and vegetables. Finally sprinkle with chopped parsley.

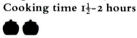 a Cahors (full-bodied red)

Preparation time 25 minutes
Cooking time 1½–2 hours

Serves 6

AMERICAN
6 artichoke hearts
juice of ½ lemon
12 button onions
12 small carrots
6 tablespoons butter
1 rolled boneless veal loin
(about 3lb)
1 cup dry white wine
salt and pepper
2 cups noodles
¾ cup grated Parmesan cheese
6oz cooked ham
1 sprig of tarragon
Garnish
chopped parsley

Veal jardinière

(Veau en jardinière)

Preparation time 30 minutes
Cooking time 1¼–1½ hours

Serves 6

METRIC/IMPERIAL
6 veal loin chops
100g/4oz butter
4 onions, finely sliced
1.5kg/3lb fresh green peas
225g/8oz new carrots
225g/8oz new turnips
225g/8oz button onions
225g/8oz small new potatoes
1 small bouquet garni
450ml/¾ pint stock
1 sugar lump
salt and pepper
3 tablespoons dry white wine
Garnish
chopped parsley

Trim and season the chops. Heat half the butter in a flame-proof casserole and brown the meat on all sides over a moderate heat. Add the finely sliced onions and cook until golden.

Shell the green peas, peel the carrots and turnips. Trim and peel the button onions and scrape the potatoes. Soften all of these vegetables in the remaining butter over a gentle heat; add the bouquet garni, cover and stir from time to time. After 15 minutes add the stock and sugar lump, bring to the boil, season and simmer for 10 minutes.

Moisten the well browned veal with the white wine, cook over a moderate heat until evaporated and the sauce begins to caramelise slightly. Finish cooking over a gentle heat for about 1 hour, moistening with a little stock from the vegetables if necessary.

Arrange the meat in the centre of a heated serving dish and surround with the vegetables. Pour over the juices from the meat and sprinkle with chopped parsley.

 a red Côtes-de-Provence

Preparation time 30 minutes
Cooking time 1¼–1½ hours

Serves 6

AMERICAN
6 veal loin chops
½ cup butter
4 onions, finely sliced
3lb fresh green peas
½lb new carrots
½lb new turnips
½lb button onions
½lb small new potatoes
1 small bouquet garni
2 cups stock
1 sugar cube
salt and pepper
¼ cup dry white wine
Garnish
chopped parsley

Veal olives

(Paupiettes de veau)

Preparation time 30 minutes
Cooking time 1¼–1½ hours

Serves 6

METRIC/IMPERIAL
6 thin veal escalopes
40 g/1½ oz butter
2 large onions
1 small bouquet garni
3 tomatoes
100 ml/4 fl oz dry white wine
200 ml/7 fl oz stock
24 button onions
1 tablespoon butter
2 teaspoons sugar
1 tablespoon potato flour
or 2 teaspoons cornflour
100 ml/4 fl oz Madeira
Stuffing
225 g/8 oz sausagemeat
150 g/5 oz minced veal
100 g/4 oz dried breadcrumbs,
moistened with milk
2 shallots
2 spring onions
pinch of dried thyme
2 tablespoons chopped parsley
salt and pepper
1 egg
Garnish
chopped parsley

Prepare the stuffing. Mix the sausagemeat with the minced veal, breadcrumbs, the chopped shallots and spring onions, thyme, parsley and seasoning. Bind this stuffing with the beaten egg.

Flatten the escalopes with a rolling pin or meat mallet. Place the stuffing in the centre of each and roll up into a parcel so that the stuffing is firmly enclosed. Tie with string.

Heat the butter in a flameproof casserole. Sauté the veal olives with the chopped large onions, let them brown well on all sides. Add the bouquet garni and the tomatoes, peeled, deseeded and crushed. Leave to cook for 10 minutes then moisten with the wine and stock. Season, cover and cook in a moderate oven (180°C, 350°F, Gas Mark 4) for 1–1¼ hours.

Remove the papery outer skin of the button onions, and cook with 4 tablespoons water, the tablespoon of butter and the sugar. Leave until the juice caramelises then coat the onions with this glaze. Transfer the veal olives to a heated serving dish and surround with the glazed onions.

Strain the sauce from the veal through a sieve and thicken over a gentle heat, stirring in the potato flour or cornflour mixed with the Madeira. Bring to the boil, stirring continuously, and pour over the veal olives. Sprinkle with chopped parsley to serve.

 a Chinon (light fruity red)

Preparation time 30 minutes
Cooking time 1¼–1½ hours

Serves 6

AMERICAN
6 thin veal scallops
3 tablespoons butter
2 large onions
1 small bouquet garni
3 tomatoes
½ cup dry white wine
¾ cup stock
24 button onions
1 tablespoon butter
2 teaspoons sugar
1 tablespoon potato flour or
2 teaspoons cornstarch
½ cup Madeira
Stuffing
½ lb sausage meat
5 oz ground veal
1 cup dry bread crumbs,
moistened with milk
2 shallots
2 scallions
dash of dried thyme
3 tablespoons chopped parsley
salt and pepper
1 egg
Garnish
chopped parsley

Veal paprika

(Flanchet de veau)

Preparation time 20 minutes
Cooking time 1 hour 20 minutes

Serves 4

METRIC/IMPERIAL
0.5kg/1lb onions
50g/2oz butter
2 tablespoons oil
salt and pepper
1kg/2lb breast of veal, sliced
1 teaspoon paprika
1 tablespoon flour
300ml/½ pint stock or water
2 tablespoons vinegar
1 sugar lump
1 small bouquet garni
Garnish
chopped parsley

Peel the onions and cut into thin segments. Heat the butter and oil in a frying pan and soften the onions over a medium heat. Cook until pale gold without browning. Drain and keep hot.

In the same butter cook the seasoned slices of veal. Turn often until golden all over. Sprinkle with the paprika and flour, mix over a high heat and remove the meat. Rinse the pan juices with the stock over a high heat, scraping the pan thoroughly to incorporate all the meat juices.

Place the veal and onions in a flameproof casserole. Pour over the stock from the frying pan and the vinegar. Add the sugar and bouquet garni, cover and simmer gently for 1 hour.

Serve very hot after removing the bouquet garni. Sprinkle chopped parsley to garnish.

 a Bourgueil (fruity red)

Preparation time 20 minutes
Cooking time 1 hour 20 minutes

Serves 4

AMERICAN
1lb onions
¼ cup butter
3 tablespoons oil
salt and pepper
2lb breast of veal, sliced
1 teaspoon paprika pepper
1 tablespoon all-purpose flour
1¼ cups stock or water
3 tablespoons vinegar
1 sugar cube
1 small bouquet garni
Garnish
chopped parsley

Osso buco with mushrooms (Osso buco aux champignons)

Preparation time 20 minutes
Cooking time 1¾ - 2¼ hours

Serves 4

METRIC/IMPERIAL
2 onions
2 shallots
2 carrots
4 tomatoes
225g/8oz mushrooms
3 tablespoons oil
25g/1oz butter
4 slices shin of veal
2 tablespoons tomato purée
2 tablespoons flour
salt and pepper
250ml/8fl oz dry white wine
100ml/4fl oz stock or water
1 whole bulb garlic
1 bouquet garni
To serve
450g/1lb spaghetti

Peel then chop the onions, shallots and carrots. Peel the tomatoes, quarter and remove seeds. Clean the mushrooms and slice finely.

Heat the oil and butter in a flameproof casserole. Add the veal slices and turn to seal well, then tip in the chopped vegetables. Reduce the heat and leave to brown slightly for 4–5 minutes.

Now add the tomato quarters and the purée, then the mushrooms. Sprinkle the whole with flour, stir in well and season to taste. Moisten with the wine and stock. Wash the garlic bulb and drop it whole into the casserole with the bouquet garni. Cover and simmer over a low heat for 1½–2 hours.

15 minutes before serving, cook the spaghetti in plenty of boiling salted water for 10–12 minutes. Drain.

To serve, transfer the spaghetti to a heated serving dish and place the veal slices on top. Remove the bouquet garni and garlic and pour over the sauce.

a Valpolicella (Italian light red)

Preparation time 20 minutes
Cooking time 1¾ - 2¼ hours

Serves 4

AMERICAN
2 onions
2 shallots
2 carrots
4 tomatoes
½lb mushrooms
¼ cup oil
2 tablespoons butter
4 slices veal shin
3 tablespoons tomato paste
3 tablespoons all-purpose flour
salt and pepper
1 cup dry white wine
½ cup stock or water
1 whole head garlic
1 bouquet garni
To serve
1lb spaghetti

Saltimbocca

(Les saltimbocca)

Preparation time 30 minutes
Cooking time 30 minutes

Serves 5

METRIC/IMPERIAL
5 thin veal escalopes
15 sage leaves
5 thin slices Parma ham
40 g/1½ oz butter
150 ml/¼ pint stock
100 ml/4 fl oz Marsala
2 teaspoons tomato purée
1 tablespoon cornflour
salt and pepper
To serve
1 kg/2 lb fresh green peas
40 g/1½ oz butter
250 ml/8 fl oz stock

First prepare the peas. Shell and braise over a gentle heat in a covered saucepan with the butter for 10 minutes. Then add the stock, season and leave to finish cooking.

Prepare the saltimbocca. Flatten the escalopes with a rolling pin or meat mallet, season them. Place on each one 2 sage leaves then a slice of ham; fold the escalopes over double and secure each with a wooden cocktail stick. Heat the butter in a frying pan and cook the veal; brown on one side before turning over. When golden brown on both sides, remove and keep warm.

Make a sauce in the pan with the stock and Marsala, scraping the pan well to incorporate all the meat juices; the sauce must be golden in colour. Add the tomato purée and thicken with the cornflour combined with a little cold water. Season and cook for 7–8 minutes, stirring continuously.

Put the veal back in this sauce for a moment to heat through. Transfer the cooked peas to a heated serving dish. Place the veal over them, pour over the sauce and finally garnish each with a sage leaf. Serve hot.

🍇 a red Bordeaux

Preparation time 30 minutes
Cooking time 30 minutes

Serves 5

AMERICAN
5 thin veal scallops
15 sage leaves
5 thin slices Parma ham
3 tablespoons butter
⅔ cup stock
½ cup Marsala
2 teaspoons tomato paste
1 tablespoon cornstarch
salt and pepper
To serve
2 lb fresh green peas
3 tablespoons butter
1 cup stock

Veal with sorrel

(Veau à l'oseille)

Preparation time 25 minutes
Cooking time 40 minutes

Serves 4

METRIC/IMPERIAL
0.75kg/1½lb shoulder of veal
salt and pepper
75g/3oz butter
225g/8oz button onions
100ml/4fl oz dry white wine
300ml/½ pint stock
1 teaspoon potato flour or
cornflour
1kg/2lb sorrel or spinach
3 tablespoons double cream

Trim and cut the veal into even pieces. Season with salt and pepper and brown in a shallow pan in 50g/2oz (US ¼ cup) butter. Lower the heat and continue to cook for 5 minutes.

Clean the onions and peel if necessary. Add them to the veal and brown well. Moisten with the white wine, and leave to evaporate completely and caramelise. Add the stock to make a sauce and thicken this sauce with the potato flour mixed with 3 tablespoons cold water.

Clean the sorrel, cutting off the stalks. Wash in plenty of water, drain well and chop. Soften in the remaining butter, stirring with a wooden spoon. Season, add the cream and cook gently for 5 minutes. Do not allow to boil.

Drain the veal and the onions and keep hot. Add the sorrel to the veal sauce and mix well. Pour into a heated serving dish and arrange the veal and onions on top. Serve immediately.

🍇 a Chinon (light fruity red)

Preparation time 25 minutes
Cooking time 40 minutes

Serves 4

AMERICAN
1½lb veal shoulder
salt and pepper
6 tablespoons butter
½lb button onions
½ cup dry white wine
1¼ cups stock
1 teaspoon potato flour or
cornstarch
2lb sorrel or spinach
¼ cup heavy cream

Sauté of veal

(Sauté de veau)

Preparation time 15 minutes
Cooking time 50-60 minutes

Serves 4

METRIC/IMPERIAL
1 kg/2 lb leg of veal
salt and pepper
6 onions
2 carrots
50 g/2 oz butter
1 small bouquet garni
2 tablespoons tomato purée
250 ml/8 fl oz stock
3 tablespoons double cream
pinch of cayenne
Garnish
chopped parsley

Cut the veal into even pieces and season with salt and pepper.

Peel the onions and carrots. Coarsely chop the onions, finely slice the carrots.

Heat the butter in a shallow frying pan. Add the meat, onions, carrots and bouquet garni and brown well, turning over on all sides.

When these ingredients are well browned, mix in the tomato purée, stirring for 5 minutes over a moderate heat. Moisten with the stock (it must scarcely cover the meat) and cook over a very gentle heat until the stock is almost completely reduced, about 30–40 minutes.

Add the cream, stir to mix well with the reduced sauce. Season to taste and add a pinch of cayenne.

Sprinkle with chopped parsley and serve very hot.

 a Chinon (light fruity red)

Preparation time 15 minutes
Cooking time 50-60 minutes

Serves 4

AMERICAN
2 lb leg of veal
salt and pepper
6 onions
2 carrots
¼ cup butter
1 small bouquet garni
3 tablespoons tomato paste
1 cup stock
¼ cup heavy cream
dash of cayenne pepper
Garnish
chopped parsley

Veal with grapefruit

(Veau au pamplemousse)

Preparation time 20 minutes
Cooking time 45-55 minutes

Serves 6

METRIC/IMPERIAL
1.5 kg/3 lb shoulder of veal
3 shallots
40 g/1½ oz butter
2 tablespoons brandy
salt and pepper
450 ml/¾ pint dry white wine
2 grapefruit

Trim the veal and cut into even pieces. Peel and chop the shallots.

Heat the butter in a flameproof casserole and brown the pieces of veal in it. Turn over to seal on all sides then sprinkle with the brandy and flame. Scatter the whole with the chopped shallots, season and pour in the white wine. Lower the heat and cook for about 30–40 minutes.

Meanwhile, squeeze the juice from 1 grapefruit, peel and segment the second.

When the veal is cooked, pour the grapefruit juice into the casserole and simmer for a further 5 minutes.

To serve, arrange the pieces of meat on a heated serving dish, sprinkle with the sauce and garnish with the grapefruit segments.

 a Chinon (light fruity red)

Preparation time 20 minutes
Cooking time 45-55 minutes

Serves 6

AMERICAN
3 lb veal shoulder
3 shallots
3 tablespoons butter
3 tablespoons brandy
salt and pepper
2 cups dry white wine
2 grapefruit

Spring lamb

(Sauté d'agneau Nantaise)

Preparation time 20 minutes
Cooking time 1½ hours

Serves 6

METRIC/IMPERIAL
350 g/12 oz button onions
350 g/12 oz new carrots
1.5 kg/3 lb fresh green peas
1 lettuce
100 g/4 oz butter
2 sprigs of savory
1 sugar lump
salt and pepper
450 ml/¾ pint stock
about 1.5 kg/3 lb lamb, cut into
pieces (shoulder, neck, etc.)

Peel the onions, scrape the carrots, shell the peas and wash the lettuce.

Lightly brown the onions in half the hot butter before adding the other vegetables, together with the savory and sugar lump. Season, cover and cook over a very gentle heat. The vegetables must cook in their own juices with no water added: if they seem likely to catch, moisten with a very little stock.

Season the pieces of lamb with salt and pepper and sauté them in the rest of the hot butter. Let them brown well, turning over on all sides. When they are browned, pour in the stock, cover and cook over a gentle heat for about 45 minutes.

Drain the pieces of lamb and add to the vegetables. Reduce the stock by two-thirds before pouring it over the meat and vegetables. Cover and cook for a further 30 minutes.

Serve very hot.

 a Bourgueil (fruity red)

Preparation time 20 minutes
Cooking time 1½ hours

Serves 6

AMERICAN
¾ lb button onions
¾ lb new carrots
3 lb fresh green peas
1 head lettuce
½ cup butter
2 sprigs of savory
1 sugar cube
salt and pepper
2 cups stock
about 3 lb lamb, cut into pieces
(shoulder, neck slices, etc.)

Stuffed shoulder of lamb

(Épaule d'agneau farcie)

Preparation time 1 hour
Cooking time 2–3 hours on a spit
or 1½–2 hours in the oven

Serves 6

METRIC/IMPERIAL
1 (1.75-kg/4-lb) shoulder of lamb
salt and pepper
1 rasher streaky bacon
3 tablespoons oil
Stuffing
4 slices stale bread
4 shallots
2 cloves garlic
1 small bunch parsley
100g/4oz slightly salted butter
½ teaspoon freshly ground black
pepper

Ask the butcher to bone the shoulder of lamb and leave flat without rolling.

Prepare the stuffing. Trim the crusts off the bread and make the bread into crumbs. Chop the shallots very finely with the garlic and parsley. Mix with the breadcrumbs. Cut the butter into small pieces, put into a basin and work with a wooden spoon until creamy. Beat in the breadcrumb mixture and freshly ground pepper. Add a little salt if necessary.

Season the lamb and spread the inside of the shoulder with this stuffing, filling the cavity left by the bone. Roll the shoulder, wrap in the bacon rasher and tie with string.

Light the barbecue and wait until the charcoal has turned red and then is covered with grey ashes. Place the lamb on the spit, brush with oil, season and turn in front of the charcoal over a dripping pan. Cook for about 2–3 hours, basting the lamb occasionally with the pan drippings.

Alternatively cook the lamb in a hot oven (220°C, 425°F, Gas Mark 7) for 20 minutes, then reduce the temperature to moderately hot (190°C, 375°F, Gas Mark 5) for the remaining time, allowing 20 minutes per half kilo/ per lb plus 20 minutes extra.

Serve very hot with green beans or creamed potatoes.

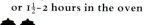 a Châteauneuf-du-Pape (red)

Preparation time 1 hour
Cooking time 2–3 hours on a spit
or 1½–2 hours in the oven

Serves 6

AMERICAN
1 (4-lb) lamb shoulder
salt and pepper
1 bacon slice
¼ cup oil
Stuffing
4 slices stale bread
4 shallots
2 cloves garlic
1 small bunch parsley
½ cup slightly salted butter
½ teaspoon freshly ground black
pepper

Spit-roasted leg of lamb

(Gigot Cabrières)

Preparation time 1 hour
Cooking time 2–3 hours

Serves 6

METRIC/IMPERIAL
1 leg of lamb (about 2 kg/4½ lb)
2 tablespoons olive oil
salt and pepper
1 tablespoon Provence herbs (mixed)
2 medium aubergines
6 small courgettes
6 round tomatoes
flour to coat
oil for deep frying
Stuffing
225 g/8 oz minced lamb
100 ml/4 fl oz olive oil
½ teaspoon powdered thyme
2 cloves garlic, chopped
2 onions, chopped
225 g/8 oz long-grain rice
450 ml/¾ pint stock
pinch of saffron
salt and pepper

Prepare the stuffing. Brown the minced lamb in 1 tablespoon olive oil. Add the thyme and garlic. In the remaining oil brown the onions and the rice, stirring continuously. Add the stock, saffron and seasoning. When the rice is barely cooked, mix into the minced lamb.

Rub the leg of lamb with oil, season and sprinkle with the herbs.

Wash and wipe the aubergines. Cut each into 3 equal slices. Scoop out the insides to form cups and sprinkle with salt. Leave upside down to drain for 30 minutes. Wash and wipe the courgettes. Cut into two lengthwise, scoop out the seeds and fill with part of the rice stuffing. Place the halves together and tie with string. Wash and wipe the tomatoes and cut a cross in the top of each with a knife.

Brush the courgettes and tomatoes with oil, place in a pan and put under the rôtisserie. Cook the leg of lamb on a spit above these vegetables, basting often, until well browned, about 2½–3 hours.

Alternatively cook the lamb in a moderately hot oven (190 C, 375 F, Gas Mark 5) allowing 20 minutes per half kilo/per lb, plus 20 minutes extra. Place the vegetables around the meat 30 minutes before the end of the cooking time.

Rinse, wipe and flour the aubergine cups. Cook in hot oil. Drain on absorbent paper and fill with the rest of the rice stuffing.

Arrange the cooked leg of lamb on a warmed serving dish. Surround with the courgettes (removing the string), tomatoes and aubergines. Serve very hot.

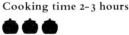 a Brouilly (fruity red)

Preparation time 1 hour
Cooking time 2–3 hours

Serves 6

AMERICAN
1 leg of lamb (about 4½ lb)
3 tablespoons olive oil
salt and pepper
1 tablespoon Provence herbs (mixed)
2 medium eggplant
6 small zucchini
6 round tomatoes
flour to coat
oil for deep frying
Stuffing
½ lb ground lamb
½ cup olive oil
½ teaspoon powdered thyme
2 cloves garlic, chopped
2 onions, chopped
1 cup long-grain rice
2 cups stock
dash of saffron
salt and pepper

Continental roast lamb

(Agneau à l'Occitane)

Preparation time 20 minutes
Cooking time 1½ hours

Serves 4

METRIC/IMPERIAL
50g/2oz butter
1 shoulder of lamb (about
1.5kg/3½lb)
salt and pepper
2 tablespoons oil
1kg/2lb small new potatoes
2 cloves garlic
4 large shallots
2 tablespoons chopped parsley
50g/2oz fresh breadcrumbs

Rub 15g/½oz (US 1 tablespoon) butter into the lamb, season and cook in a moderately hot oven (200°C, 400°F, Gas Mark 6) for the first 20 minutes, then reduce to moderate (180°C, 350°F, Gas Mark 4) for the remaining time. Allow 20 minutes cooking time per half kilo/per lb of meat, plus 20 minutes extra.

Heat the remaining butter and the oil in a frying pan, add the scraped new potatoes and cook over a medium heat for 20–25 minutes, shaking the pan. Do not use a spoon or fork to turn them over as this would squash them.

Chop the garlic and shallots very finely and mix with the parsley and breadcrumbs.

When the potatoes are cooked and golden, season, add the parsley mixture, shake well together and allow the breadcrumbs to brown.

Put the shoulder of lamb on a heated serving dish. Surround with the potatoes and serve with a green salad.

🍇 a Médoc (red)

Preparation time 20 minutes
Cooking time 1½ hours

Serves 4

AMERICAN
¼ cup butter
1 lamb shoulder (about 3½lb)
salt and pepper
3 tablespoons oil
2lb small new potatoes
2 cloves garlic
4 large shallots
3 tablespoons chopped parsley
1 cup fresh soft bread crumbs

Lamb with Moroccan sauce

(Agneau sauce Marocaine)

Preparation time 30 minutes
Cooking time 1¼ hours

Serves 6

METRIC/IMPERIAL
3 onions
4 tablespoons olive oil
2 cloves garlic
2 teaspoons cinnamon
1 teaspoon turmeric
6 tablespoons tomato purée
salt and pepper
50g/2oz raisins
50g/2oz pine nuts
1kg/2lb piece lamb fillet, rolled
To serve
275g/10oz long-grain rice
pinch of saffron or turmeric
50g/2oz raisins
25g/1oz pine nuts
Garnish
sprigs of parsley

First prepare the sauce. Brown the chopped onions well in most of the heated oil, add the crushed garlic and when it begins to turn golden add the cinnamon and turmeric. Stir in the tomato purée and 600ml/1 pint (US 2½ cups) boiling water. Add salt to taste. Reduce from boiling and mix in the raisins and pine nuts. Simmer for 1 hour to let the sauce thicken.

Brush the lamb fillet with oil and season well. Cook in a moderately hot oven (190°C, 375°F, Gas Mark 5) for 40–50 minutes.

At the same time cook the rice in twice its volume of water with the saffron or turmeric. Halfway through cooking add the raisins and pine nuts and season to taste. When cooked, cool slightly and shape into small balls.

Place the lamb on a heated serving dish. Arrange the rice balls around it and garnish with parsley. Serve very hot, accompanied by the sauce.

 a Provence rosé

Preparation time 30 minutes
Cooking time 1¼ hours

Serves 6

AMERICAN
3 onions
⅓ cup olive oil
2 cloves garlic
2 teaspoons cinnamon
1 teaspoon turmeric
½ cup tomato paste
salt and pepper
⅓ cup seeded raisins
½ cup pine nuts
2lb piece lamb fillet, rolled
To serve
1¼ cups long-grain rice
dash of saffron or turmeric
⅓ cup seeded raisins
¼ cup pine nuts
Garnish
sprigs of parsley

Lamb chops with garlic

(Côtes d'agneau Provençale)

Preparation time 20 minutes
Cooking time 20 minutes

Serves 3

METRIC/IMPERIAL
2 cloves garlic
sea salt
3 sprigs of basil
4-5 tablespoons olive oil
pepper
6 small lamb fillet chops
50g/2oz butter

Peel the garlic and crush lightly. Place in a kitchen mortar with a small pinch of sea salt and most of the basil leaves, reserving 6 for garnish. Pound these ingredients to a paste, then slowly add the olive oil. The mixture should be smooth.

Lightly pepper the chops on both sides and spread each with a little of the above mixture. Place under a preheated grill and cook for about 10 minutes on each side.

Transfer the chops to a heated serving dish. Place a pat of butter and a basil leaf on each. Serve immediately, accompanied by buttered green beans.

 a red Côtes-de-Ventoux (light and fruity)

Preparation time 20 minutes
Cooking time 20 minutes

Serves 3

AMERICAN
2 cloves garlic
coarse salt
3 sprigs of basil
5-6 tablespoons olive oil
pepper
6 small lamb fillet chops
¼ cup butter

Loin of pork with prunes

(Carré de porc à la Limousine)

**Preparation time 30 minutes
plus overnight soaking
Cooking time 1½–1¾ hours**

Serves 5-6

METRIC/IMPERIAL
1 kg/2 lb chestnuts
1 litre/1¾ pints stock
1 stick celery
50 g/2 oz butter
1 pork loin (5-6 cutlets)
0.5 kg/1 lb prunes, soaked overnight
350 ml/12 fl oz red wine
1 small piece cinnamon stick
1 tablespoon potato flour or
2 teaspoons cornflour
salt and pepper
Garnish
chopped parsley

With a very sharp knife slit the chestnuts through both layers of skin. Toss into a pan of boiling water. Simmer for 5 minutes then drain. Peel; the two skins will come off together.

Heat the stock in a saucepan with the celery. Add the peeled chestnuts and cook for 30–35 minutes, until tender. Drain and discard the stock and celery.

Meanwhile melt the butter in a large flameproof casserole. Brown the loin of pork, turning until golden all over. Transfer to a hot oven (220°C, 425°F, Gas Mark 7) for 20 minutes, then reduce to moderately hot (190°C, 375°F, Gas Mark 5) for a further 55 minutes.

Put the prunes into a saucepan with the red wine and cinnamon stick. Bring slowly to the boil and simmer for 20 minutes. Drain the prunes and reserve the cooking liquor.

Fifteen minutes before serving add the chestnuts and prunes to the pork.

Meanwhile reduce the prune cooking liquor by half, by open boiling over a high heat. Mix the potato flour with 1 tablespoon of this liquor and pour back into the saucepan, stirring to make a smooth sauce.

Arrange the pork loin on a heated serving dish. Surround with the chestnuts and prunes. Keep hot. Add the prune sauce to the casserole dish to incorporate the pork juices. Scrape the bottom with a wooden spoon and stir over a gentle heat. Season to taste. Pour over the serving dish and sprinkle with a little chopped parsley. Serve immediately.

a Madiran (vigorous red)

**Preparation time 30 minutes
plus overnight soaking
Cooking time 1½–1¾ hours**

Serves 5-6

AMERICAN
2 lb chestnuts
4¼ cups stock
1 stalk celery
¼ cup butter
1 pork loin (5-6 chops)
1 lb prunes, soaked overnight
1½ cups red wine
1 small piece cinnamon stick
1 tablespoon potato flour or
2 teaspoons cornstarch
salt and pepper
Garnish
chopped parsley

Braised pork in wine sauce (Rôti de porc en venaison)

**Preparation time 45 minutes
plus 24 hours marinating time
Cooking time 1½ hours**

Serves 6

METRIC/IMPERIAL
1 (1.5-kg/3-lb) pork loin, boned
and rolled
50 g/2 oz butter
2 carrots
2 onions
1 small stick celery
1 small bouquet garni
1 tablespoon flour
Marinade
1 carrot
1 onion, finely sliced
sage, rosemary, thyme, bay leaf
2 cloves
salt and black pepper
1 bottle dry white wine
1 tablespoon vinegar
2 tablespoons brandy
2 tablespoons oil
To serve
1 celeriac
3 tablespoons double cream
40 g/1½ oz butter
450 g/1 lb mashed potato
300 ml/½ pint apple sauce
sprigs of watercress

The previous day, line an earthenware dish with the aromatic marinade ingredients (vegetables, herbs and cloves). Place the pork loin on top and season. Pour over the white wine, vinegar, brandy and oil. Cover and marinate for 24 hours, turning the meat occasionally.

The following day wipe the meat. Brown on all sides in a flameproof casserole in the butter. Remove. In the same butter, brown the diced carrots, chopped onions and celery, with the bouquet garni. Sprinkle over the flour and stir to make a brown roux. Strain the marinade, heat to boiling and stir into the vegetable roux. Cover and cook for 15 minutes, stirring occasionally. Return the meat to this sauce, season and cover. Cook in a moderately hot oven (190°C, 375°F, Gas Mark 5) for 1¼–1½ hours, until the meat is tender.

Meanwhile, cut the celeriac into pieces and cook in boiling salted water for 20–30 minutes. Drain and mash to a purée. Place over a gentle heat and mix with the cream and butter, beating well.

Arrange the meat on a serving dish. Pour over the sauce and surround with mounds of celeriac and mashed potato. Garnish with watercress and serve the apple sauce separately.

 a Cahors (full-bodied red)

**Preparation time 45 minutes
plus 24 hours marinating time
Cooking time 1½ hours**

Serves 6

AMERICAN
1 (3-lb) rolled boneless pork
loin roast
¼ cup butter
2 carrots
2 onions
1 small stalk celery
1 small bouquet garni
1 tablespoon all-purpose flour
Marinade
1 carrot
1 onion, finely sliced
sage, rosemary, thyme, bay leaf
2 cloves
salt and black pepper
1 bottle dry white wine
1 tablespoon vinegar
3 tablespoons brandy
3 tablespoons oil
To serve
1 celeriac
¼ cup heavy cream
3 tablespoons butter
2 cups mashed potato
1¼ cups applesauce
sprigs of watercress

Roulades of pork

(Roulades de porc)

Preparation time 50 minutes
Cooking time 1 hour

Serves 6

METRIC/IMPERIAL
1 kg/2 lb floury potatoes
about 150 ml/¼ pint hot milk
salt and freshly ground pepper
2 shallots
1 clove garlic
50 g/2 oz butter
2 tablespoons chopped parsley
6 (100-g/4-oz) slices pork fillet
(cut lengthwise)

Peel the potatoes and cook in boiling salted water. Mash well with just enough hot milk to obtain a smooth thick purée. Season to taste, spread into a buttered ovenproof dish and keep warm.

Peel and finely chop the shallots and crush the garlic.

Cut the butter into small pieces and work with a wooden spoon, combining it with freshly ground pepper, the garlic, shallots and parsley.

Lay out the slices of pork, flatten with a rolling pin and spread on one side with a thick layer of this butter mixture.

Roll up the slices, keeping the butter inside, and fasten with a wooden cocktail stick or skewer.

Arrange upright on the potato purée. Place in a hot oven (220°C, 425°F, Gas Mark 7) for 20–25 minutes, until the meat is cooked through. Serve immediately.

🍇 a Gamay (red Beaujolais)

Preparation time 50 minutes
Cooking time 1 hour

Serves 6

AMERICAN
2 lb floury potatoes
about ⅔ cup hot milk
salt and freshly ground pepper
2 shallots
1 clove garlic
¼ cup butter
3 tablespoons chopped parsley
6 (¼-lb) slices pork tenderloin
(cut lengthwise)

Pork with lentils

(Petit salé aux lentilles)

Preparation time 20 minutes plus 24 hours soaking time
Cooking time 2½ hours

Serves 6-8

METRIC/IMPERIAL
1 kg/2 lb brown lentils
1 piece smoked streaky bacon (about 600–700 g/1¼–1½ lb)
1 knuckle of pork
3 carrots
2 small leeks
3 cloves garlic
1 onion stuck with 3 cloves
1 bouquet garni
salt and pepper

Soak the lentils in cold water for 4–5 hours.

Soak the meats in cold water for 24 hours. Rinse in fresh water and drain.

Place the meats in a large saucepan, cover with cold water and bring gently to the boil. Skim, add 2 of the peeled carrots and the leeks, previously trimmed and washed. Leave to simmer for 1½ hours.

During this time, drain the lentils and rinse them. Pour into another saucepan, cover with cold water. Add the remaining carrot cut into slices, the cloves of garlic, the onion stuck with cloves and the bouquet garni. Bring to the boil and simmer for 30 minutes.

When the meat has been simmering for 1½ hours, add the drained lentils and cook for a further 1 hour over a very low heat. Taste to correct the seasoning 20 minutes before the end of cooking.

To serve, remove the bouquet garni and transfer to a heated serving dish. Serve very hot with a farmhouse loaf.

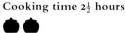 a Juliénas (fruity red Beaujolais)

Preparation time 20 minutes plus 24 hours soaking time
Cooking time 2½ hours

Serves 6-8

AMERICAN
4 cups brown lentils
1¼–1½-lb bacon piece
1 pork hock
3 carrots
2 small leeks
3 cloves garlic
1 onion stuck with 3 cloves
1 bouquet garni
salt and pepper

Pork with garlic

(Porc sauté à l'ail)

Preparation time 20 minutes
Cooking time 40 minutes

Serves 6-8

METRIC/IMPERIAL
1.5 kg/3 lb pork spare rib
50 g/2 oz butter
2 tablespoons oil
salt and pepper
2 cloves garlic
1 bunch parsley

Cut the pork into equal-sized pieces.

In a frying pan heat half the butter with the oil. When the fat is very hot, brown the meat on all sides over a medium heat. Season and continue cooking for 20–25 minutes.

Meanwhile, peel the cloves of garlic and chop finely with the parsley.

When the meat is cooked, discard all but 1 tablespoon of the cooking fat. Melt the remaining butter in the pan and add the chopped garlic and parsley. Stir for a moment over a high heat, mixing with the meat but taking care not to let the garlic brown.

Place the meat on a heated serving dish. Serve immediately with flageolets or green beans.

 a Pécharmant (light red)

Preparation time 20 minutes
Cooking time 40 minutes

Serves 6-8

AMERICAN
3 lb pork shoulder butt
$\frac{1}{4}$ cup butter
3 tablespoons oil
salt and pepper
2 cloves garlic
1 bunch parsley

Barbecued sucking pig

(Cochon de lait au barbecue)

Preparation time 2½ hours
Cooking time 7 hours

Serves about 20

METRIC/IMPERIAL
1 sucking pig (about 10 kg/22 lb)
and its lights (liver, spleen, heart
and lungs)
0.5 kg/1 lb onions
3 cloves garlic
2.5 kg/5½ lb sausagemeat
225 g/8 oz dried breadcrumbs,
moistened with milk and
squeezed
50 g/2 oz parsley, chopped
1 tablespoon powdered thyme
salt and pepper
2 bay leaves
about 1 litre/1¾ pints oil
1 bunch dried herbs

Prepare the stuffing the day before. Finely chop the pig's lights, the onions and garlic. Work these ingredients with the sausagemeat, breadcrumbs, parsley, thyme and seasoning. Knead the mixture well together. Season the inside of the pig and fill with the stuffing. Add the bay leaves.

Join the skin on the underside of the belly with short pieces of string tied every 2.5 cm/1 inch, so that the stuffing does not spill out. Brush the pig with oil, season with salt and pepper and leave until the following day.

The following day light the barbecue fire several hours in advance. Thread the pig on to a spit and again brush with oil. Place in front of the fire, not too close for the pig must not brown too quickly. Baste frequently with the bunch of dried herbs dipped in oil, and turn by hand if you have no electric spit. Take care to constantly feed the fire during cooking. When almost cooked place the pig nearer the fire to crisp the skin.

With the barbecued pig serve grilled tomatoes, jacket potatoes, baked apples and mixed salads.

 a Chinon (light fruity red)

Preparation time 2½ hours
Cooking time 7 hours

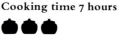

Serves about 20

AMERICAN
1 suckling pig (about 22 lb) and its
lights (liver, spleen, heart and
lungs)
1 lb onions
3 cloves garlic
5½ lb sausage meat
2 cups fine dry bread crumbs,
moistened with milk and
squeezed
1½ cups chopped parsley
1 tablespoon powdered thyme
salt and pepper
2 bay leaves
about 4¼ cups oil
1 bunch dried herbs

Farmhouse stew

(La potée)

**Preparation time 30 minutes
plus 8–12 hours soaking time
Cooking time 4 hours**

Serves 8–10

METRIC/IMPERIAL
275g/10oz dried haricot beans
1 bouquet garni
3 cloves garlic
1 onion stuck with 2 cloves
1 stick celery
1kg/2lb beef topside
1 knuckle of pork
1kg/2lb belly of pork
2–3 bacon rinds, tied together
4 carrots
3 turnips
3 leeks
$\frac{1}{2}$ white cabbage
4 large potatoes
1 sausage
sea salt
few slices French bread

The evening before, soak the beans in cold water.

Put the drained and rinsed beans into a large saucepan. Add the bouquet garni, crushed garlic, the onion stuck with cloves, celery, beef, pork knuckle, belly of pork and the bacon rinds. Fill the saucepan with cold water, bring to the boil; skim then add the peeled and quartered carrots and turnips. Cover and simmer for 3 hours over a gentle heat, skimming occasionally.

At the end of this time add the trimmed leeks and the cabbage, then, 15 minutes later, the halved potatoes and the sausage. Season with sea salt if necessary, and cook for a further 30 minutes.

To serve, strain the stock into a heated soup tureen over thin slices of French bread. Serve the meats cut into pieces and surrounded by the beans and vegetables.

 a Côtes-de-Ventoux (light fruity red)

**Preparation time 30 minutes
plus 8–12 hours soaking time
Cooking time 4 hours**

Serves 8–10

AMERICAN
1$\frac{1}{2}$ cups dried navy beans
1 bouquet garni
3 cloves garlic
1 onion stuck with 2 cloves
1 stalk celery
2lb beef top round
1 pork hock
2lb salt pork
2–3 bacon rinds, tied together
4 carrots
3 turnips
3 leeks
$\frac{1}{2}$ head white cabbage
4 large potatoes
1 sausage
coarse salt
few slices French bread

Sauerkraut with bacon

(La choucroute)

Preparation time 30 minutes
Cooking time 1-1¼ hours

Serves 10

METRIC/IMPERIAL
50g/2oz lard
225-g/8-oz piece smoked streaky
bacon
2 onions
1 (810-g/1lb 12-oz) can sauerkraut
1 piece pork rind (from the chops)
1 tablespoon juniper berries
1 bouquet garni
4 cloves
8 peppercorns
salt
1 bottle medium dry white wine
1 saveloy
12 rashers smoked streaky bacon
6 Strasburg sausages
6 pork loin chops, cooked
6 frankfurters

Melt the lard in a flameproof casserole and lightly brown the chopped bacon piece and onions. Add the drained sauerkraut and in the centre place the pork rind, juniper berries, bouquet garni, cloves and peppercorns. Salt lightly. Pour over the wine, bring to the boil, cover and cook for 5–10 minutes.

Add the saveloy and cook for a further 30 minutes. Then place over the sauerkraut the rashers of bacon, the sausages, pork chops and frankfurters. Cover again and cook for a further 20–30 minutes.

Just before serving, remove the bouquet garni and cloves and place the sauerkraut in a serving dish. Cut the saveloy into rounds and arrange the different meats over the sauerkraut. Serve very hot.

a Riesling (fruity white)

Preparation time 30 minutes
Cooking time 1-1¼ hours

Serves 10

AMERICAN
¼ cup shortening
½-lb bacon piece
2 onions
1 (28-oz) can sauerkraut
1 piece pork rind (from the chops)
1 tablespoon juniper berries
1 bouquet garni
4 cloves
8 peppercorns
salt
1 bottle medium dry white wine
1 saveloy
12 bacon slices
6 Strasburg sausages
6 pork loin chops, cooked
6 frankfurters

Pâté en croûte

(Pâté en croûte)

**Preparation time 1¼ hours
plus 2 hours standing time
Cooking time 3 hours**

Serves 8–10

METRIC/IMPERIAL
450 g/1 lb ham
5 tablespoons brandy (or port and brandy)
salt and pepper
225 g/8 oz pork fillet
225 g/8 oz lean veal
350 g/12 oz streaky bacon
1 onion
6 shallots
2 eggs plus 1 egg yolk
3 tablespoons double cream
pinch of allspice
few shelled hazelnuts
15 g/½ oz powdered gelatine
300 ml/½ pint stock
Pastry
400 g/15 oz plain flour
1 teaspoon salt
1 egg plus 1 egg yolk
100 g/4 oz butter
75 g/3 oz lard
4 tablespoons water
Garnish
sprigs of watercress

First make the pastry. Sift the flour and salt into a bowl. Drop the egg plus yolk into the centre and cover with flour. Heat the butter, lard and water in a pan; bring to the boil and pour immediately into the flour. Beat thoroughly with a wooden spoon. Turn out on to a floured surface and knead until smooth. Cover and stand for 2 hours.

Prepare the filling. Cut half the ham into thin strips. Sprinkle with 1 tablespoon brandy and season. Finely mince the rest of the ham with the pork, veal and bacon.

Peel and finely chop the onion and shallots, mix into the minced meats. Bind with the whole eggs and the cream, beaten with the rest of the brandy. Season with salt, pepper and allspice. Knead to obtain an even mixture.

Roll out two-thirds of the pastry to line a 1-kg/2-lb loaf tin. Fill with the pâté mixture, layering with the ham strips and the hazelnuts. Finish with a layer of pâté mixture. Roll out the rest of the pastry to form a lid. Press the edges of the pastry together and flute. Mix the egg yolk with 2 tablespoons (US 3 tablespoons) water and use to brush the top of the pie.

Make a small opening in the centre of the lid and keep it open with a piece of foil. Cook in a moderately hot oven (200°C, 400°F, Gas Mark 6) for 30 minutes, then reduce to moderate (180°C, 350°F, Gas Mark 4) for 2½ hours.

Dissolve the gelatine in 3 tablespoons (US ¼ cup) stock, then add the remaining stock and leave to cool, but not set.

When cooked, remove the pâté from the oven. Carefully pour the liquid jelly through the opening to fill the pie. Cool for 24 hours then garnish with watercress.

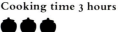 a Côtes Canon-Fronsac (red Bordeaux)

**Preparation time 1¼ hours
plus 2 hours standing time
Cooking time 3 hours**

Serves 8–10

AMERICAN
1 lb cooked ham
6 tablespoons brandy (or port and brandy)
salt and pepper
½ lb pork tenderloin
½ lb lean veal
18 bacon slices
1 onion
6 shallots
2 eggs plus 1 egg yolk
¼ cup heavy cream
dash of allspice
few shelled hazelnuts
2 envelopes gelatin
1¼ cups stock
Dough
3¾ cups all-purpose flour
1 teaspoon salt
1 egg plus 1 egg yolk
½ cup butter
6 tablespoons shortening
⅓ cup water
Garnish
sprigs of watercress

Ham in cream sauce

(Tranches de jambon au raisin)

Preparation time 15 minutes
Cooking time 7–8 minutes

Serves 6

METRIC/IMPERIAL
0.5 kg/1 lb seedless green grapes
40 g/1½ oz butter
6 thick slices ham
100 ml/4 fl oz grape juice
1 tablespoon lemon juice
150 ml/¼ pint double cream
1 tablespoon tomato purée
salt and pepper
small pinch of cayenne
Garnish
parsley

Wash and dry the grapes.

Melt the butter in a shallow frying pan, do not allow it to brown. Quickly heat through the slices of ham in this butter, then arrange them overlapping on a serving dish and keep hot in a low oven.

Stir the grape juice and lemon juice into the frying pan. Add the grapes and heat through for 1 minute. Drain and place round the ham.

Mix the cream with the tomato purée and pour into the frying pan. Thicken by beating with a wire whisk, season with salt, pepper and a little cayenne.

Pour this sauce over the ham. Garnish with the parsley leaves and serve immediately.

 a Chablis (dry white)

Preparation time 15 minutes
Cooking time 7–8 minutes

Serves 6

AMERICAN
1 lb seedless white grapes
3 tablespoons butter
6 thick slices cooked ham
½ cup grape juice
1 tablespoon lemon juice
⅔ cup heavy cream
1 tablespoon tomato paste
salt and pepper
small dash of cayenne pepper
Garnish
parsley

Ham in wine sauce

(Jambon au vin blanc)

Preparation time 15 minutes
Cooking time 20 minutes

Serves 4

METRIC/IMPERIAL
300 ml/½ pint dry white wine
3 sprigs of tarragon
40 g/1½ oz butter
4 thick slices ham
3 shallots
2 tablespoons vinegar
1 teaspoon crushed peppercorns
300 ml/½ pint double cream
1 tablespoon tomato purée
1 tablespoon butter and flour
thickening (beurre manié)
salt and pepper

Put the wine and tarragon (reserving a little for garnish) in a pan over a low heat. When beginning to boil, remove from the heat and leave to infuse for 10 minutes.

Generously grease an ovenproof dish with the butter and place in the slices of ham. Pour over the strained wine. Cover the dish with buttered greaseproof paper or foil and put in a moderate oven (180°C, 350°F, Gas Mark 4) for 10 minutes.

In a small pan boil the very finely chopped shallots with the vinegar and crushed peppercorns until the liquid is almost completely evaporated.

When the ham is heated through, strain the wine into a saucepan and reduce by one-third. Add the shallots, cream and tomato purée. Place over a medium heat and beat with a wire whisk. Thicken this sauce with the beurre manié (butter and flour worked together) and adjust seasoning to taste.

Pour over the ham slices and sprinkle with chopped tarragon.

 a Meursault (dry white)

Preparation time 15 minutes
Cooking time 20 minutes

Serves 4

AMERICAN
1¼ cups dry white wine
3 sprigs of tarragon
3 tablespoons butter
4 thick slices cooked ham
3 shallots
3 tablespoons vinegar
1 teaspoon crushed peppercorns
1¼ cups heavy cream
1 tablespoon tomato paste
1 tablespoon butter and flour
thickening (beurre manié)
salt and pepper

Couscous

(Couscous maison)

**Preparation time 1½ hours
plus overnight soaking
Cooking time 2 hours**

Serves 8-10

METRIC/IMPERIAL
1.25 kg/2½ lb leg of lamb
1 small chicken
oil and butter to fry
3 onions
4 cloves
3 cloves garlic
225 g/8 oz carrots
225 g/8 oz turnips
150 g/5 oz chick peas, soaked
overnight
1 teaspoon cayenne
salt and pepper
225 g/8 oz medium semolina
0.5 kg/1 lb tomatoes
3 green, red or yellow peppers
½ head celery
0.5 kg/1 lb courgettes
75 g/3 oz sultanas
150 g/5 oz minced beef
150 g/5 oz minced lamb
2 teaspoons chopped mixed herbs
flour to coat
1 egg
6 sausages

Cut the lamb and chicken into pieces and fry gently in hot oil until sealed. Place in a saucepan with 2 onions stuck with cloves, the chopped garlic, sliced carrots, diced turnips, drained chick peas and cayenne. Cover with water, season and cook for about 1 hour, skimming. Keep hot.

Prepare the couscous. Spread the semolina grains on a napkin, sprinkle with 100 ml/4 fl oz (US ½ cup) lightly salted water and roll flat with the palm of the hand so that the grains separate completely. Cook the semolina in a wide metal sieve placed over the meat and vegetables. Cover the sieve with foil and take care that the stock does not touch the base of the sieve. After 30 minutes pour the semolina back on to the napkin and fluff up with a fork, adding a little more water if necessary. Return the semolina to the sieve and cover with foil.

Place the remaining vegetables in a saucepan; the peeled and deseeded tomatoes, diced peppers, chopped celery and courgettes. Cook gently for 30 minutes, steaming the semolina over the vegetables at the same time.

Soak the sultanas in warm water. Prepare the meat balls by mixing the minced meats with the herbs, seasoning and the last onion, chopped and softened in butter. Flour them, dip in beaten egg and fry in very hot oil. Grill the sausages. Arrange over the couscous and sprinkle with the sultanas and a few of the chick peas.

Serve all the other meat and vegetables in a separate dish and accompany with fresh tomato sauce, if liked.

 a Mascara (full-bodied Moroccan red)

**Preparation time 1½ hours
plus overnight soaking
Cooking time 2 hours**

Serves 8-10

AMERICAN
2½ lb leg of lamb
1 small chicken
oil and butter to fry
3 onions
4 cloves
3 cloves garlic
½ lb carrots
½ lb turnips
⅔ cup garbanzos, soaked overnight
1 teaspoon cayenne pepper
salt and pepper
1⅓ cups semolina flour
1 lb tomatoes
3 green, red or yellow peppers
½ bunch celery
1 lb zucchini
½ cup seedless white raisins
⅔ cup ground beef
⅔ cup ground lamb
2 teaspoons chopped mixed herbs
flour to coat
1 egg
6 sausages

Tongue with gherkin sauce

(Langue sauce piquante)

**Preparation time 40 minutes
plus 2 hours soaking time
Cooking time 2 hours**

Serves 4

METRIC/IMPERIAL
**1 calf's tongue
salt and pepper
1 onion stuck with 3 cloves
1 bouquet garni
2 leeks
2 carrots
1 turnip
75 g/3 oz butter
40 g/1½ oz flour
3 shallots, chopped
1 tablespoon vinegar
100 ml/4 fl oz white wine
225 g/8 oz mushrooms
8 gherkins
1 tablespoon tomato purée**
Garnish
chopped parsley

Soak the tongue for 2 hours in cold water. Trim and blanch for 20 minutes in boiling salted water. Cool in cold water.

Place the tongue in a flameproof casserole with the onion and bouquet garni. Cover with cold water and bring to the boil before adding the halved leeks, sliced carrots and diced turnip. Salt and leave to simmer gently for 1½ hours. Drain the tongue and remove the outer skin and any small bones. Keep hot in the cooking stock.

Prepare the sauce. Melt 50 g/2 oz (US ¼ cup) butter and stir in the flour. Brown well and thin this roux with 450 ml/¾ pint (US 2 cups) of the tongue stock. Cook gently for 20 minutes, stirring to make a smooth sauce.

Into a small saucepan put the chopped shallots, vinegar, white wine and a little pepper. Boil and reduce by two-thirds. Soften the sliced mushrooms in the rest of the butter. Slice 4 gherkins.

Add the reduced shallots, mushrooms, gherkin slices and tomato purée to the sauce. Adjust seasoning and cook for a further 5 minutes. Add some of the vegetables from cooking the tongue, if liked.

Arrange the tongue, whole or cut into slices, on a heated serving dish. Top with the sauce. Surround with the rest of the gherkins cut into fan shapes and sprinkle with chopped parsley. Serve immediately.

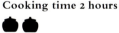 a Beaujolais (light fruity red)

**Preparation time 40 minutes
plus 2 hours soaking time
Cooking time 2 hours**

Serves 4

AMERICAN
**1 calf tongue
salt and pepper
1 onion stuck with 3 cloves
1 bouquet garni
2 leeks
2 carrots
1 turnip
6 tablespoons butter
6 tablespoons all-purpose flour
3 shallots, chopped
1 tablespoon vinegar
½ cup white wine
½ lb mushrooms
8 sweet dill pickles
1 tablespoon tomato paste**
Garnish
chopped parsley

Calf's head ravigote

(Tête de veau en tortue)

**Preparation time 1 hour
plus 24 hours soaking time
Cooking time 3½ hours**

Serves 8

METRIC/IMPERIAL
1 whole calf's head (tongue, brains
and sweetbreads removed)
flour, vinegar and salt
100 g/4 oz green olives
225 g/8 oz mushrooms
90 g/3½ oz butter
1 carrot
2 onions
75 g/3 oz smoked streaky bacon
25 g/1 oz flour
600 ml/1 pint dry white wine
1 bunch mixed herbs (thyme,
parsley, bay leaf, basil, rosemary
and sage)
3 tablespoons tomato purée
salt and pepper
6 gherkins
½ slice ham
100 ml/4 fl oz Madeira
Garnish
chopped parsley

Soak the calf's head, tongue, brains and sweetbreads in cold water for 24 hours. Pour off water and fill with fresh, salt lightly, bring to the boil and simmer for 20 minutes.

Estimate how much water you will need to cover and cook the calf's head in a large saucepan. Then blend 1 tablespoon flour, 1 tablespoon vinegar and 1 teaspoon salt to each 1 litre/1¾ pints (US 4¼ cups) and sieve. Place the calf's head in the saucepan and cover with this mixture. Cook for 1 hour, add the tongue, then cook for a further 1½ hours.

Poach the brains and the sweetbreads separately for 10 minutes in boiling salted water. Drain and cool the sweetbreads and press them between two plates.

Blanch the olives for 5 minutes in boiling water and soften the finely sliced mushrooms in 25 g/1 oz (US 2 tablespoons) butter.

Prepare the sauce. Brown in the remaining butter the diced carrot, chopped onions and diced bacon. Sprinkle with the flour and stir with a wooden spoon until coloured. Simmer the white wine with the bunch of herbs for 10 minutes, then strain into the vegetable roux together with a little stock from the calf's head. Add the tomato purée, season and cook for 10 minutes, stirring frequently.

Strain this sauce through a sieve or blend in a liquidiser; add the sliced gherkins, blanched olives, mushrooms and diced ham. Remove the skin from the calf's head and tongue and slice. Dice the brains and sweetbreads and add all the meats to the sauce. Add the Madeira and simmer for 10 minutes. Garnish with parsley.

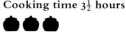 a Beaujolais Villages (light red)

**Preparation time 1 hour
plus 24 hours soaking time
Cooking time 3½ hours**

Serves 8

AMERICAN
1 whole calf head (tongue, brains
and sweetbreads removed)
flour, vinegar and salt
¼ lb green olives
½ lb mushrooms
7 tablespoons butter
1 carrot
2 onions
4–5 bacon slices
¼ cup all-purpose flour
2½ cups dry white wine
1 bunch mixed herbs (thyme,
parsley, bay leaf, basil, rosemary
and sage)
¼ cup tomato paste
salt and pepper
6 sweet dill pickles
½ slice cooked ham
½ cup Madeira
Garnish
chopped parsley

Casserole of tripe

(Tripes à la mode de Caen)

Preparation time 30 minutes
Cooking time 11–12 hours

Serves 8

METRIC/IMPERIAL
100 g/4 oz beef dripping
0.5 kg/1 lb onions
0.5 kg/1 lb carrots
2 leeks (white parts only)
2 kg/4½ lb tripe, blanched
2 calf's feet, split in two (optional)
1 onion stuck with 2 cloves
2 cloves garlic
1 bouquet garni
100 ml/4 fl oz calvados or brandy
600 ml/1 pint dry cider
salt and pepper
pinch of allspice
75 g/3 oz flour

Cut the dripping into small pieces. Finely slice the onions, carrots and leeks. Wash and wipe the tripe, cut into pieces about 3.5 cm/1½ inches square.

In the bottom of a large ovenproof casserole, place half the dripping. Cover with the onions, carrots and leeks. Place the halved calf's feet over these ingredients then the pieces of tripe. Add the onion stuck with cloves, the peeled garlic and the bouquet garni, then cover with the rest of the dripping. Pour over the calvados and cider, add enough water to cover the tripe. Season with salt, pepper and allspice.

Cover the casserole and secure the lid with a fairly soft paste of flour mixed with a little water. Place for 1 hour in a hot oven (220°C, 425°F, Gas Mark 7) then continue to cook for at least 10 hours in a cool oven (140°C, 275°F, Gas Mark 1).

To serve, remove the bones from the calf's foot and discard the bouquet garni. Skim the fat from the casserole and serve on heated plates.

 a Graves (dry white)

Preparation time 30 minutes
Cooking time 11–12 hours

Serves 8

AMERICAN
½ cup beef drippings
1 lb onions
1 lb carrots
2 leeks (white parts only)
4½ lb tripe, blanched
2 calf feet, split in two (optional)
1 onion stuck with 2 cloves
2 cloves garlic
1 bouquet garni
½ cup calvados or brandy
2½ cups dry cider
salt and pepper
dash of allspice
¾ cup all-purpose flour

Brains au gratin

(Croustade de cervelle)

**Preparation time 45 minutes
plus 2 hours soaking time
Cooking time 35 minutes**

Serves 4

METRIC/IMPERIAL
2 calf's brains
salt and pepper
peppercorns, 1 bay leaf, vinegar
3 large potatoes
75 g/3 oz butter
1 egg
freshly grated nutmeg
2 shallots
15 g/½ oz flour
1 tablespoon tomato purée
100 ml/4 fl oz stock or water
100 ml/4 fl oz dry white wine
2 tablespoons dried breadcrumbs
1 lemon

Soak the brains in cold water for at least 2 hours, changing the water two or three times.

Drain and wipe the brains. Remove the outer membrane. Place in a saucepan and cover with boiling salted water. Add a few peppercorns, the bay leaf and a large dash of vinegar. Boil gently for 15 minutes. Remove from the heat and leave until warm in the stock.

Meanwhile, peel the potatoes and cook in boiling salted water. Drain and mash. Add half the butter, the beaten egg, salt, pepper and a little nutmeg. Beat briskly with a wooden spoon and tip on to a floured surface. Spoon into a sausage shape and join the ends to make a circle, or pipe using a plain vegetable nozzle on to a round ovenproof dish.

Chop the shallots and cook in the remaining butter without browning. Sprinkle with the flour, add the tomato purée, stock and wine. Season. Boil for 1 minute then add the sliced brains. Leave to heat through for 10 minutes before turning into the potato ring.

Sprinkle the whole with breadcrumbs and place under the grill for 5 minutes to brown. Serve with lemon quarters.

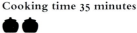 a dry Saumur (white)

**Preparation time 45 minutes
plus 2 hours soaking time
Cooking time 35 minutes**

Serves 4

AMERICAN
2 calf brains
salt and pepper
peppercorns, 1 bay leaf, vinegar
3 large potatoes
6 tablespoons butter
1 egg
freshly grated nutmeg
2 shallots
2 tablespoons all-purpose flour
1 tablespoon tomato paste
½ cup stock or water
½ cup dry white wine
3 tablespoons dry bread crumbs
1 lemon

Calf's brains meunière

(Cervelles meunière)

**Preparation time 15 minutes
plus 2 hours soaking time
Cooking time 25 minutes**

Serves 4

METRIC/IMPERIAL
**2 calf's brains
150 ml/¼ pint vinegar
salt and pepper
1 bouquet garni
flour to coat
75 g/3 oz butter**
Garnish
**1 lemon
chopped parsley**

Clean the brains by soaking for 2 hours in the vinegar and water to cover. Rinse under a cold running tap. Skin and remove blood vessels. Rinse again.

Poach in salted water with the bouquet garni, simmering for 20 minutes. Drain and pat dry on absorbent paper. Leave to cool.

Cut into slices, season and coat with flour. Heat the butter in a frying pan and brown the slices all over.

Arrange the brains on a heated serving dish, and surround with halved lemon slices. Sprinkle with parsley and serve very hot.

🍇 a dry Saumur (white)

**Preparation time 15 minutes
plus 2 hours soaking time
Cooking time 25 minutes**

Serves 4

AMERICAN
**2 calf brains
⅔ cup vinegar
salt and pepper
1 bouquet garni
flour to coat
6 tablespoons butter**
Garnish
**1 lemon
chopped parsley**

Sweetbreads in Madeira

(Ris de veau braisés)

**Preparation time 35 minutes
plus 2 hours soaking time
Cooking time 1¾ hours**

Serves 4

METRIC/IMPERIAL
675 g/1½ lb calf's sweetbreads
sea salt
juice of 1 lemon
thyme, bay leaf, parsley
225 g/8 oz mushrooms
75 g/3 oz butter
3 onions
1 carrot
2 sticks celery
100 g/4 oz ham
100 ml/4 fl oz dry white wine
4 large tomatoes or 1 (227-g/8-oz)
can tomatoes
1 small bouquet garni
250 ml/8 fl oz Madeira
salt and pepper
1 tablespoon potato flour or
2 teaspoons cornflour
Garnish
chopped parsley

Soak the sweetbreads for at least 2 hours in cold water until they become white. Rinse, drain and place in a saucepan of cold water with the salt, lemon juice, thyme, bay leaf and parsley. Bring to the boil and simmer for 1 hour, until tender. Drain, trim and cool, pressing the sweetbreads between two boards or two plates with a weight on top.

Lightly sauté the finely chopped mushrooms in 25 g/1 oz (US 2 tablespoons) butter. Heat the rest of the butter in a flameproof casserole and soften the chopped onions, carrot and celery with the diced ham. When golden, stir in the white wine and bring to the boil. Place the sweetbreads over these ingredients, surround with the peeled and diced tomatoes, and add the bouquet garni and mushrooms. Pour in half the Madeira, season, cover and cook for 45 minutes over a very gentle heat.

Drain the sweetbreads and arrange on a heated serving dish. Reduce the sauce over a brisk heat and thicken with the potato flour mixed with the remaining Madeira.

Pour this sauce over the sweetbreads and sprinkle with chopped parsley.

 a Médoc (red Bordeaux)

**Preparation time 35 minutes
plus 2 hours soaking time
Cooking time 1¾ hours**

Serves 4

AMERICAN
1½ lb calf sweetbreads
coarse salt
juice of 1 lemon
thyme, bay leaf, parsley
½ lb mushrooms
6 tablespoons butter
3 onions
1 carrot
2 stalks celery
¼ lb cooked ham
½ cup dry white wine
4 large tomatoes or 1 (8-oz) can
tomatoes
1 small bouquet garni
1 cup Madeira
salt and pepper
1 tablespoon potato flour or
2 teaspoons cornstarch
Garnish
chopped parsley

Liver with onions

(Foie aux oignons)

Preparation time 15 minutes
Cooking time 20 minutes

Serves 4

METRIC/IMPERIAL
4 large slices liver (calf's or lamb's)
salt and pepper
flour to coat
50g/2oz butter
2 onions
1 teaspoon vinegar
4 tablespoons white wine
Garnish
chopped parsley

Season the slices of liver with salt and pepper and flour both sides.

Melt the butter in a frying pan. Peel and finely slice the onions and soften in the hot butter. When beginning to turn golden, push to one side of the pan and place the liver slices in the centre. Seal over a fairly high heat, turning half-way through cooking. (The inside should remain pink.)

Drain and place on a warmed serving dish.

Add the vinegar and white wine to the juices in the pan. Bring to the boil, scraping the base of the pan well. Season.

Pour this sauce over the liver, sprinkle with chopped parsley and serve very hot.

 a Beaujolais (light fruity red)

Preparation time 15 minutes
Cooking time 20 minutes

Serves 4

AMERICAN
4 large slices liver (calf or lamb)
salt and pepper
flour to coat
¼ cup butter
2 onions
1 teaspoon vinegar
⅓ cup white wine
Garnish
chopped parsley

Liver and bacon kebabs

(Brochettes gourmandes)

Preparation time 20 minutes
Cooking time 10-15 minutes

Serves 6

METRIC/IMPERIAL
275 g/10 oz liver (lamb's, calf's or ox)
275 g/10 oz kidney (lamb's, calf's or ox)
275 g/10 oz lamb's heart
12 rashers smoked streaky bacon
(3 mm/⅛ inch thick)
6 small onions
12 bay leaves
4 tablespoons oil
salt and pepper

Cut the liver into bite-sized pieces. Skin the kidneys, cut into small pieces. Cut the heart into similar pieces. Cut each rasher of bacon into four.

Peel the onions and cut in half lengthwise.

Thread the different ingredients alternately on to six metal skewers or twelve smaller wooden skewers, beginning with half an onion. Between the pieces of offal place 8 pieces of bacon and 2 bay leaves per skewer. Finish with another onion half.

Brush the kebabs with oil and season well.

Grill gently over charcoal or under a preheated grill for 10–15 minutes. Serve very hot. Pilaf rice is a good accompaniment to these kebabs.

 a red Côtes-de-Provence

Preparation time 20 minutes
Cooking time 10-15 minutes

Serves 6

AMERICAN
10 oz liver (lamb, calf or pork)
10 oz kidney (lamb, veal or pork)
10 oz lamb heart
12 bacon slices (⅛ inch thick)
6 small onions
12 bay leaves
⅓ cup oil
salt and pepper

Savoury kebabs (Brochettes mixed grill)

Preparation time 8 minutes
Cooking time 20 minutes

Serves 4

METRIC/IMPERIAL
8 small chipolata sausages
8 lamb's kidneys
8 thin rashers smoked streaky
bacon
4 small tomatoes
8 bay leaves
4 lamb cutlets
4 small white onions
salt and pepper
2 tablespoons oil

Carefully prick the sausages and grill lightly for 7–8 minutes, as these require more cooking than the other ingredients. Clean and skin the kidneys. Roll up the bacon rashers.

Thread on to each skewer a small tomato, then alternately the kidneys, sausages, bacon rolls, bay leaves and cutlets, ending with a small onion. Season with salt and pepper and brush with a little oil.

Grill over charcoal or under the grill for 10–15 minutes. Serve very hot.

 a Médoc (red Bordeaux)

Preparation time 8 minutes
Cooking time 20 minutes

Serves 4

AMERICAN
8 small sausage links
8 lamb kidneys
8 thin bacon slices
4 small tomatoes
8 bay leaves
4 rib lamb chops
4 small white onions
salt and pepper
3 tablespoons oil

Spring chicken with olives

(Coquelets aux olives)

Preparation time 25 minutes
Cooking time 50 minutes

Serves 4

METRIC/IMPERIAL
2 small spring chickens
salt and pepper
50 g/2 oz butter
100 g/4 oz streaky bacon
2 onions
1 stick celery
1 carrot
1 tablespoon flour
250 ml/8 fl oz stock
100 ml/4 fl oz Madeira
1 small bouquet garni
1 tablespoon tomato purée
100 g/4 oz green olives
Garnish
chopped parsley

Clean the chickens. Cleave in two from the base of the neck to the parson's nose. Trim the chicken halves, cutting off any small bones. Flatten slightly and season.

Heat the butter in a frying pan and cook the diced bacon. When golden remove from the pan. In the same butter cook the chicken halves until golden brown all over. Take out of the pan and keep hot.

Put the chopped onions, sliced celery and finely diced carrot into the same pan. Cook until golden and sprinkle with the flour. Stir in well then moisten with the stock and 2 tablespoons (US 3 tablespoons) Madeira. Add the bouquet garni and simmer gently for 20 minutes. Strain the sauce through a conical sieve and mix in the tomato purée.

Stone the olives and blanch for 5 minutes in boiling water. Drain. Replace the chicken and bacon in the frying pan and add the olives. Pour over the sauce. Cover the pan and simmer gently for 20 minutes. Five minutes before serving add the rest of the Madeira. Do not allow to boil.

To serve, arrange the chicken halves side by side on a heated serving dish. Surround with the olives and bacon and pour over the sauce. Sprinkle with chopped parsley and serve very hot.

a Médoc (red Bordeaux)

Preparation time 25 minutes
Cooking time 50 minutes

Serves 4

AMERICAN
2 small spring chickens
salt and pepper
¼ cup butter
6 bacon slices
2 onions
1 stalk celery
1 carrot
1 tablespoon all-purpose flour
1 cup stock
½ cup Madeira
1 small bouquet garni
1 tablespoon tomato paste
¾ cup green olives
Garnish
chopped parsley

Spring chicken with chives

(Coquelets à la ciboulette)

Preparation time 25 minutes
Cooking time 1 hour

Serves 4

METRIC/IMPERIAL
2 small spring chickens
salt and freshly ground pepper
50 g/2 oz butter
1 tablespoon oil
200 ml/7 fl oz chicken stock
450 ml/¾ pint double cream
Garnish
chopped chives

Clean the chickens. Cleave in two lengthwise from the base of the neck to the parson's nose. Trim the chicken halves, cutting off any small bones that stick out. Flatten the halves slightly and season with salt and pepper.

Heat the butter and oil in a frying pan. When hot but not brown add the chicken halves. Cook for 50 minutes, turning frequently. Do not have the heat too high or the butter will burn. Moisten occasionally with stock. When cooked, remove the chicken from the pan and keep hot.

Pour the cream into the frying pan. Thicken over a high heat, beating continuously with a wire whisk. Add the chicken to this sauce to reheat for a few moments. Season.

Arrange the chicken on a heated serving dish. Pour over the sauce and sprinkle generously with chopped chives. Serve very hot.

a Chinon (light fruity red)

Preparation time 25 minutes
Cooking time 1 hour

Serves 4

AMERICAN
2 small spring chickens
salt and freshly ground pepper
¼ cup butter
1 tablespoon oil
¾ cup chicken stock
2 cups heavy cream
Garnish
chopped chives

Chicken in white wine

(Coq au vin blanc)

Preparation time 20 minutes
Cooking time 1 hour

Serves 4-5

METRIC/IMPERIAL
1 (1.5-kg/3½-lb) chicken
4 shallots
225g/8oz mushrooms
75g/3oz butter
1 bottle dry white wine
1 small bouquet garni
½ teaspoon French mustard
300 ml/½ pint double cream
salt and pepper
Garnish
chopped chives and parsley

Clean the chicken. Cut into portions and season.

Peel and chop the shallots. Clean the mushrooms, cutting off the tips of the stalks, and slice them finely.

Heat the butter in a frying pan. Add the mushrooms. Cook until golden then remove and keep warm.

In the same butter cook the chicken portions over a gentle heat. They should turn slightly golden but not brown. Add the shallots and stir well. Moisten with 2–3 tablespoons (US 3–4 tablespoons) wine. When this has evaporated, add a further 2–3 tablespoons (US 3–4 tablespoons). Cook in this way for 40 minutes then remove the chicken.

Rinse the juices from the frying pan with the rest of the wine, and add the bouquet garni. Reduce the sauce by half, by open boiling.

Mix the mustard with the cream and pour into the sauce, stirring well. Finally add the mushrooms and chicken portions and adjust the seasoning.

To serve, remove the bouquet garni, turn into a heated serving dish and sprinkle with chopped chives and parsley.

🍇 a white Mâcon (dry)

Preparation time 20 minutes
Cooking time 1 hour

Serves 4-5

AMERICAN
1 (3½-lb) chicken
4 shallots
½lb mushrooms
6 tablespoons butter
1 bottle dry white wine
1 small bouquet garni
½ teaspoon French mustard
1¼ cups heavy cream
salt and pepper
Garnish
chopped chives and parsley

Chicken pot-roast with herbs

(Poulet Varoise)

**Preparation time 25 minutes
Cooking time 1½ hours**

Serves 4-5

METRIC/IMPERIAL
1 (1.5-kg/3½-lb) chicken
salt and pepper
100ml/4fl oz olive oil
1 sprig of rosemary
3-4 sprigs of dried fennel
2 bay leaves
1 bunch thyme
2 sage leaves
1 bulb garlic
150ml/¼ pint dry red wine

Season the chicken inside with salt and pepper, truss it and brown on all sides in half the hot oil. Set the oven to moderately hot (200°C, 400°F, Gas Mark 6).

Pour the rest of the oil into an ovenproof earthenware dish, scatter with all the herbs and place the chicken on top.

Split the garlic bulb, separating the cloves, but do not peel them. Arrange around the chicken, season and sprinkle with the red wine. Cover and cook in the oven for 1–1½ hours.

Remove the dish from the oven, bring to the table and uncover just before serving.

 a red Côtes-de-Provence

**Preparation time 25 minutes
Cooking time 1½ hours**

Serves 4-5

AMERICAN
1 (3½-lb) chicken
salt and pepper
½ cup olive oil
1 sprig of rosemary
3-4 sprigs of dried fennel
2 bay leaves
1 bunch thyme
2 sage leaves
1 head garlic
⅔ cup dry red wine

Chicken with tarragon

(Poulet à l'estragon)

Preparation time 20 minutes
Cooking time 55 minutes

Serves 4

METRIC/IMPERIAL
1 (1.5-kg/3-lb) chicken
salt and freshly ground pepper
1 bunch tarragon
100 ml/4 fl oz dry white wine
40 g/1½ oz butter
300 ml/½ pint double cream

Joint the chicken into 4 portions, each including one of the limbs, and season.

Set aside 2 sprigs of tarragon; place the remainder in the white wine with freshly ground pepper and simmer gently for 7–8 minutes.

Melt the butter in a shallow frying pan and brown the chicken portions over a low heat until golden. Turn several times and take care they do not overcook.

Cook for 40–45 minutes, sprinkling from time to time with a little of the tarragon wine. Wait until it has evaporated each time before adding more.

When the chicken is cooked, remove and keep warm. Pour the cream into the pan juices and beat over a brisk heat for 2 minutes with a wire whisk. The sauce must be slightly golden in colour.

Pour this sauce over the chicken and sprinkle with the rest of the tarragon. Serve very hot.

 a Tavel (rosé)

Preparation time 20 minutes
Cooking time 55 minutes

Serves 4

AMERICAN
1 (3-lb) chicken
salt and freshly ground pepper
1 bunch tarragon
½ cup dry white wine
3 tablespoons butter
1¼ cups heavy cream

Basque chicken

(Poulet Basquaise)

Preparation time 20 minutes
Cooking time 1 hour

Serves 6

METRIC/IMPERIAL
1 (1.75-kg/4-lb) chicken
salt and pepper
100g/4oz smoked streaky bacon
4 onions
2 cloves garlic
4 green or red peppers
4 tablespoons olive oil
0.75kg/1½lb tomatoes
300ml/½ pint chicken stock
Garnish
chopped parsley

Cut the chicken into portions and season with salt and pepper. Dice the bacon. Peel and finely slice the onions, crush the garlic. Discard the cores and seeds from the peppers and cut into thin strips.

Heat the oil in a large frying pan and brown the pieces of bacon. When they are well done, remove and keep hot.

In the same oil, fry the chicken pieces, turning over on all sides. When golden brown, remove also.

Still in the same pan, soften the onions and cook until transparent, stirring with a wooden spoon. Add the peppers and garlic and cook for 10 minutes, stirring often.

Meanwhile, peel and halve the tomatoes. Remove seeds.

Return the chicken and bacon to the frying pan. Stir in the tomatoes and stock. Season, cover and cook over a very gentle heat for about 40 minutes.

Serve sprinkled with chopped parsley and accompany with a dish of plain boiled rice.

🍇 an Irouléguy (Basque dry white)

Preparation time 20 minutes
Cooking time 1 hour

Serves 6

AMERICAN
1 (4-lb) chicken
salt and pepper
6 bacon slices
4 onions
2 cloves garlic
4 green or red peppers
⅓ cup olive oil
1½lb tomatoes
1¼ cups chicken stock
Garnish
chopped parsley

Chicken Véronique

(Poulet Véronique)

Preparation time 15 minutes
plus overnight marinating
Cooking time 1 hour

Serves 4–5

METRIC/IMPERIAL
1 (1.5-kg/3½-lb) chicken
100 g/4 oz butter
salt and pepper
100 ml/4 fl oz brandy
25 g/1 oz flour
150 ml/¼ pint double cream
225 g/8 oz seedless green grapes
Marinade
1 tablespoon oil
250 ml/8 fl oz grape juice
100 ml/4 fl oz sweet white wine
1 sprig of thyme
freshly ground pepper

The day before place the chicken, cut into pieces, in an earthenware dish. Sprinkle with the oil, grape juice and wine. Add the thyme and pepper and leave to marinate overnight.

The following day, carefully drain the chicken pieces and lightly brown in a shallow frying pan in 75 g/3 oz (US 6 tablespoons) butter. Strain the marinade through a conical sieve and pour over the chicken. Season, cover and cook for 40 minutes.

Drain the chicken pieces again and flame in a separate pan with the brandy. Transfer to a serving dish and keep warm in the oven. Add the flamed brandy to the marinade stock.

Prepare the sauce. Melt the remaining butter in a saucepan, stir in the flour to make a roux. Add the marinade stock and bring to the boil, stirring continuously. Reduce the heat and mix in the cream and grapes. Heat through for 2 minutes, stirring, without allowing to boil.

Pour over the chicken and serve immediately.

 a dry Jurançon (white)

Preparation time 15 minutes
plus overnight marinating
Cooking time 1 hour

Serves 4–5

AMERICAN
1 (3½-lb) chicken
½ cup butter
salt and pepper
½ cup brandy
¼ cup all-purpose flour
⅔ cup heavy cream
½ lb seedless white grapes
Marinade
1 tablespoon oil
1 cup grape juice
½ cup sweet white wine
1 sprig of thyme
freshly ground pepper

New Orleans fried chicken
(Poulet frit New Orleans)

Preparation time 35 minutes
Cooking time 40–50 minutes

Serves 6

METRIC/IMPERIAL
1 (1.5-kg/3½-lb) chicken
freshly ground pepper
4 tablespoons paprika
2 teaspoons celery salt
4 tablespoons flour
about 150ml/¼ pint oil
9 chipolata sausages
18 thin rashers bacon
1 cucumber
4 bananas
1 (326-g/11½-oz) can sweetcorn
with peppers
6 pineapple rings
To serve
350g/12oz long-grain rice

Cut the chicken into 12 pieces, season generously with freshly ground pepper.

Put 3 tablespoons (US ¼ cup) paprika, the celery salt and flour into a large plastic bag. Seal the bag and shake to mix. Add the chicken pieces a few at a time and shake to coat them with the mixture.

Heat some of the oil for frying in a large pan and cook the chicken pieces for 30–40 minutes, browning well but taking care not to burn. Drain on absorbent paper and keep hot. Then fry the chipolatas, each cut into 3 pieces. Drain and keep hot in a low oven with the chicken.

Add a little more oil to the pan if necessary and brown the bacon rashers briefly on both sides. Drain and roll them.

Arrange the chicken pieces in a serving dish with the chipolatas and bacon rolls. Surround with halved cucumber slices, banana wedges, drained sweetcorn and halved pineapple rings. Return to the oven and keep warm.

Mix the remaining paprika with 4 tablespoons (US ⅓ cup) oil and spoon over the dish. Serve immediately, accompanied by the cooked rice.

 a Médoc (red Bordeaux)

Preparation time 35 minutes
Cooking time 40–50 minutes

Serves 6

AMERICAN
1 (3½-lb) chicken
freshly ground pepper
⅓ cup paprika pepper
2 teaspoons celery salt
⅓ cup all-purpose flour
about ⅔ cup oil
9 link sausages
18 bacon slices
1 cucumber
4 bananas
1 (11½-oz) can corn with peppers
6 pineapple rings
To serve
1½ cups long-grain rice

Chicken curry

(Le curry de poulet)

Preparation time 45 minutes
Cooking time 1 hour

Serves 6

METRIC/IMPERIAL
1 (1.75-kg/4-lb) chicken
salt and pepper
1 tablespoon freshly grated root
ginger or ground ginger
5 tablespoons oil
4 large onions
1 apple
1 tablespoon curry powder
50g/2oz desiccated coconut
450–600ml/$\frac{3}{4}$–1 pint chicken stock
150ml/$\frac{1}{4}$ pint natural yogurt
1 clove garlic
To serve
350g/12oz long-grain rice
$\frac{1}{4}$ white cabbage
225g/8oz green runner beans
1 tablespoon castor sugar
175ml/6fl oz vinegar
5 tablespoons water
pinch each of salt and cayenne
3 bananas
6 pineapple rings, diced
100g/4oz desiccated coconut
chutneys, pickles and relishes

Divide the chicken into portions, season and rub with the ginger. Brown in hot oil with the finely chopped onions.

Grate the peeled apple. Add to the chicken, sprinkle with the curry powder and 50g/2oz (US $\frac{2}{3}$ cup) coconut and mix with a wooden spoon over a high heat.

Stir in the chicken stock, yogurt and crushed garlic. Season and cook for about 40 minutes.

Wash the rice and cook for 15 minutes in plenty of boiling salted water. Drain and keep warm in a low oven.

Prepare the sweet and sour vegetables. Shred the cabbage and green beans. Boil the sugar, vinegar and water with a pinch of salt and cayenne. Add the beans and cook for 5 minutes. Drain. Boil the shredded cabbage in the same mixture for 5 minutes, then drain.

Arrange the chicken curry in a large dish. Serve it with the rice and small bowls of sliced banana, diced pineapple, coconut, the sweet and sour vegetables and assorted chutneys, pickles and relishes.

 a Côtes-de-Provence rosé

Preparation time 45 minutes
Cooking time 1 hour

Serves 6

AMERICAN
1 (4-lb) chicken
salt and pepper
1 tablespoon freshly grated ginger
root or ground ginger
6 tablespoons oil
4 large onions
1 apple
1 tablespoon curry powder
$\frac{2}{3}$ cup shredded coconut
2–2$\frac{1}{2}$ cups chicken stock
$\frac{2}{3}$ cup plain yogurt
1 clove garlic
To serve
1$\frac{1}{2}$ cups long-grain rice
$\frac{1}{4}$ head white cabbage
$\frac{1}{2}$ lb green beans
1 tablespoon sugar
$\frac{3}{4}$ cup vinegar
6 tablespoons water
dash each of salt and cayenne
pepper
3 bananas
6 pineapple rings, diced
1$\frac{1}{3}$ cups shredded coconut
chutneys, pickles and relishes

Spiced chicken with saffron

(La poule aux oeufs d'or)

Preparation time 30 minutes
Cooking time 1½ hours

Serves 6

METRIC/IMPERIAL
1 (1.5-kg/3½-lb) boiling fowl
2 lemons
1 small piece fresh root ginger
2 cloves
salt and pepper
40g/1½oz butter
100ml/4fl oz olive oil
575g/1¼lb onions
1 clove garlic
250ml/8fl oz chicken stock
generous pinch of saffron or
turmeric
pinch of cayenne
6 eggs
To serve
oriental rice (see page 252) made
with 350g/12oz long-grain rice,
etc.

Prepare and clean the fowl. Put inside 1 lemon cut into quarters, half the grated ginger and the cloves, crushed with a little salt and pepper. Truss the bird.

Heat the butter with 2 tablespoons (US 3 tablespoons) oil in a flameproof casserole. Place the bird in it and brown well on all sides.

Peel then finely slice the onions and garlic. Add to the well-browned chicken and leave to soften. Pour over the chicken stock and season to taste.

Put the saffron, cayenne, remaining grated ginger and the rest of the olive oil in a bowl. Beat the mixture with a wooden spoon then gradually incorporate the juice of the second lemon. Pour this sauce over the chicken, cover the casserole and cook over a very gentle heat for 1–1¼ hours.

During this time, prepare the oriental rice.

Hard-boil the eggs, plunge into cold water then shell them. Place around the chicken 10 minutes before the end of cooking, mixing in well with the sauce to give the eggs a good colour.

Transfer the chicken to a heated serving dish and coat it with the sauce. Surround with the onions and eggs, coloured golden by the saffron, and serve accompanied by the oriental rice.

 a Tavel (rosé) or a Beaujolais (light fruity red)

Preparation time 30 minutes
Cooking time 1½ hours

Serves 6

AMERICAN
1 (3½-lb) stewing chicken
2 lemons
1 small piece fresh ginger root
2 cloves
salt and pepper
3 tablespoons butter
½ cup olive oil
1¼lb onions
1 clove garlic
1 cup chicken stock
generous dash of saffron or
turmeric
dash of cayenne pepper
6 eggs
To serve
oriental rice (see page 252) made
with 1½ cups long-grain rice, etc.

Béarnaise chicken

(La poule au pot Béarnaise)

Preparation time 1 hour
Cooking time 1¼–1½ hours

Serves 6

METRIC/IMPERIAL
1 (1.5-kg/3½-lb) boiling fowl
1 bouquet garni
2 cloves garlic
1 stick celery
1 onion stuck with 3 cloves
6 leeks
6 carrots
3 turnips
1 cabbage
Stuffing
4 shallots
1 onion
2 cloves garlic
2 chicken livers
75g/3oz dried breadcrumbs, soaked
in milk and squeezed
2 eggs
450g/1lb sausagemeat
2 tablespoons chopped parsley
pinch of allspice
salt and pepper

Prepare the stuffing. Peel and finely chop the shallots, onion and garlic. Mince the chicken livers. Bind the breadcrumbs with the eggs. Mix all these ingredients with the sausagemeat, chopped parsley, allspice and seasoning. Knead well to obtain an even stuffing.

Fill the inside of the chicken with a third of this stuffing, sew up the openings. Truss the chicken, place in a large saucepan and cover with plenty of cold water. Add the bouquet garni, garlic, celery and onion stuck with cloves. Bring to the boil then skim before seasoning.

Peel and wash the leeks, carrots and turnips. Add to the pan after having skimmed the stock. (Tie the leeks in a bundle if preferred.) Cover and cook over a gentle heat for 30–40 minutes.

Meanwhile, remove 12 large leaves from the cabbage. Wash these and the remaining cabbage, quartered. Blanch the 12 leaves for 2 minutes only in boiling water, drain and wipe them. Place 2 cabbage leaves on top of each other, to make 6 parcels in all. Spread each parcel with a little of the stuffing. Secure each by folding the leaves over, then tie with string.

Remove the chicken from the saucepan and finish cooking in a moderately hot oven (190 C, 375 F, Gas Mark 5) for 30 minutes.

Meanwhile, place the stuffed cabbage leaves and cabbage quarters in the stock in the saucepan, and simmer for 30 minutes.

Strain the stock into a soup tureen and serve the chicken on a dish with the stuffed cabbage leaves and vegetables.

 a Beaujolais (light fruity red)

Preparation time 1 hour
Cooking time 1¼–1½ hours

Serves 6

AMERICAN
1 (3½-lb) stewing chicken
1 bouquet garni
2 cloves garlic
1 stalk celery
1 onion stuck with 3 cloves
6 leeks
6 carrots
3 turnips
1 head cabbage
Stuffing
4 shallots
1 onion
2 cloves garlic
2 chicken livers
¾ cup dry bread crumbs, soaked in
milk and squeezed
2 eggs
1lb sausage meat
3 tablespoons chopped parsley
dash of allspice
salt and pepper

Chicken with rice

(La poule au riz)

Preparation time 30 minutes
Cooking time 1¼–1½ hours

Serves 6

METRIC/IMPERIAL
1 (1.5-kg/3½-lb) boiling fowl
1 onion stuck with 2 cloves
1 stick celery
1 bouquet garni
sea salt and freshly ground black
pepper
3 carrots
2 turnips
6 leeks
350g/12oz long-grain rice
Sauce
50g/2oz butter
50g/2oz flour
150ml/¼ pint double cream

Prepare and clean the fowl. Place in a large saucepan, cover with at least 3 litres/5 pints (US 6½ pints) cold water and add the onion, celery and bouquet garni. Bring gently to the boil, skim carefully, bring to the boil again and season.

Peel and wash the carrots and turnips, cut into chunks and toss into the boiling stock. Cover and simmer for about 30–40 minutes. At the end of this time, transfer the chicken to a moderately hot oven (190°C, 375°F, Gas Mark 5) and cook for a further 30 minutes. Add the cleaned leeks to the stock with the other vegetables and continue to simmer for 30 minutes.

Measure the rice, wash until the water is clear. Cook for 15 minutes in twice its volume of water with a little salt.

Prepare the sauce. Melt the butter and stir in the flour. Cook for 1 minute, stirring, until it begins to bubble. Thin with 450ml/¾ pint (US 2 cups) cooking stock and cook for 5 minutes, stirring continuously. Add the cream, continue cooking for 5 minutes and adjust seasoning to taste. Do not boil.

To serve, arrange the chicken on a serving dish and surround with the vegetables. Accompany with the rice and the cream sauce; the rest of the stock will make an excellent soup.

 a Côtes-du-Rhône (red)

Preparation time 30 minutes
Cooking time 1¼–1½ hours

Serves 6

AMERICAN
1 (3½-lb) stewing chicken
1 onion stuck with 2 cloves
1 stalk celery
1 bouquet garni
coarse salt and freshly ground
black pepper
3 carrots
2 turnips
6 leeks
1½ cups long-grain rice
Sauce
¼ cup butter
½ cup all-purpose flour
⅔ cup heavy cream

Chicken chaudfroid

(Chaud-froid de volailles)

Preparation time 1½ hours
Cooking time 4¾ hours

Serves 6

METRIC/IMPERIAL
1 small knuckle of veal
1 calf's foot, split
275g/10oz chicken giblets
1 bouquet garni
1 onion, stuck with 2 cloves
1 stick celery
4 leeks (white parts only)
3 carrots
2 turnips
salt and pepper
1 (1.75-kg/4-lb) chicken
Sauce
2 (35-g/1¼-oz) packets aspic jelly powder
50g/2oz butter
50g/2oz flour
·150ml/¼ pint double cream
2 egg yolks
Garnish
1 bunch tarragon

Prepare the consommé. Put the knuckle of veal, calf's foot and chicken giblets into a large saucepan. Cover with cold water. Add the bouquet garni, onion and celery. Bring to the boil. Remove the scum and add the remaining vegetables. Cook for 3 hours, seasoning halfway through cooking. Strain the stock, cool and skim off the fat.

Clean and truss the chicken. Place in the stock and bring to the boil. Simmer gently for 1¼–1½ hours. The cooked chicken should remain firm. Drain and allow to cool. Skim the fat from the surface of the cooled stock.

Prepare the sauce. Pour 1 litre/1¾ pints (US 4¼ cups) stock into a saucepan and reduce to 450 ml/¾ pint (US 2 cups) over a high heat. Cool slightly and mix half this stock with the aspic jelly powder, stirring until dissolved. Reserve. Make a white roux with the butter and flour. When it begins to bubble stir in the remaining reduced stock. Cook over a low heat for 2 minutes, stirring continuously. Mix the cream with the egg yolks and a little of the hot sauce. Add to the rest of the sauce. Thicken for a few moments over a gentle heat, still stirring vigorously. Stir in the dissolved aspic jelly powder and leave to cool.

Carve the chicken into 6 portions. Remove the skin and trim. Place on a baking sheet lined with greaseproof paper.

As soon as the sauce is cool, and before it forms a jelly, pour a little over each chicken portion. Repeat several times until covered in a layer of aspic sauce.

Pour the rest of the sauce over the base of a serving dish. Arrange the chicken pieces on it. Garnish with tarragon and keep cool until required.

 a Chablis (dry white)

Preparation time 1½ hours
Cooking time 4¾ hours

Serves 6

AMERICAN
1 small veal shank
1 calf's foot, split
10oz chicken giblets
1 bouquet garni
1 onion, stuck with 2 cloves
1 stalk celery
4 leeks (white parts only)
3 carrots
2 turnips
salt and pepper
1 (4-lb) chicken
Sauce
2 (1¼-oz) packages aspic jelly powder
¼ cup butter
½ cup all-purpose flour
⅔ cup heavy cream
2 egg yolks
Garnish
1 bunch tarragon

Roast turkey English style

(Dinde à l'Anglaise)

Preparation time 45 minutes
Cooking time about 2½ hours

Serves 10

METRIC/IMPERIAL
1 (3.5-kg/8-lb) turkey
100g/4oz butter
salt and pepper
1 thin rasher streaky bacon
20 small chipolata sausages
10 rashers bacon, halved
2kg/4½lb chestnuts
2 litres/3½ pints chicken stock
Stuffing
350g/12oz onions, finely chopped
75g/3oz butter
150g/5oz chicken livers
225g/8oz sausagemeat
50g/2oz fresh breadcrumbs
4 tablespoons double cream
1 egg
2 tablespoons chopped parsley and chives
salt and pepper
freshly grated nutmeg
Garnish
sprigs of watercress

Clean the turkey carefully. Trim the liver and reserve. Boil up the remaining giblets to make stock.

Prepare the stuffing. Cook the onions in 50g/2oz (US ¼ cup) butter over a gentle heat, until soft but not browned. Before they begin to colour, sieve or liquidise to reduce to a purée. In the remaining hot butter seal the chicken livers and reserved turkey liver and mince finely.

Mix together the onion, minced liver, sausagemeat, breadcrumbs, cream, beaten egg, parsley and chives. Season with salt, pepper and nutmeg. Work the whole together well to give a uniform stuffing.

Fill the inside of the turkey with this stuffing and sew up the openings. Truss and place in a large buttered roasting pan. Season, place the slice of bacon over it and baste with half the melted butter. Cook in a moderately hot oven (200°C, 400°F, Gas Mark 6) for 2¼–2½ hours. Baste again several times during cooking. Thirty minutes before the end of the cooking time roll each chipolata sausage in a halved bacon rasher and place around the edge of the turkey.

Meanwhile, slit the chestnuts and cook for 5–10 minutes in boiling water. Drain and peel. Cook in the chicken stock until tender then drain carefully and brown in the remaining butter.

Arrange the turkey on a large serving dish. Surround with the bacon rolls and chestnuts and garnish with watercress sprigs. Make a gravy with the pan juices and turkey stock and serve in a sauceboat.

🍇 a Châteauneuf-du-Pape (red)

Preparation time 45 minutes
Cooking time about 2½ hours

Serves 10

AMERICAN
1 (8-lb) turkey
½ cup butter
salt and pepper
1 thin bacon slice
20 small link sausages
10 bacon slices, halved
4½ lb chestnuts
4½ pints chicken stock
Stuffing
3 cups finely chopped onion
6 tablespoons butter
5oz chicken livers
1 cup sausage meat
1 cup fresh soft bread crumbs
⅓ cup heavy cream
1 egg
3 tablespoons chopped parsley and chives
salt and pepper
freshly grated nutmeg
Garnish
sprigs of watercress

Normandy turkey

(Dinde Normande)

Preparation time 25 minutes
Cooking time 2¼-2½ hours

Serves 8-10

METRIC/IMPERIAL
12-14 dessert apples
3 tablespoons calvados or brandy
1 (3.5-4-kg/8-9-lb) turkey
salt and pepper
200g/7oz butter
1 rasher streaky bacon
1kg/2lb pork chipolata sausages

Peel 4 apples, cut each into 8 segments and sprinkle with the calvados.

Clean the turkey and place the apple segments inside. Add salt and pepper, truss the turkey and brush with a little melted butter.

Butter a large ovenproof dish. Place the turkey in the dish, cover with the bacon rasher and cook in a moderately hot oven (200°C, 400°F, Gas Mark 6) for 1½ hours.

Remove the bacon rasher, melt the rest of the butter and arrange the remaining apples, peeled and cored, around the turkey. Return to the oven for a further 45–60 minutes. Baste the apples and turkey frequently with the melted butter.

Prick the sausages so they do not burst. Place in the dish 30 minutes before the end of cooking. Serve the turkey hot, garnished with a sliced cooked apple.

🍇 a Côtes-du-Rhône (red)

Preparation time 25 minutes
Cooking time 2¼-2½ hours

Serves 8-10

AMERICAN
12-14 dessert apples
¼ cup calvados or brandy
1 (8-9-lb) turkey
salt and pepper
¾ cup plus 2 tablespoons butter
1 bacon slice
2lb pork link sausages

Duck with orange sauce

(Canard à l'orange)

Preparation time 30 minutes
Cooking time 1 hour

Serves 4

METRIC/IMPERIAL
1 duck or duckling
salt and pepper
50g/2oz butter
3 tablespoons brandy
3 oranges
2 tablespoons sugar
few drops of vinegar
1 teaspoon lemon juice

Prepare and clean the duck. Season the inside and truss. Heat the butter in a flameproof casserole and brown the duck all over. Sprinkle with the brandy and flame.

Wash and finely peel 1 orange. Shred the peel and blanch for 5 minutes in boiling water. Cool under running water then dry. Squeeze the juice from this orange.

Prepare a caramel by dissolving the sugar and vinegar in a heavy-bottomed saucepan, very slowly over a low heat. Do not stir.

Sprinkle the duck with this caramel. Add the orange and lemon juice, cover the casserole and finish cooking. Peel the remaining oranges with a knife, slice into rounds, collect the juice and add to the duck sauce.

Place the duck on a heated serving dish and surround with the orange slices. Pour the sauce over the duck, garnish with the shredded orange peel and serve very hot.

a red Bordeaux

Preparation time 30 minutes
Cooking time 1 hour

Serves 4

AMERICAN
1 duck or duckling
salt and pepper
¼ cup butter
¼ cup brandy
3 oranges
3 tablespoons sugar
few drops of vinegar
1 teaspoon lemon juice

Duck with peaches

(Canard aux pêches)

Preparation time 25 minutes
Cooking time 1–1¼ hours

Serves 5–6

METRIC/IMPERIAL
1 large duck
2 small cloves
pinch of sea salt
6 black peppercorns
pinch of cinnamon
40g/1½oz butter
10–12 peaches
1 bottle sweet white wine
salt and pepper
1 tablespoon potato flour or
2 teaspoons cornflour
Garnish
chopped parsley

Prepare and clean the duck.

In a kitchen mortar pound the cloves, sea salt, peppercorns and cinnamon. Use to season the duck inside and out. Truss.

Heat the butter in a flameproof casserole and brown the duck all over.

Continue cooking in a moderately hot oven (200°C, 400°F, Gas Mark 6) for 1–1¼ hours.

Wipe the peaches with a damp cloth but do not peel. Leave whole and poach for 15 minutes in the wine.

When the duck has been cooking for about 35 minutes remove any excess fat. Arrange the peaches around the duck.

Reduce the wine by half, by boiling in an open pan. Reserve 3 tablespoons (US ¼ cup) and pour the remainder over the duck. Season and finish cooking.

Arrange the duck on a heated serving dish and surround with the peaches. Thicken the casserole juices over a gentle heat, stirring in the potato flour mixed with the reserved wine. Pour over the duck and peaches and sprinkle with chopped parsley.

 a red Bordeaux

Preparation time 25 minutes
Cooking time 1–1¼ hours

Serves 5–6

AMERICAN
1 large duck
2 small cloves
dash of coarse salt
6 black peppercorns
dash of cinnamon
3 tablespoons butter
10–12 peaches
1 bottle sweet white wine
salt and pepper
1 tablespoon potato flour or
2 teaspoons cornstarch
Garnish
chopped parsley

Duckling with cherries

(Caneton aux cerises)

Preparation time 25 minutes
Cooking time 1-1¼ hours

Serves 4

METRIC/IMPERIAL
1 duckling
salt and pepper
40g/1½oz butter
0.75kg/1½ lb cherries
450ml/¾ pint red wine
50g/2oz brown sugar
1 small piece cinnamon stick
1 clove
3-4 tablespoons cherry liqueur
2 teaspoons potato flour or
1 teaspoon cornflour
1 tablespoon Kirsch

Prepare and clean the duckling. Season the inside with salt and pepper. Truss.

Heat the butter in a flameproof casserole and brown the duckling all over, turning several times. Transfer to a moderately hot oven (200°C, 400°F, Gas Mark 6) and cook for 30 minutes.

Wipe the cherries and remove stalks and stones. Pour the wine into a saucepan with the brown sugar, cinnamon and clove. Bring to the boil and add the cherries. Poach for 15 minutes and then add the cherry liqueur.

Pour the cherries and sauce around the duckling. Season to taste and return to the oven for a further 20 minutes.

Place the duckling on a heated serving dish and surround with the cherries. Thicken the sauce over a gentle heat, stirring in the potato flour mixed with the Kirsch. Pour over the dish and serve immediately.

 a red Bordeaux

Preparation time 25 minutes
Cooking time 1-1¼ hours

Serves 4

AMERICAN
1 duckling
salt and pepper
3 tablespoons butter
1½ lb cherries
2 cups red wine
¼ cup light brown sugar
1 small piece cinnamon stick
1 clove
¼-⅓ cup cherry liqueur
2 teaspoons potato flour or
1 teaspoon cornstarch
1 tablespoon Kirsch

Duckling with peas

(Caneton aux petits pois)

Preparation time 45 minutes
Cooking time 1–1¼ hours

Serves 4

METRIC/IMPERIAL
1.5 kg/3 lb fresh young peas
6 large spring onions
100 g/4 oz butter
1 bunch savory
1 sugar lump
200 ml/7 fl oz stock
1 duckling
salt and pepper

Shell the peas and trim the spring onions.

Melt 65 g/2½ oz (US 5 tablespoons) butter in a flame-proof casserole. Add the peas, onions, three-quarters of the savory and the sugar lump. Cover and cook over a low heat for 40–45 minutes. If necessary moisten with the stock.

Meanwhile, prepare and clean the duckling. Put a knob of butter inside with salt, pepper and the rest of the savory. Brush the outside with the remaining butter, melted, and season. Place in an ovenproof dish.

Cook in a moderately hot oven (200°C, 400°F, Gas Mark 6) for 1–1¼ hours. Baste occasionally with the cooking juices, adding 1–2 tablespoons hot water if necessary.

Drain any excess fat from the cooked duck and surround with the peas. Serve at once.

🍇 a Médoc (red Bordeaux)

Preparation time 45 minutes
Cooking time 1–1¼ hours

Serves 4

AMERICAN
3 lb fresh young peas
6 large scallions
½ cup butter
1 bunch savory
1 sugar cube
¾ cup stock
1 duckling
salt and pepper

Duck in foil parcels

(Canard en chemise)

Preparation time 20 minutes
Cooking time 50 minutes

Serves 4

METRIC/IMPERIAL
1 (1.5-kg/3½-lb) duck
2 tablespoons olive oil
1 can green peppercorns
1 bunch chives
salt

Cut the duck into 4 portions.

Heat the olive oil in a frying pan. Add the duck portions and brown all over for 5 minutes.

Drain and chop the peppercorns. Chop the chives.

Place each portion of duck on a sheet of foil. Sprinkle with a little salt and the peppercorns and chives. Fold up and seal the foil parcels.

Place in a roasting pan and cook in a hot oven (230°C, 450°F, Gas Mark 8) for 45 minutes.

To serve, open the parcels, fold back the foil and drain off any excess fat. Arrange on a serving dish and accompany with buttered potatoes.

 a Saint-Nicolas-de-Bourgueil (light fruity red)

Preparation time 20 minutes
Cooking time 50 minutes

Serves 4

AMERICAN
1 (3½-lb) duck
3 tablespoons olive oil
1 can green peppercorns
1 bunch chives
salt

Normandy duck

(Canard sauvage aux pommes)

Preparation time 25 minutes
Cooking time 1-1¼ hours

Serves 4

METRIC/IMPERIAL
1 wild duck
8 peppercorns
pinch of sea salt
2 cloves
pinch of cinnamon
2 dessert apples
75g/3oz butter
1 small rasher bacon
3 tablespoons calvados or brandy
Garnish
6 dessert apples
50g/2oz butter
pinch of cinnamon
salt and pepper
about 20 cloves

Prepare and clean the duck.

In a kitchen mortar pound the peppercorns, sea salt, cloves and cinnamon. Peel, core and dice the apples. Mix with the ground spices and half the butter. Combine the mixture thoroughly and fill the inside of the duck. Cover with the bacon rasher and truss.

Peel and core the 6 apples for garnish. Fill the core cavity with the butter, beaten with the cinnamon and a little seasoning. Stick cloves into each apple.

Place the duck in a well-buttered ovenproof dish and arrange the apples around it. Sprinkle with the rest of the melted butter and cook in a moderately hot oven (200°C, 400°F, Gas Mark 6) for 1–1¼ hours.

Serve in the cooking dish and flame with calvados at the table.

 a Morgon (red Beaujolais)

Preparation time 25 minutes
Cooking time 1-1¼ hours

Serves 4

AMERICAN
1 wild duck
8 peppercorns
dash of coarse salt
2 cloves
dash of cinnamon
2 dessert apples
6 tablespoons butter
1 small bacon slice
¼ cup calvados or brandy
Garnish
6 dessert apples
¼ cup butter
dash of cinnamon
salt and pepper
about 20 cloves

Wild duck and wine casserole (Daube de canard sauvage)

Preparation time 30 minutes
Cooking time 1¼ hours

Serves 4-8

METRIC/IMPERIAL
2 wild ducks
salt and pepper
75 g/3 oz butter
100 g/4 oz small bacon pieces
2 onions
1 carrot
4 shallots
½ stick celery
2 sage leaves
1 tablespoon flour
250 ml/8 fl oz stock
100 ml/4 fl oz red wine
3 tablespoons brandy
2 oranges
1 lemon

Prepare, clean and joint the ducks. Season.

Heat 50 g/2 oz (US ¼ cup) butter in a flameproof casserole. Add the bacon, brown and remove from the pan. Keep warm. In the same butter, brown the duck portions over a medium heat. Remove and keep warm.

Peel the onions, carrot and shallots, chop very finely with the celery. Soften these ingredients in the casserole, adding the sage leaves for flavour. When golden, sprinkle with the flour. Brown and stir in the stock and red wine. After cooking for 15 minutes strain through a conical sieve.

Wash and dry the casserole. Heat the remaining butter, add the duck portions, sprinkle with brandy and flame. Add the sauce and bacon, cover and cook over a low heat for about 1 hour.

Wash and dry the oranges. Remove the peel thinly from one of them and cut into narrow strips. Blanch for 5 minutes in boiling water and drain. Squeeze the juice from this orange and add to the duck sauce.

When the duck is cooked, drain and arrange on a heated serving dish. Cut the second orange into slices and dip into the hot sauce. Arrange around the duck. Pour over the sauce, sprinkle with the peel and garnish the dish with halved lemon quarters. Serve immediately.

 a Médoc (red Bordeaux)

Preparation time 30 minutes
Cooking time 1¼ hours

Serves 4-8

AMERICAN
2 wild ducks
salt and pepper
6 tablespoons butter
¼ lb small bacon pieces
2 onions
1 carrot
4 shallots
½ stalk celery
2 sage leaves
1 tablespoon all-purpose flour
1 cup stock
½ cup red wine
¼ cup brandy
2 oranges
1 lemon

Rabbit with lemon

(Lapin au citron)

**Preparation time 30 minutes
plus 2 hours marinating time
Cooking time 1 hour**

🟤🟤

Serves 4

METRIC/IMPERIAL
1 rabbit (about 1.25 kg/2½ lb)
salt and pepper
1 teaspoon ground ginger
3 lemons
5 tablespoons olive oil
pinch of saffron
1 stock cube
1 kg/2 lb new potatoes

Cut the rabbit into pieces. Season with salt, pepper and ground ginger. Mix the juice of 2 lemons with 3 tablespoons (US ¼ cup) olive oil. Spoon over the rabbit and leave to marinate for 2 hours, turning the pieces occasionally with a wooden spoon.

Drain the rabbit pieces and fry in the rest of the olive oil. When they begin to turn golden sprinkle with a pinch of saffron and add the marinade. Turn up the heat.

Dissolve the stock cube in 300 ml/½ pint (US 1¼ cups) boiling water. Pour over the rabbit and finish cooking over a low heat for about 40 minutes.

Meanwhile, peel the potatoes and cook in boiling salted water.

Five minutes before serving cut the last lemon into slices and add to the rabbit.

Arrange the rabbit on a serving dish, surround with the potatoes and pour over the sauce.

 a red Côtes-de-Provence

**Preparation time 30 minutes
plus 2 hours marinating time
Cooking time 1 hour**

🟤🟤

Serves 4

AMERICAN
1 rabbit (about 2½ lb)
salt and pepper
1 teaspoon ground ginger
3 lemons
6 tablespoons olive oil
dash of saffron
1 bouillon cube
2 lb new potatoes

Rabbit with mustard

(Lapin à la moutarde)

Preparation time 20 minutes
Cooking time 1 hour

Serves 4

METRIC/IMPERIAL
salt and pepper
1 saddle of rabbit
50 g/2 oz butter
2 carrots
1 large onion
2 sticks celery
6 tablespoons French mustard
3 sprigs of parsley
1 sprig of thyme
½ bay leaf
pinch of rosemary
100 ml/4 fl oz dry white wine
150 ml/¼ pint double cream

Salt and pepper the saddle of rabbit, rub with the butter and cook in a hot oven (220°C, 425°F, Gas Mark 7) for 20 minutes, basting frequently.

Peel or wash the vegetables and slice.

Take the rabbit out of the oven. Coat generously with mustard.

Return to a moderate oven (180°C, 350°F, Gas Mark 4) and surround with the sliced vegetables. Add the parsley, thyme, bay leaf and rosemary, and cook for a further 40 minutes, basting from time to time.

Transfer the rabbit and vegetables to a serving dish and keep warm. Stir the white wine into the pan juices, boil for 2 minutes then stir in the cream. Heat through without boiling. Taste and adjust seasoning. Strain the sauce through a conical sieve and serve in a sauceboat to accompany the rabbit.

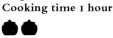 a Bourgueil (fruity red)

Preparation time 20 minutes
Cooking time 1 hour

Serves 4

AMERICAN
salt and pepper
1 saddle of rabbit
¼ cup butter
2 carrots
1 large onion
2 stalks celery
½ cup French mustard
3 sprigs of parsley
1 sprig of thyme
½ bay leaf
dash of rosemary
½ cup dry white wine
⅔ cup heavy cream

Stuffed rabbit

(Lapereau farci)

Preparation time 1 hour
Cooking time 1 hour

Serves 6

METRIC/IMPERIAL
1 young rabbit (about 1.25kg/2½lb)
2–3 tablespoons French mustard
1 bay leaf
salt and pepper
40g/1½oz butter
3 tablespoons dry white wine
Stuffing
3 medium pieces of rabbit
(each about 100g/4oz)
1 young rabbit liver
100g/4oz smoked streaky bacon
200g/7oz unsmoked streaky bacon
2 onions
4 shallots
2 cloves garlic
1 small bunch parsley
pinch of thyme
1 egg
50g/2oz fresh breadcrumbs,
moistened in milk and squeezed
1 bay leaf
Garnish
2–3 bunches watercress

Ask your butcher to bone the rabbit, except for the legs, and to remove the head.

Prepare the stuffing. Mince the pieces of rabbit (after removing bones), the rabbit liver, previously fried in a little hot butter, and the smoked and unsmoked bacon. Finely chop the onions, shallots, garlic and parsley and mix with the minced meats in a large bowl. Add the thyme, beaten egg and breadcrumbs. Season and knead to give a uniform stuffing. Form into a roll and place inside the rabbit with the bay leaf. Sew up the skin of the stomach to retain the stuffing then coat the rabbit all over with mustard. Place a bay leaf on top and season with salt and pepper.

Set the oven to hot (220°C, 425°F, Gas Mark 7). Butter a roasting pan and place the rabbit in it, dotted with small pieces of butter. Cook in the oven for 1 hour, basting from time to time with the white wine and several tablespoons hot water. When cooked the rabbit should be golden brown.

Cut up and arrange on a heated serving dish. Garnish with sprigs of watercress. Rinse out the juices from the roasting pan with a little boiling water and pour into a sauceboat. This stuffed rabbit is equally delicious served cold.

 a Bourgueil (fruity red)

Preparation time 1 hour
Cooking time 1 hour

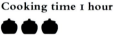

Serves 6

AMERICAN
1 young rabbit (about 2½lb)
3–4 tablespoons French mustard
1 bay leaf
salt and pepper
3 tablespoons butter
¼ cup dry white wine
Stuffing
3 medium pieces of rabbit
(each about ¼lb)
1 young rabbit liver
6 smoked bacon slices
9–10 unsmoked bacon slices
2 onions
4 shallots
2 cloves garlic
1 small bunch parsley
dash of thyme
1 egg
1 cup fresh soft bread crumbs,
moistened in milk and squeezed
1 bay leaf
Garnish
2–3 bunches watercress

Bohemian rabbit

(Lapin à la bohémienne)

Preparation time 1 hour
Cooking time 1 hour

Serves 4

METRIC/IMPERIAL
1 rabbit (about 1.25kg/2½lb)
salt and pepper
4 onions
0.75kg/1½lb tomatoes
3 aubergines
3 courgettes
175ml/6fl oz oil
1 small bouquet garni
2 cloves garlic
2 peppers
24 slices chorizo sausage
225g/8oz long-grain rice
pinch of saffron or turmeric
50g/2oz black olives
Garnish
3 eggs, hard-boiled

Cut the rabbit into pieces and season.

Peel and finely slice the onions. Peel the tomatoes and quarter. Wash the aubergines and courgettes (do not peel), cut into slices.

Sprinkle the aubergine slices with salt and leave to sweat.

Fry the rabbit pieces in a frying pan with 4 tablespoons (US ⅓ cup) hot oil, half the onions and the bouquet garni. Brown well and moisten if necessary with a little hot water.

Brown the rest of the onions in 2 tablespoons (US 3 tablespoons) hot oil. Add the tomatoes, the aubergines (rinsed and wiped) and courgettes. Season and add the crushed garlic. Add this tomato mixture to the browned rabbit and continue cooking over a low heat for 40–50 minutes.

Wash the peppers, remove the core and seeds. Cut into strips and fry in the rest of the oil with the slices of chorizo sausage. Wash the rice and cook with the saffron or turmeric in one and a half times its volume of boiling water.

Drain the rabbit pieces and place the tomato mixture in the centre of a serving dish. Surround with the cooked rice and place the rabbit pieces on the rice. Add the olives, chorizo sausage and pepper strips and garnish the dish with quartered hard-boiled eggs.

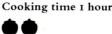 a Corbières (full-bodied red)

Preparation time 1 hour
Cooking time 1 hour

Serves 4

AMERICAN
1 rabbit (about 2½lb)
salt and pepper
4 onions
1½lb tomatoes
3 eggplant
3 zucchini
¾ cup oil
1 small bouquet garni
2 cloves garlic
2 peppers
24 slices chorizo sausage
1 cup long-grain rice
dash of saffron or turmeric
2oz ripe olives
Garnish
3 eggs, hard-cooked

Rabbit with olives

(Lapin aux olives)

Preparation time 25 minutes
Cooking time 1¼–1½ hours

Serves 4

METRIC/IMPERIAL
1 rabbit (about 1.25 kg/2½ lb)
salt and pepper
50 g/2 oz butter
2 tablespoons oil
3 onions
2 cloves garlic
1 tablespoon flour
300 ml/½ pint dry white wine
250 ml/8 fl oz stock
3 tablespoons tomato purée
1 bouquet garni
100 g/4 oz green olives
100 ml/4 fl oz Madeira
Garnish
chopped parsley

Cut the rabbit into 8 pieces and season.

Heat 40 g/1½ oz (US 3 tablespoons) butter and the oil in a large frying pan, add the rabbit pieces and brown well. Add the chopped onions and crushed garlic and turn to brown all over.

Heat the rest of the butter and stir in the flour. Add half the white wine and stock and bring to the boil, stirring continuously. Add the tomato purée and bouquet garni and cook for 20 minutes, simmering gently.

Blanch the olives for 5 minutes in boiling water.

When the rabbit is well browned, add the remaining wine and stock and cook for 30 minutes. Stir in the tomato wine sauce and cook gently for a further 20 minutes.

Add the strained olives and 10 minutes later the Madeira. Remove the bouquet garni, sprinkle with parsley and serve very hot.

 a Bandol (red)

Preparation time 25 minutes
Cooking time 1¼–1½ hours

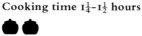

Serves 4

AMERICAN
1 rabbit (about 2½ lb)
salt and pepper
¼ cup butter
3 tablespoons oil
3 onions
2 cloves garlic
1 tablespoon flour
1¼ cups dry white wine
1 cup stock
¼ cup tomato paste
1 bouquet garni
¼ lb green olives
½ cup Madeira
Garnish
chopped parsley

Spanish rabbit

(Lapin à l'Espagnole)

**Preparation time 25 minutes
Cooking time 1 hour**

Serves 4

METRIC/IMPERIAL
1 rabbit (about 1.25 kg/2½ lb)
salt and pepper
3 green peppers
4 tablespoons olive oil
3 onions
2 cloves garlic
150 ml/¼ pint stock or water
350 g/12 oz long-grain rice
pinch of saffron or turmeric

Cut the rabbit into pieces and season. Clean the peppers, remove cores and seeds and cut into strips.

Heat the oil in a frying pan and soften the pepper strips. Remove and place on one side.

In the same oil brown the rabbit pieces. When they begin to turn golden add the sliced onions and crushed garlic. Brown. Moisten with the stock or water. Adjust seasoning and continue to cook for 40–50 minutes.

Carefully wash the rice, place in a saucepan and add twice its volume of boiling water. Toss in a pinch of saffron or turmeric, add a little salt and cook for 15 minutes.

Ten minutes before serving, add the pepper strips to the rabbit.

Transfer the rice to a heated serving dish. Arrange the rabbit pieces over the rice with the onions, garlic and pepper strips. Serve immediately.

 a Corbières (full-bodied red)

**Preparation time 25 minutes
Cooking time 1 hour**

Serves 4

AMERICAN
1 rabbit (about 2½ lb)
salt and pepper
3 green peppers
⅓ cup olive oil
3 onions
2 cloves garlic
⅔ cup stock or water
1½ cups long-grain rice
dash of saffron or turmeric

Paprika rabbit

(Lapin au paprika)

Preparation time 20 minutes
Cooking time 50–60 minutes

Serves 4

METRIC/IMPERIAL
1 rabbit (about 1.25 kg/2½ lb)
salt and pepper
50 g/2 oz butter
2 tablespoons oil
0.5 kg/1 lb onions
1 tablespoon paprika
pinch of cayenne
1 bouquet garni
300 ml/½ pint stock
100 ml/4 fl oz double cream
Garnish
chopped parsley

Cut the rabbit into portions. Season with salt and pepper.

Heat the butter and oil in a frying pan. Brown the rabbit portions on all sides over a moderate heat. Remove and keep warm.

In the same frying pan cook the sliced onions. Fry until golden, stirring with a wooden spoon.

Return the rabbit portions to the pan, sprinkle the whole with the paprika and mix over a high heat for 2–3 minutes. Add the cayenne, bouquet garni and stock. Cook for 30–40 minutes, by which time the sauce should be thickened and well reduced.

Add the cream, adjust seasoning and simmer for 5–6 minutes, stirring continuously.

Transfer to a serving dish, sprinkle with chopped parsley and serve immediately. Creamed potatoes or noodles go well with this dish.

 a red Côtes-de-Provence

Preparation time 20 minutes
Cooking time 50–60 minutes

Serves 4

AMERICAN
1 rabbit (about 2½ lb)
salt and pepper
¼ cup butter
3 tablespoons oil
1 lb onions
1 tablespoon paprika pepper
dash of cayenne pepper
1 bouquet garni
1¼ cups stock
½ cup heavy cream
Garnish
chopped parsley

Country-style rabbit

(Lapin à la paysanne)

Preparation time 25 minutes
Cooking time 1½ hours

Serves 4

METRIC/IMPERIAL
1 young rabbit (about 1.25kg/2½lb)
salt and pepper
3 onions
3 cloves garlic
100g/4oz butter
3 tablespoons oil
1 bunch thyme
250ml/8fl oz stock
100ml/4fl oz dry white wine
150g/5oz button onions
1kg/2lb new potatoes
Garnish
chopped parsley

Cut the rabbit into 8 pieces and season. Peel and slice the onions. Peel and crush the garlic.

Heat half the butter and half the oil in a frying pan. Add the rabbit pieces, sliced onions and two-thirds of the thyme. Fry the meat over a moderate heat, turning often to brown well all over. When the rabbit is well coloured add one-third of the stock and allow to evaporate completely. When the rabbit has become slightly caramelised add half the remaining stock and then the rest when this has evaporated.

When all the stock is completely evaporated add the white wine, garlic, button onions and the rest of the thyme. Season and leave to finish cooking over a fairly low heat. The sauce should be a good brown colour.

Scrape the potatoes and halve if necessary. Cook in a flameproof casserole with the rest of the very hot oil and butter. Shake often but do not use a fork or spoon to stir.

Arrange the rabbit and onions in a serving dish, spoon over the sauce, surround with the potatoes and sprinkle with chopped parsley. Serve very hot with a green salad.

a Bourgueil (fruity red)

Preparation time 25 minutes
Cooking time 1½ hours

Serves 4

AMERICAN
1 young rabbit (about 2½lb)
salt and pepper
3 onions
3 cloves garlic
½ cup butter
¼ cup oil
1 bunch thyme
1 cup stock
½ cup dry white wine
5oz button onions
2lb new potatoes
Garnish
chopped parsley

Rabbit with prunes

(Lapin aux pruneaux)

**Preparation time 30 minutes
plus 24 hours marinating time
Cooking time 1 hour 20 minutes**

Serves 4

METRIC/IMPERIAL
1 rabbit (about 1.25 kg/2½ lb)
275 g/10 oz prunes
75 g/3 oz butter
225 g/8 oz bacon pieces
2 large onions
25 g/1 oz flour
3 tablespoons brandy
salt and pepper
1 bouquet garni
36 button onions or shallots
1 tablespoon castor sugar
225 g/8 oz button mushrooms
rabbit (or pork) blood
3 tablespoons double cream
Marinade
1 litre/1¾ pints good red wine
2 onions, chopped
1 carrot, sliced
thyme, bay leaves, rosemary
salt and pepper
3 tablespoons brandy
3 tablespoons oil
Garnish
chopped parsley

In a large bowl mix together all the ingredients for the marinade. Cut the rabbit into pieces, reserving any blood, and marinate for 24 hours. At the same time soak the prunes in water.

The following day fry the drained rabbit in 50 g/2 oz (US ¼ cup) hot butter. Brown with the bacon pieces and the large sliced onions. Sprinkle with the flour, mix in well then add the strained marinade. Bring to the boil, add the brandy and flame. Season, add the bouquet garni and continue cooking for 40 minutes.

Drain the prunes and remove stones.

Peel the button onions. Place in a saucepan to glaze with the castor sugar, 7 g/¼ oz (US 2 teaspoons) butter and water to just cover. Reduce the juice until the onions caramelise.

Fry the cleaned mushrooms in the remaining butter.

Remove the bouquet garni from the rabbit and add the prunes, glazed onions and mushrooms. Simmer for a further 15 minutes.

Just before serving, thicken the sauce over a low heat with 2 tablespoons (US 3 tablespoons) rabbit blood mixed with the cream and a little hot sauce. Take care that it does not boil. Sprinkle with chopped parsley.

 a Saint-Émilion (red Bordeaux)

**Preparation time 30 minutes
plus 24 hours marinating time
Cooking time 1 hour 20 minutes**

Serves 4

AMERICAN
1 rabbit (about 2½ lb)
10 oz prunes
6 tablespoons butter
½ lb bacon pieces
2 large onions
¼ cup all-purpose flour
¼ cup brandy
salt and pepper
1 bouquet garni
36 button onions or shallots
1 tablespoon sugar
½ lb button mushrooms
rabbit (or pork) blood
¼ cup heavy cream
Marinade
4¼ cups good red wine
2 onions, chopped
1 carrot, sliced
thyme, bay leaves, rosemary
salt and pepper
¼ cup brandy
¼ cup oil
Garnish
chopped parsley

Rabbit with rosemary

(Lapin au romarin)

Preparation time 25 minutes
Cooking time 1 hour

Serves 4

METRIC/IMPERIAL
1 saddle of rabbit
salt and pepper
8 thin rashers smoked streaky bacon
8 sprigs of rosemary
50g/2oz butter
2 tablespoons oil
225g/8oz smoked streaky bacon, diced
225g/8oz button onions
2 cloves garlic
150ml/¼ pint dry white wine
2 tablespoons tomato purée
Garnish
chopped parsley

Cut the saddle and rabbit thighs into 8 pieces. Season with salt and pepper. Wrap each piece in a rasher of bacon and tuck under a sprig of rosemary.

Heat the butter and oil in a frying pan and place in the rabbit pieces side by side. Add the diced smoked bacon and the peeled onions. Brown over a moderate heat, turning to cook on all sides, for about 15 minutes. When everything is well browned add the crushed garlic, wine, tomato purée and 4 tablespoons (US ⅓ cup) hot water. Adjust seasoning and finish cooking over a low heat for 40–45 minutes.

Just before serving transfer the rabbit to a heated serving dish. Surround with the onions and bacon and keep warm.

Rinse the juices from the frying pan with 4 tablespoons (US ⅓ cup) water, mixing well. Pour this sauce over the rabbit, and sprinkle with chopped parsley.

 a Gigondas (full-bodied red)

Preparation time 25 minutes
Cooking time 1 hour

Serves 4

AMERICAN
1 saddle of rabbit
salt and pepper
8 thin bacon slices
8 sprigs of rosemary
¼ cup butter
3 tablespoons oil
½-lb bacon piece, diced
½ lb button onions
2 cloves garlic
⅔ cup dry white wine
3 tablespoons tomato paste
Garnish
chopped parsley

Flambéed quails with grapes

(Cailles aux raisins)

Preparation time 20 minutes
plus 2–3 hours steeping time
Cooking time 25 minutes

Serves 4

METRIC/IMPERIAL
36 green grapes
100 ml/4 fl oz brandy
4 quails
pinch of sea salt
8 peppercorns
4 vine leaves (optional)
4 small rashers bacon
40 g/1½ oz butter
4 shallots
3 tablespoons meat juices or stock
salt and pepper

Peel the grapes and steep for 2–3 hours in half the brandy.

Prepare and clean the quails. Pound the sea salt with the peppercorns and use to season the insides of the birds. Also place 3 grapes inside each.

Cover each quail with a vine leaf, if used, and wrap around a rasher of bacon. Tie with string.

Heat the butter in a frying pan. Soften the chopped shallots, but do not allow to brown. Add the quails. Brown all over, sprinkle with the rest of the brandy and flame. Cook in a moderately hot oven (200°C, 400°F, Gas Mark 6) for 15 minutes.

Three minutes before serving add the grapes and brandy. Flame again. Stir in the meat juices and season to taste. Serve very hot.

 a Châteauneuf-du-Pape (red)

Preparation time 20 minutes
plus 2–3 hours steeping time
Cooking time 25 minutes

Serves 4

AMERICAN
36 white grapes
½ cup brandy
4 quails
dash of coarse salt
8 peppercorns
4 grape leaves (optional)
4 small bacon slices
3 tablespoons butter
4 shallots
¼ cup meat juices or stock
salt and pepper

Quails Rossini

(Cailles sur canapé)

Preparation time 25 minutes
Cooking time 25 minutes

Serves 4

METRIC/IMPERIAL
4 quails
salt and pepper
100 g/4 oz pâté de foie gras
75 g/3 oz butter
3 tablespoons brandy
1 onion
1 carrot
1 small sprig of thyme
½ bay leaf
2 teaspoons flour
200 ml/7 fl oz stock
3 tablespoons dry white wine
100 ml/4 fl oz port
1 small can truffles
4 slices white bread

Prepare and clean the quails. Season and place a teaspoon of pâté inside each.

Brown the quails in a frying pan in half the hot butter. Sprinkle over the brandy, flame and cook for 18–20 minutes.

Meanwhile, peel and chop the onion and carrot. Brown in the remaining butter with the thyme and bay leaf.

Sprinkle the flour over this mixture and stir until it is absorbed. Moisten with the stock and white wine and cook over a low heat, stirring continuously, for 10 minutes. Strain, return to the pan then add the port and three-quarters of the chopped truffles. Season to taste. Heat through but do not allow the sauce to boil.

Toast the slices of bread. Spread with the rest of the pâté and arrange on a heated serving dish. Place a quail on each slice of toast.

Add the sauce to the frying pan to incorporate all the quail juice and pour over the quails. Sprinkle with the rest of the chopped truffles and serve immediately.

a Médoc (red Bordeaux)

Preparation time 25 minutes
Cooking time 25 minutes

Serves 4

AMERICAN
4 quails
salt and pepper
¼ lb pâté de foie gras
6 tablespoons butter
¼ cup brandy
1 onion
1 carrot
1 small sprig of thyme
½ bay leaf
2 teaspoons all-purpose flour
¾ cup stock
¼ cup dry white wine
½ cup port
1 small can truffles
4 slices white bread

Quails in aspic

(Cailles en gelée)

Preparation time 40 minutes
Cooking time 40 minutes

Serves 4

METRIC/IMPERIAL
6 quails
2 chicken livers
75 g/3 oz pork fillet
50 g/2 oz streaky bacon
3 shallots
25 g/1 oz butter
100 g/4 oz mushrooms
1 slice stale bread
150 ml/¼ pint milk
100 ml/4 fl oz brandy
1 small can truffles (optional)
salt and pepper
3 tablespoons white port
300 ml/½ pint stock
300 ml/½ pint aspic jelly (see method)
1 green olive
Garnish
lettuce leaves

Prepare and clean the quails. Remove the bones from 2 of them and mince the meat very finely with the chicken livers, pork fillet and bacon.

Peel and finely chop the shallots. Brown in the hot butter. Clean and slice the mushrooms. Add to the shallots and dry out over a gentle heat, stirring with a wooden spoon. Leave to cool then add to the minced meats.

Crumble the bread, moisten with the milk then squeeze out the liquid before adding to the stuffing with 3 table-spoons (US ¼ cup) brandy and most of the chopped truffles, if used. Season to taste, combine well together and divide the stuffing between the 4 quails.

Put the quails in a small ovenproof casserole and cover with the port, remaining brandy and stock. Place in a hot oven (220°C, 425°F, Gas Mark 7) and cook for 25 minutes. When cooked remove the quails and cool. Make the cooking liquor from the casserole up to 300 ml/½ pint (US 1¼ cups) with stock or water, if necessary, and season to taste. Use this liquor to make up the aspic jelly according to the instructions on the packet. Leave to cool until just on setting.

Plunge the quails into this aspic jelly several times, waiting each time for the jelly around the quail to set. Before dipping for the last time stick a piece of truffle, if used, and a slice of olive on each quail.

Arrange the well-coated quails on a dish garnished with lettuce leaves and the rest of the chopped jelly.

 a dry Champagne.

Preparation time 40 minutes
Cooking time 40 minutes

Serves 4

AMERICAN
6 quails
2 chicken livers
3 oz pork tenderloin
3 bacon slices
3 shallots
2 tablespoons butter
¼ lb mushrooms
1 slice stale bread
⅔ cup milk
½ cup brandy
1 small can truffles (optional)
salt and pepper
¼ cup white port
1¼ cups stock
1¼ cups aspic jelly (see method)
1 green olive
Garnish
lettuce leaves

Périgord pigeons

(Pigeons Périgourdine)

Preparation time 30 minutes
Cooking time 50-60 minutes

Serves 4

METRIC/IMPERIAL
2 pigeons
50 g/2oz butter
450 ml/¾ pint stock
2 teaspoons potato flour or
1 teaspoon cornflour
100 ml/4 fl oz Madeira
salt and freshly ground pepper
Stuffing
225 g/8 oz unsmoked streaky bacon
50 g/2 oz fresh breadcrumbs
150 ml/¼ pint milk
75 g/3 oz pâté de foie gras
1 egg
Garnish
potato chips
sprigs of watercress

Prepare the stuffing. Mince the bacon twice. Moisten the breadcrumbs with milk and squeeze.

Work together with a wooden spoon the minced bacon, breadcrumbs and the pâté de foie gras. Bind all together with sufficient beaten egg and season.

Prepare and clean the pigeons. Fill with the stuffing, sewing up the openings so that it does not escape. Heat the butter in a flameproof casserole and sauté the pigeons, turning so that they brown on all sides. Cover the casserole, reduce the heat and cook for 35–45 minutes, moistening from time to time with 1–2 tablespoons (US 2–3 tablespoons) of stock. During this cooking, turn the pigeons two or three times more.

When cooked, arrange the pigeons on a serving dish and keep hot.

Mix the potato flour with 2 tablespoons (US 3 tablespoons) stock. Add the rest of the stock to the juices in the casserole, then stir in the moistened potato flour and the Madeira.

Thicken over a gentle heat, stirring constantly with a wooden spoon. Season.

Coat the pigeons with this sauce and garnish the dish with potato chips and watercress sprigs. Serve immediately.

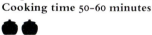 a red Bordeaux

Preparation time 30 minutes
Cooking time 50-60 minutes

Serves 4

AMERICAN
2 pigeons
¼ cup butter
2 cups stock
2 teaspoons potato flour or
1 teaspoon cornstarch
½ cup Madeira
salt and freshly ground pepper
Stuffing
½ lb unsmoked bacon
1 cup fresh soft bread crumbs
⅔ cup milk
3 oz pâté de foie gras
1 egg
Garnish
French fries
sprigs of watercress

Normandy pheasant

(Faisan aux pommes)

**Preparation time 30 minutes
Cooking time 1 hour–1 hour
10 minutes**

Serves 4

METRIC/IMPERIAL
**1 pheasant
6 dessert apples
3 petits suisses (small cream
cheeses)
½ teaspoon freshly ground pepper
salt
75 g/3 oz butter
3 tablespoons calvados or brandy**

Prepare and clean the pheasant.

Peel and core the apples. Cut 4 in half and dice the remaining 2. Work the diced apple into the cream cheese and season with the pepper and a pinch of salt. Fill the inside of the pheasant with this stuffing and sew up the opening.

Set the oven to moderately hot (200°C, 400°F, Gas Mark 6). Grease an ovenproof dish, place the pheasant in it, brush with melted butter and cook in the oven for 30 minutes.

Remove the pheasant from the oven and surround with the halved apples. Sprinkle them with melted butter. Replace in the oven and cook for a further 30–40 minutes.

Just before serving heat the calvados, spoon over the pheasant and flame at the table.

 a Chinon (light fruity red)

**Preparation time 30 minutes
Cooking time 1 hour–1 hour
10 minutes**

Serves 4

AMERICAN
**1 pheasant
6 dessert apples
1 (3-oz) package full-fat cream
cheese
½ teaspoon freshly ground pepper
salt
6 tablespoons butter
¼ cup calvados or brandy**

Casserole of partridge

(Perdrix en cocotte)

Preparation time 30 minutes
Cooking time 1 hour 10 minutes

Serves 4

METRIC/IMPERIAL
2 young partridges
salt and pepper
150 g/5 oz smoked bacon
2 onions
1 carrot
225 g/8 oz mushrooms
75 g/3 oz butter
1 small bouquet garni
1 tablespoon flour
100 ml/4 fl oz dry white wine
300 ml/½ pint stock
100 ml/4 fl oz Madeira

Prepare and clean the partridges. Season with salt and pepper. Cut the bacon into small pieces. Finely chop the onions and carrot. Clean then finely slice the mushrooms.

Heat 50 g/2 oz (US ¼ cup) butter in a flameproof casserole, toss in the pieces of bacon and cook until golden.

Sauté the mushrooms in a separate pan in the remaining butter.

Remove the bacon and keep hot. In the same casserole, brown the partridges on all sides. Remove and keep warm.

Still in the same casserole, brown the onions and carrots with the bouquet garni. Sprinkle with the flour and stir to obtain a brown roux. Add the white wine and stock and cook over a gentle heat for 8 minutes, stirring from time to time. Strain the sauce through a sieve.

Return the partridges to the casserole with the sauce, bacon pieces and mushrooms. Cover and finish cooking for 50 minutes–1 hour over a gentle heat.

Two minutes before serving, add the Madeira and heat through without boiling.

Cut the partridges in two, arrange on a heated serving dish with the bacon pieces and mushrooms. **Pour** over the sauce or serve separately, very hot.

 a Morgon (red Beaujolais)

Preparation time 30 minutes
Cooking time 1 hour 10 minutes

Serves 4

AMERICAN
2 young partridges
salt and pepper
8 bacon slices
2 onions
1 carrot
½ lb mushrooms
6 tablespoons butter
1 small bouquet garni
1 tablespoon all-purpose flour
½ cup dry white wine
1¼ cups stock
½ cup Madeira

Young guinea fowl with mushrooms (Pintadeaux aux girolles)

Preparation time 40 minutes
Cooking time 50-60 minutes

Serves 4

METRIC/IMPERIAL
2 small young guinea fowl, with
livers
2 chicken livers
1kg/2lb mushrooms
100g/4oz butter
5 shallots
salt and pepper
3 petits suisses (small cream
cheeses)
100g/4oz dried breadcrumbs,
moistened in milk and squeezed
2 tablespoons chopped parsley
1 slice ham
1 egg
150ml/¼ pint stock
Garnish
chopped parsley

Prepare and clean the young guinea fowl. Trim all the livers to use for the stuffing. Clean the mushrooms, wash quickly and wipe. Chop a quarter of them into small pieces.

Prepare the stuffing. Quickly sauté the guinea fowl and chicken livers in 25g/1oz (US 2 tablespoons) butter. Sieve them or blend in the liquidiser. Next brown 3 chopped shallots in the same butter, add the chopped mushrooms, season and cook for 5 minutes.

Mix together all the ingredients for the stuffing: the livers, chopped mushrooms and shallots, petits suisses, breadcrumbs, parsley and minced ham. Bind well together with the beaten egg. Season.

Fill the guinea fowl with this stuffing and tie up with string. Heat 50g/2oz (US ¼ cup) butter in a flameproof casserole and brown the birds on all sides. Add the stock, cover and cook over a moderate heat for 40–50 minutes.

Brown the remaining chopped shallots in the rest of the butter, add the whole mushrooms and cook for 10 minutes. Add to the guinea fowl 15 minutes before the end of cooking.

Arrange the guinea fowl in a heated serving dish and surround with the mushrooms. Serve at once, sprinkled with chopped parsley.

 a light Bordeaux (red)

Preparation time 40 minutes
Cooking time 50-60 minutes

Serves 4

AMERICAN
2 small young guinea fowl, with
livers
2 chicken livers
2lb mushrooms
½ cup butter
5 shallots
salt and pepper
1 (3-oz) package full-fat cream
cheese
1 cup dry bread crumbs, moistened
in milk and squeezed
3 tablespoons chopped parsley
1 slice cooked ham
1 egg
⅔ cup stock
Garnish
chopped parsley

Guinea fowl Italian style

(Pintade à l'Italienne)

Preparation time 30 minutes
Cooking time 50-60 minutes

Serves 4

METRIC/IMPERIAL
1 guinea fowl
salt and pepper
1 small rasher bacon
50 g/2 oz butter
2 onions
100 ml/4 fl oz dry white vermouth
3 shallots
2 cloves garlic
1 small bunch parsley
1 (396-g/14-oz) can tomatoes
1 (200-g/7-oz) can artichoke hearts
225 g/8 oz button mushrooms
100 ml/4 fl oz oil
1 tablespoon potato flour or
2 teaspoons cornflour

Prepare and clean the guinea fowl. Season and wrap with the bacon rasher. Secure with string and brown in a flame-proof casserole in the melted butter.

Peel and chop the onions and add to the casserole, turning with the guinea fowl to brown on all sides. Cover and cook over a low heat for 40–50 minutes. Moisten from time to time with a little vermouth (waiting for it to evaporate each time before adding more).

Peel and finely chop the shallots, garlic and parsley. Drain the can of tomatoes and reserve the juice. Cut the artichoke hearts into thin strips. Clean and chop the mushrooms.

Quickly heat the tomatoes in 2–3 tablespoons (US 3–4 tablespoons) oil, remove and add separately to the pan the artichoke hearts and mushrooms; leave to turn slightly golden. Sprinkle each with the chopped garlic, shallots and parsley.

Arrange the guinea fowl on a hot dish, surround with the vegetables and keep hot.

Add the tomato juice to the juices in the casserole, thickening over a gentle heat with the potato flour and remaining vermouth, mixed together. Strain this sauce through a sieve and pour over the guinea fowl.

Serve very hot.

 a Chianti (Italian red)

Preparation time 30 minutes
Cooking time 50-60 minutes

Serves 4

AMERICAN
1 guinea fowl
salt and pepper
1 small bacon slice
¼ cup butter
2 onions
½ cup dry white vermouth
3 shallots
2 cloves garlic
1 small bunch parsley
1 (14-oz) can tomatoes
1 (7-oz) can artichoke hearts
½ lb button mushrooms
½ cup oil
1 tablespoon potato flour or
2 teaspoons cornstarch

Normandy guinea fowl

(Pintadeaux Normandy)

Preparation time 25 minutes
Cooking time 1-1¼ hours

Serves 6 - 8

METRIC/IMPERIAL
2 young guinea fowl, with livers
2 sage leaves
2 sprigs of parsley
1 small sprig of rosemary
75 g/3 oz butter
salt and pepper
3 tablespoons whisky
200 ml/7 fl oz stock
2 tablespoons sherry
3 tablespoons port
4 tablespoons double cream
To serve
1 (340-g/12-oz) packet frozen mixed vegetables

Prepare and clean the young guinea fowl. Set aside the livers. Chop the sage and parsley, strip off the rosemary leaves. Work these herbs with 40 g/1½ oz (US 3 tablespoons) butter, salt and pepper. Put half this herb butter inside each guinea fowl. Truss with string. Set the oven to hot (220°C, 425°F, Gas Mark 7).

Place the birds in a roasting pan, rub well with the remaining butter, season with salt and pepper. Cook in the oven for 10 minutes, turning over once. Then sprinkle with half the whisky and flame. Add the stock to the roasting pan and return to the oven.

Continue cooking for 45 minutes, basting frequently. After 30 minutes add the chopped livers.

When ready to serve, remove the guinea fowl and livers and keep hot on a serving dish. Add the rest of the whisky, the sherry and the port to the pan juices. Place over a brisk heat for 5 minutes to reduce the sauce, stirring constantly. Reduce the heat, stir in the cream and heat through without boiling.

Pour this sauce over the guinea fowl and surround with the cooked mixed vegetables. Serve immediately.

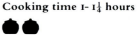 an Arbois (light red)

Preparation time 25 minutes
Cooking time 1-1¼ hours

Serves 6 - 8

AMERICAN
2 young guinea fowl, with livers
2 sage leaves
2 sprigs of parsley
1 small sprig of rosemary
6 tablespoons butter
salt and pepper
¼ cup whiskey
¾ cup stock
3 tablespoons sherry
¼ cup port
⅓ cup heavy cream
To serve
1 (12-oz) package frozen mixed vegetables

Goose in mustard sauce

(Oie à la sauce moutarde)

Preparation time 20 minutes
Cooking time 1½ hours

Serves 6

METRIC/IMPERIAL
4 onions
salt and pepper
6 goose portions (each about 175-225g/6-8oz)
40g/1½oz goose fat, butter or lard
250ml/8fl oz chicken stock or hot water
1 small bouquet garni
225g/8oz mushrooms
20g/¾oz butter
150ml/¼ pint double cream
2 tablespoons French mustard
Garnish
chopped parsley

Peel and chop the onions. Season the goose portions. Heat the goose fat in a flameproof casserole and add the goose and onions. Cook very gently, turning frequently, but do not let them become too brown.

Moisten with the hot stock, add the bouquet garni and continue cooking over a gentle heat for about 30–40 minutes.

Clean and finely slice the mushrooms. Soften them in the hot butter and when half-cooked add to the goose mixture.

When ready to serve, drain the portions of goose, arrange in a fairly deep dish and keep hot. Mix the cream with the mustard then pour into the casserole juices. Thicken over a very gentle heat, whisking continually. Do not boil. Correct the seasoning and remove the bouquet garni.

Pour this sauce over the goose, sprinkle with chopped parsley and serve very hot.

 a Beaujolais (light fruity red)

Preparation time 20 minutes
Cooking time 1½ hours

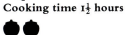

Serves 6

AMERICAN
4 onions
salt and pepper
6 goose portions (each about 6-8oz)
3 tablespoons goose fat, butter or shortening
1 cup chicken stock or hot water
1 small bouquet garni
½lb mushrooms
1½ tablespoons butter
⅔ cup heavy cream
3 tablespoons French mustard
Garnish
chopped parsley

Potted goose

(Confit d'oie)

Preparation time 1 hour
plus 36 hours standing time
Cooking time 3 hours

METRIC/IMPERIAL
1 fat goose
2 teaspoons salt for each 1kg/2lb of
goose
pinch of dried thyme
2 bay leaves, crumbled
1 teaspoon allspice
350ml/12fl oz water

Prepare and clean the goose, keeping any fat from the entrails. Cut up the goose, leaving the legs and wings whole. Trim them into shape. Keep any fat and cut into small pieces.

Sprinkle the goose pieces with a mixture of salt, thyme, bay leaves and allspice. Place in a large bowl, cover and leave to stand for 36 hours.

Just before cooking pour the water into a flameproof casserole. Add all the goose fat and melt it over a medium heat. Wipe the goose pieces, plunge into the melted fat, cover and simmer gently for about $2\frac{1}{2}$ hours.

Drain the portions of goose and remove any bones which are loose.

Heat the fat again until it is liquid. Pour a layer of fat into a stoneware pot and then add the pieces of goose. Cover with the remaining fat.

Stored covered in the refrigerator, this will keep for a few days.

Preparation time 1 hour
plus 36 hours standing time
Cooking time 3 hours

AMERICAN
1 fat goose
2 teaspoons salt for each 2lb of
goose
dash of dried thyme
2 bay leaves, crumbled
1 teaspoon allspice
$1\frac{1}{2}$ cups water

Potted goose with garlic

(Confit d'oie Landaise)

Preparation time 25 minutes
Cooking time 30 minutes

Serves 4

METRIC/IMPERIAL
2 potted thighs and drumsticks of
goose (see page 190)
1 kg/2lb small potatoes
4 tablespoons of the goose
preserving fat
salt and pepper
3 shallots
3 cloves garlic
2 tablespoons chopped parsley

Preheat the oven to moderate (180°C, 350°F, Gas Mark 4).
Place the pieces of preserved goose, covered with their fat,
in an ovenproof dish. Heat through in the oven.

Peel the potatoes. Brown well in a flameproof casserole
in the hot preserving fat and continue cooking over a
gentle heat. Ten minutes before the potatoes are cooked,
season them and cover the casserole.

Peel and finely chop the shallots and garlic. Add the
chopped parsley. Tip this mixture over the potatoes 2
minutes before serving and stir quickly.

Turn the potatoes into a heated serving dish and place
the well-drained pieces of goose over them. Serve very hot.

 a Pécharmant (light red)

Preparation time 25 minutes
Cooking time 30 minutes

Serves 4

AMERICAN
2 potted thighs and drumsticks of
goose (see page 190)
2lb small potatoes
⅓ cup of the goose preserving fat
salt and pepper
3 shallots
3 cloves garlic
3 tablespoons chopped parsley

Young wild boar Vosges style (Marcassin à la Vosgienne)

Preparation time 30 minutes
Cooking time 1½–2 hours

Serves 6

METRIC/IMPERIAL
2 onions
1 carrot
75 g/3 oz butter
1 (1.5-kg/3-lb) joint of young wild boar or top leg of pork (see note)
1 small bouquet garni
3 tablespoons brandy
1 teaspoon castor sugar
1 tablespoon lemon juice
200 ml/7 fl oz stock
salt and pepper
0.75 kg/1½ lb bilberries or cranberries
75 g/3 oz castor sugar
6 dessert apples
12 cloves

Peel the onions and the carrot. Chop the onions, cut the carrot into very small dice. Melt 50 g/2 oz (US ¼ cup) butter in a flameproof casserole. In this hot butter, brown the meat, onions and carrot with the bouquet garni, turning until well coloured on all sides. Pour on the brandy and flame. Remove the meat and keep hot.

Sprinkle the teaspoon of castor sugar over the vegetables and let the whole caramelise slightly. Add the lemon juice and stock and simmer for 5 minutes. Strain through a sieve.

Return this sauce to the casserole with the meat. Season, cover and cook in a moderately hot oven (190°C, 375°F, Gas Mark 5) for 1½–1¾ hours, basting often.

Meanwhile, wash the bilberries or cranberries, place in a saucepan, cover with cold water and add the castor sugar. Bring to the boil and simmer gently for 15 minutes.

Peel and core the apples, halve and stick 2 cloves into each half. Baste with the remaining melted butter and place around the meat 30 minutes before the end of cooking.

Arrange the cooked meat on a heated serving dish. Surround with apple halves, removing the cloves, and fill the cavity of each with bilberries. Serve the rest of the bilberries separately, along with the sauce from the meat.

Note If using pork, remove rind and trim off any excess fat. Crush 3 juniper berries and rub the meat with them. Place the meat in a bowl and cover with red wine. Peel 1 onion and stick it with 4 cloves. Peel 1 clove garlic and add to the bowl with the onion, a few sprigs of parsley, a sprig of thyme, 3 bay leaves, salt and pepper and a little lemon rind. Marinate overnight.

 a Châteauneuf-du-Pape (red)

Preparation time 30 minutes
Cooking time 1½–2 hours

Serves 6

AMERICAN
2 onions
1 carrot
6 tablespoons butter
1 (3-lb) joint of young wild boar or top leg of pork (see note)
1 small bouquet garni
¼ cup brandy
1 teaspoon sugar
1 tablespoon lemon juice
¾ cup stock
salt and pepper
1½ lb blueberries or cranberries
6 tablespoons sugar
6 dessert apples
12 cloves

Venison Saint-Hubert

(Chevreuil Saint-Hubert)

Preparation time 40 minutes
Cooking time 40 minutes

Serves 4

METRIC/IMPERIAL
8 small venison steaks, trimmed
(see method)
100g/4oz smoked streaky bacon
2 onions
1 stick celery
1 carrot
1 bouquet garni
100g/4oz butter
1 tablespoon flour
350ml/12fl oz stock
175ml/6fl oz dry white wine
1 (440-g/15½-oz) can unsweetened
chestnut purée
100ml/4fl oz double cream
2 tablespoons redcurrant jelly
1 teaspoon lemon juice
100ml/4fl oz port
salt and pepper
pinch of cayenne
Garnish
sprigs of watercress

Prepare the sauce. Cut the venison trimmings into very small pieces, dice the bacon, chop the onions and celery, finely dice the carrot. Brown these ingredients with the bouquet garni in half the butter. When well browned sprinkle on the flour and stir in. Reserve a few tablespoons of stock, and add the remainder with the wine to the vegetables. Bring to the boil, stirring, and simmer gently for 30 minutes. Strain this sauce through a conical sieve and keep warm over a gentle heat.

Meanwhile, prepare the chestnut purée. Empty the contents of the can into a bowl over simmering water and heat through gently. Add the cream and beat together until smooth. Pipe 8 rosettes of the chestnut purée around the edge of a heated serving dish. Keep warm in a low oven.

Cook the venison steaks in a frying pan in the remaining butter for 15–20 minutes. Place on the serving dish between the mounds of purée.

Rinse the juices from the frying pan with the reserved stock and add to the sauce. Stir in the redcurrant jelly, lemon juice and port. Season with salt, pepper and cayenne. Bring to the boil and spoon a little over each steak. Garnish the centre of the dish with watercress sprigs, and serve the remaining sauce separately.

 a red Bourgogne (Burgundy)

Preparation time 40 minutes
Cooking time 40 minutes

Serves 4

AMERICAN
8 small venison steaks, trimmed
(see method)
6 bacon slices
2 onions
1 stalk celery
1 carrot
1 bouquet garni
½ cup butter
1 tablespoon all-purpose flour
1½ cups stock
¾ cup dry white wine
1 (15½-oz) can unsweetened chestnut
purée
½ cup heavy cream
3 tablespoons red currant jelly
1 teaspoon lemon juice
½ cup port
salt and pepper
dash of cayenne pepper
Garnish
sprigs of watercress

Green peas with bacon

(Petits pois au lard)

Preparation time 20 minutes
Cooking time 35 minutes

Serves 6

METRIC/IMPERIAL
1 bunch large spring onions
2 lettuces
150 g/5 oz smoked streaky bacon
75 g/3 oz butter
1 kg/2 lb shelled green peas
1 bunch savory
1 sugar lump
salt and pepper

Trim the spring onions, leaving only the bulbs. Wash the lettuces and cut in two. Finely dice the bacon.

Heat the butter in a flameproof casserole, add the spring onions and diced bacon. Leave to braise and very slightly brown before adding the lettuces, peas, savory and sugar lump. Season, cover and simmer over a gentle heat for 30 minutes. While they are cooking, take care that the vegetables do not catch; moisten from time to time with a few tablespoons of hot water if necessary.

Transfer to a heated vegetable dish and serve very hot.

Preparation time 20 minutes
Cooking time 35 minutes

Serves 6

AMERICAN
1 bunch scallions
2 heads lettuce
8 bacon slices
6 tablespoons butter
6 cups shelled peas
1 bunch savory
1 sugar cube
salt and pepper

French beans with basil

(Haricots verts au basilic)

Preparation time 20 minutes
Cooking time 20 minutes

Serves 6

─METRIC/IMPERIAL
1 kg/2lb French beans
salt and pepper
Tomato sauce
2 onions
0.5 kg/1lb ripe tomatoes
3 tablespoons olive oil
1 small bouquet garni
Pistou sauce
4 cloves garlic
pinch of sea salt
1 bunch basil
4 tablespoons olive oil

String the French beans, wash and drain. Toss into a pan of boiling salted water and cook for 10–15 minutes.

Prepare the tomato sauce. Peel and chop the onions. Peel the tomatoes, remove the seeds and crush the flesh. Brown the onions in the hot olive oil. When well coloured add the tomatoes and bouquet garni. Season and cook for 15 minutes over a low heat.

Prepare the pistou sauce. Into a kitchen mortar put the garlic, peeled and lightly crushed, sea salt and basil leaves. Crush the whole with a pestle, gradually adding the olive oil to obtain a smooth paste.

Strain the tomato sauce through a conical sieve. Drain the green beans and turn into a heated serving dish. Spoon the pistou sauce in the centre and surround with the tomato sauce. If liked, toss all together. Serve very hot.

Preparation time 20 minutes
Cooking time 20 minutes

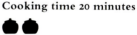

Serves 6

AMERICAN
2lb green beans
salt and pepper
Tomato sauce
2 onions
1lb ripe tomatoes
¼ cup olive oil
1 small bouquet garni
Pistou sauce
4 cloves garlic
dash of coarse salt
1 bunch basil
⅓ cup olive oil

Braised French beans

(Haricots verts braisés)

Preparation time 25 minutes
Cooking time 40 minutes

Serves 5–6

METRIC/IMPERIAL
1 kg/2lb French beans
3 onions
3 tablespoons oil
0.5kg/1lb ripe tomatoes
1 clove garlic
salt and pepper
Garnish
1 tablespoon chopped parsley
1 clove garlic, chopped (optional)

String and wash the beans, dry carefully.

Peel and finely slice the onions. Soften in a flameproof casserole in the hot oil. Do not allow to brown.

Peel the tomatoes, remove the seeds and juice. Leave 2 or 3 whole and dice the remainder.

Add the beans to the onions with the tomatoes and the crushed garlic. Season, cover and cook for 35–40 minutes over a low heat.

Just before serving tip the beans into a vegetable dish, sprinkle with the parsley and the chopped garlic.

Preparation time 25 minutes
Cooking time 40 minutes

Serves 5–6

AMERICAN
2lb green beans
3 onions
¼ cup oil
1lb ripe tomatoes
1 clove garlic
salt and pepper
Garnish
1 tablespoon chopped parsley
1 clove garlic, chopped (optional)

Peasant-style French beans (Haricots verts à la paysanne)

Preparation time 25 minutes
Cooking time 20 minutes

Serves 4

METRIC/IMPERIAL
1 kg/2 lb French beans
sea salt
100 g/4 oz smoked streaky bacon, in the piece
25 g/1 oz butter
3 tablespoons double cream
Garnish
chopped chervil

String and wash the French beans then toss into a saucepan of boiling salted water. Cook for 10–15 minutes, until tender. Do not cover the pan so the beans remain green.

Cut the bacon into thin strips, brown in the hot butter.

When the beans are cooked, drain and place them in a heated vegetable dish. Toss in the butter used to cook the bacon and arrange the bacon in a ring on top of the beans. Spoon the lightly whipped cream into the centre and sprinkle with chopped chervil. Serve very hot.

Preparation time 25 minutes
Cooking time 20 minutes

Serves 4

AMERICAN
2 lb green beans
coarse salt
$\frac{1}{4}$-lb bacon piece
2 tablespoons butter
$\frac{1}{4}$ cup heavy cream
Garnish
chopped chervil

Haricots Provençal

(Haricots à la Provençale)

**Preparation time 30 minutes
plus overnight soaking
Cooking time 1½–2 hours**

Serves 6

METRIC/IMPERIAL
1.25kg/2½lb unshelled haricot beans
or 450g/1lb dried haricots, soaked
overnight
3 onions
2 cloves
2 cloves garlic
0.5kg/1lb very ripe tomatoes
1 carrot
3 tablespoons olive oil
1 small bouquet garni
1 sprig of basil
Pistou sauce
3 cloves garlic
2 sprigs of basil
3 tablespoons olive oil

Shell the fresh haricots or drain the soaked beans. Peel the onions and slice 2 of them. Stick the cloves into the third. Peel and crush the garlic. Peel and deseed the tomatoes and cut the flesh into small dice. Slice the carrot.

Heat the oil in a flameproof casserole and cook the sliced onions without browning. Stir in the haricots, cover and cook for 10 minutes over a low heat. Then pour on boiling water to come 2cm/¾ inch above the level of the beans. Add the tomatoes, carrot, garlic, bouquet garni, basil and the onion stuck with cloves. Cover and cook over a low heat for 1½–2 hours.

Prepare the pistou sauce. In a kitchen mortar place the peeled garlic and basil leaves; pound together, gradually adding the olive oil to give a smooth sauce. Stir this sauce into the cooked haricots just before serving very hot.

**Preparation time 30 minutes
plus overnight soaking
Cooking time 1½–2 hours**

Serves 6

AMERICAN
2½lb unshelled navy beans or 2 cups
dried navy beans, soaked
overnight
3 onions
2 cloves
2 cloves garlic
1lb very ripe tomatoes
1 carrot
¼ cup olive oil
1 small bouquet garni
1 sprig of basil
Pistou sauce
3 cloves garlic
2 sprigs of basil
¼ cup olive oil

Spinach croquettes

(Croquettes d'épinards)

Preparation time 20 minutes
Cooking time 20 minutes

Serves 6

METRIC/IMPERIAL
1kg/2lb spinach or 2 (227-g/8-oz) packets frozen chopped spinach
90g/3½oz butter
20g/¾oz flour
100ml/4fl oz milk
3 eggs
freshly grated nutmeg
salt and pepper
2 tablespoons oil
4 slices bread, crusts removed
150ml/¼ pint single cream

Wash the spinach in a large amount of water, then cook for 3 minutes. Drain, squeeze to remove all excess water and chop finely with a knife. If using frozen spinach heat in a saucepan then drain thoroughly.

Melt 50g/2oz (US ¼ cup) butter in a heavy saucepan, add the spinach and allow to dry out. Sprinkle with the flour and cook for 2 minutes. Add the cold milk and cook for a further 2 minutes, stirring with a wooden spoon.

Beat the eggs and pour slowly on to the spinach, mixing in quickly. Add nutmeg, salt and pepper and cook for a further 2 minutes over a low heat. Leave to cool.

Take large spoonfuls of the spinach and place on a lightly floured board. Form into small round croquettes. Heat the oil with 15g/½oz (US 1 tablespoon) butter in a frying pan and brown the croquettes on both sides.

Meanwhile, cut the slices of bread into small triangles. Fry until golden in the remaining butter.

Arrange the spinach croquettes on a serving dish. Top with the warmed cream and garnish with the fried croûtons.

Preparation time 20 minutes
Cooking time 20 minutes

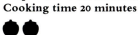

Serves 6

AMERICAN
2lb spinach or 2 (8-oz) packages frozen chopped spinach
7 tablespoons butter
3 tablespoons all-purpose flour
½ cup milk
3 eggs
freshly grated nutmeg
salt and pepper
3 tablespoons oil
4 slices bread, crusts removed
⅔ cup light cream

Cucumber in cream sauce

(Concombres à la Normande)

Preparation time 15 minutes
Cooking time 5–10 minutes

Serves 4

METRIC/IMPERIAL
2 cucumbers
salt and pepper
50g/2oz butter
20g/¾oz flour
200ml/7fl oz milk
150ml/¼ pint double cream
Garnish
1 tablespoon chopped chives

Peel the cucumbers and divide in half lengthwise. Remove the seeds with a teaspoon and cut into short lengths. Place the cucumber in a pan of boiling salted water and boil for 5 minutes. Drain and cool in cold water. Rinse and drain again very carefully and dry with absorbent paper.

Melt the butter in a frying pan and when hot add the cucumber. Sauté for 3–4 minutes, shaking the pan gently to turn the cucumber without damaging. Remove cucumber and keep hot. Stir in the flour, mix in thoroughly with a wooden spoon then moisten with the milk and cream, stirring to incorporate. Finish cooking over a low heat. Return the cucumber and just before serving adjust the seasoning and sprinkle the dish with chopped chives.

Preparation time 15 minutes
Cooking time 5–10 minutes

Serves 4

AMERICAN
2 cucumbers
salt and pepper
¼ cup butter
3 tablespoons all-purpose flour
¾ cup milk
⅔ cup heavy cream
Garnish
1 tablespoon chopped chives

Celery in Madeira sauce

(Céleri au jus)

Preparation time 25 minutes
Cooking time 1 hour

Serves 5-6

METRIC/IMPERIAL
5-6 medium heads celery
salt and pepper
2 onions
1 carrot
100g/4oz smoked streaky bacon
40g/1½oz butter
450ml/¾ pint stock
2 tablespoons meat juices
1 tablespoon cornflour
100ml/4fl oz Madeira
Garnish
chopped parsley

Clean the celery and cut off the stalks 10–13cm/4–5 inches from the base. (The rest of the stalks can be used to make a salad or soup.) Plunge the celery into a pan of boiling salted water. Simmer for 10 minutes, then drain.

Finely chop the onions, carrot and bacon. Brown well in the melted butter. Stir in the stock and simmer for 15 minutes. Add the meat juices and season.

Place the celery in this sauce. Cover and continue cooking over a low heat for 30 minutes. When the celery is cooked arrange on a heated serving dish and keep warm.

Strain the sauce and stir in the cornflour mixed with the Madeira. Thicken over a gentle heat without boiling, stirring continuously.

Pour over the celery and sprinkle with chopped parsley. Serve very hot.

Preparation time 25 minutes
Cooking time 1 hour

Serves 5-6

AMERICAN
5-6 medium bunches celery
salt and pepper
2 onions
1 carrot
6 bacon slices
3 tablespoons butter
2 cups stock
3 tablespoons meat juices
1 tablespoon cornstarch
½ cup Madeira
Garnish
chopped parsley

Braised chicory

(Endives braisées)

Preparation time 15 minutes
Cooking time 50–60 minutes

Serves 6

METRIC/IMPERIAL
1 kg/2 lb chicory
50 g/2 oz butter
1 tablespoon oil
salt and pepper
1 sugar lump
Garnish
chopped parsley

Wipe the chicory but do not wash. With a small pointed knife remove the hard part at the base of the stem. Blanch in boiling water for 3 minutes.

Melt the butter and oil in a frying pan or flameproof casserole. Place the chicory in this hot butter. Season with salt and pepper, add the sugar lump, cover and cook over a low heat for 50–60 minutes.

Turn from time to time. The chicory should cook in its own juice and brown slightly. Moisten with a little hot water if necessary.

Arrange the chicory in a vegetable dish, sprinkle with chopped parsley and serve very hot. Braised chicory is often served with the gravy of whatever roast meat it accompanies poured over it on the plate.

Preparation time 15 minutes
Cooking time 50–60 minutes

Serves 6

AMERICAN
2 lb Belgian endive
¼ cup butter
1 tablespoon oil
salt and pepper
1 sugar cube
Garnish
chopped parsley

Fennel Provençal

(Fenouils Lucia)

Preparation time 15 minutes
Cooking time 1¼ hours

Serves 5

METRIC/IMPERIAL
0.75kg/1½lb fennel
salt and pepper
2 large onions
0.5kg/1lb tomatoes or 1 (396-g/
14-oz) can tomatoes
4 tablespoons olive oil
½ teaspoon powdered thyme
1 small bay leaf
50g/2oz Gruyère cheese, grated

Trim and wash the bulbs of fennel. Cook for 15 minutes in boiling salted water. Drain and halve, reserving 150ml/¼ pint (US ⅔ cup) of the cooking liquor.

Peel the onions and chop coarsely. Peel the tomatoes, quarter and remove seeds, or drain the canned tomatoes.

Heat the oil in a flameproof casserole and brown the onions. Add the fennel halves, the reserved cooking liquor and tomato quarters. Season with salt, pepper, thyme and the bay leaf. Cover and simmer over a gentle heat for about 50 minutes, stirring occasionally.

When cooked remove the lid and turn up the heat for 5 minutes to reduce the cooking liquor.

Transfer to a heated serving dish and sprinkle with the grated Gruyère. Serve immediately.

Preparation time 15 minutes
Cooking time 1¼ hours

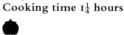

Serves 5

AMERICAN
1½lb fennel
salt and pepper
2 large onions
1lb tomatoes or 1 (14-oz) can
tomatoes
⅓ cup olive oil
½ teaspoon powdered thyme
1 small bay leaf
½ cup grated Gruyère cheese

Baked stuffed potatoes
(Pommes de terre farcies)

Preparation time 15 minutes
Cooking time 1–1¼ hours

Serves 5

METRIC/IMPERIAL
10 potatoes, long in shape
Stuffing
2 onions
75g/3oz butter
350g/12oz sausagemeat
1 clove garlic
1 tablespoon chopped parsley
**50g/2oz fresh breadcrumbs, soaked
in milk and squeezed**
1 egg
salt and pepper
Garnish
sprigs of watercress

Prepare the stuffing. Peel and finely chop the onions, lightly sauté in 25g/1oz (US 2 tablespoons) hot butter. When they begin to colour, add the sausagemeat and break up with a fork while browning it.

Peel and chop the garlic, add to the sausagemeat with the parsley and breadcrumbs. Mix over a gentle heat. Remove from the heat and bind this stuffing with the beaten egg. Season.

Preheat the oven to hot (220°C, 425°F, Gas Mark 7).

Peel the potatoes, cut a thin slice off the longest part then hollow out the insides. Fill them with the sausagemeat stuffing.

Butter an ovenproof dish. Arrange the potatoes in it and sprinkle with the rest of the melted butter. Put the dish in the oven for about 45–50 minutes, until the potatoes are cooked through.

Serve hot garnished with sprigs of watercress.

Preparation time 15 minutes
Cooking time 1–1¼ hours

Serves 5

AMERICAN
10 potatoes, long in shape
Stuffing
2 onions
6 tablespoons butter
¾ lb sausage meat
1 clove garlic
1 tablespoon chopped parsley
**1 cup fresh soft bread crumbs,
soaked in milk and squeezed**
1 egg
salt and pepper
Garnish
sprigs of watercress

Dauphine potatoes

(Pommes dauphines)

Preparation time 35 minutes
Cooking time 1 hour

Serves 6

METRIC/IMPERIAL
1 kg/2lb floury potatoes
75 g/3oz butter
3 eggs plus 3 egg yolks
salt and pepper
freshly grated nutmeg
oil for deep frying
Choux pastry
250 ml/8 fl oz water
75 g/3oz butter
pinch of salt
125 g/4½ oz plain flour, sifted
4 eggs

Wash the potatoes and cook in their jackets in boiling salted water.

While they are cooking, prepare the choux pastry. Place the water, butter and salt in a saucepan. Allow the butter to melt then bring quickly to the boil. Toss in the flour all at once and beat rapidly with a wooden spoon to obtain a smooth even paste. Continue cooking over a gentle heat, stirring constantly to dry out the paste. Remove from the heat as soon as it leaves the sides of the pan clean. Let it stand for a few moments, then add the first egg. Beat well together and add separately the 3 remaining eggs, beating well each time.

Peel the potatoes and mash or sieve them. Place this purée in a saucepan and dry out over a gentle heat, stirring with a wooden spoon. Mix in the butter, then the 3 whole eggs and the 3 yolks, one by one.

Mix this purée with the choux paste. Season with salt, pepper and freshly grated nutmeg. Leave to cool.

Form into small balls and toss into the heated frying oil. Drain the dauphine potatoes on absorbent paper as soon as they are cooked through and golden.

Preparation time 35 minutes
Cooking time 1 hour

Serves 6

AMERICAN
2lb floury potatoes
6 tablespoons butter
3 eggs plus 3 egg yolks
salt and pepper
freshly grated nutmeg
oil for deep frying
Choux paste
1 cup water
6 tablespoons butter
dash of salt
1 cup plus 2 tablespoons sifted all-
    purpose flour
4 eggs

Potato galettes

(Galettes parmentier)

Preparation time 30 minutes
Cooking time 10 minutes

Serves 6

METRIC/IMPERIAL
6 large floury potatoes
salt and freshly ground pepper
100g/4oz butter
2 egg yolks
2 tablespoons ground almonds
3 petits suisses (small cream cheeses)
1 tablespoon double cream
1 tablespoon finely chopped parsley
flour to coat
Garnish
sprigs of parsley

Peel the potatoes. Cut into quarters and cook for 20 minutes from cold in salted water.

Drain well and dry out in the oven for about 3 minutes. Pass through a vegetable mill or sieve to make a purée. Return to the saucepan and beat in 40g/1½oz (US 3 tablespoons) butter over a low heat. Mix in the egg yolks.

Remove from the heat. Add the ground almonds, petits suisses, cream and parsley. Season with pepper and mix all the ingredients well together. Taste and adjust for seasoning.

With floured hands, form into small round cakes 1cm/½ inch thick, and flour lightly. Brown in a frying pan in the remaining very hot butter. Turn when half cooked. Mark a criss-cross pattern with a knife, if liked. Garnish with parsley and serve very hot.

Preparation time 30 minutes
Cooking time 10 minutes

Serves 6

AMERICAN
6 large floury potatoes
salt and freshly ground pepper
½ cup butter
2 egg yolks
3 tablespoons ground almonds
1 (3-oz) package full-fat cream cheese
1 tablespoon heavy cream
1 tablespoon finely chopped parsley
flour to coat
Garnish
sprigs of parsley

Gratin potatoes

(Gratin Dauphinois)

Preparation time 20 minutes
Cooking time 50-60 minutes

Serves 6

METRIC/IMPERIAL
1kg/2lb potatoes
1 clove garlic
50g/2oz butter
150g/5oz cheese, grated
2 eggs
100ml/4fl oz double cream
450ml/¾ pint milk
salt and pepper
freshly grated nutmeg

Peel, wash and wipe the potatoes. Cut into slices 5mm/¼ inch thick. Set the oven to moderately hot (190°C, 375°F, Gas Mark 5).

Rub an ovenproof earthenware dish with the cut clove of garlic and grease with half the butter. Cover the base with an even layer of potatoes and sprinkle with a little grated cheese. Continue layering in this way until the potatoes are used up.

Beat the eggs with the cream. Mix in the milk and season with salt, pepper and a little nutmeg. Pour over the potatoes. Sprinkle the top of the dish with the rest of the grated cheese and dot with the remaining butter. Place in the oven for 50–60 minutes, until cooked.

Serve the potatoes well browned straight from the oven.

Preparation time 20 minutes
Cooking time 50-60 minutes

Serves 6

AMERICAN
2lb potatoes
1 clove garlic
¼ cup butter
1¼ cups grated cheese
2 eggs
½ cup heavy cream
2 cups milk
salt and pepper
freshly grated nutmeg

Braised spring vegetables (Jardinière de printemps)

Preparation time 25 minutes
Cooking time 50 minutes

Serves 6

METRIC/IMPERIAL
24 button onions
225g/8oz small new turnips
0.5kg/1lb new carrots
1 lettuce
350g/12oz French beans
100g/4oz bacon
50g/2oz butter
0.5kg/1lb shelled peas
250ml/8fl oz stock
salt and pepper
1 sugar lump

Peel the onions and turnips. Scrape the carrots and cut in half. Wash and dry the lettuce. String the beans and cut each into 2 or 3 pieces, according to length. Dice the bacon.

Heat the butter in a flameproof casserole and cook the bacon and onions. When beginning to turn golden add the turnips and carrots. Allow to colour slightly before adding the peas, lettuce leaves and beans. Cover the pan and cook for 10 minutes over a low heat.

Add the stock. Season with salt and pepper and add the sugar lump. Continue to cook for about 30 minutes. Serve very hot in a warmed vegetable dish.

Preparation time 25 minutes
Cooking time 50 minutes

Serves 6

AMERICAN
24 button onions
½lb new turnips
1lb new carrots
1 head lettuce
¾lb green beans
¼lb Canadian bacon
¼ cup butter
3 cups shelled peas
1 cup stock
salt and pepper
1 sugar cube

Braised lettuce

(Laitues braisées)

Preparation time 15 minutes
Cooking time 30–35 minutes

Serves 6

METRIC/IMPERIAL
6 lettuces
salt and pepper
50g/2oz butter
1 bunch savory or 2 teaspoons dried savory
150ml/¼ pint stock

Remove any wrinkled leaves and trim the stem from the lettuces. Leave whole and wash carefully.

Boil salted water in a large pan. Plunge the lettuces into it for 5 minutes to blanch. Remove with a draining spoon and pass under the cold tap. Drain well, squeezing gently to extract all the water. Place on a tea towel to dry.

Preheat the oven to moderately hot (190°C, 375°F, Gas Mark 5).

Grease an ovenproof dish with part of the butter. Arrange the lettuces side by side in the dish, placing a sprig of savory between each, or sprinkling with dried savory. Dot the top with butter and sprinkle all over with stock. Season moderately. Butter a sheet of foil and cover the lettuces.

Cook in the oven for 30 minutes until the stock has reduced slightly. Serve hot.

Preparation time 15 minutes
Cooking time 30–35 minutes

Serves 6

AMERICAN
6 heads lettuce
salt and pepper
¼ cup butter
1 bunch savory or 2 teaspoons dried savory
⅔ cup stock

Courgettes au gratin

(Courgettes au gratin)

Preparation time 25 minutes
Cooking time 30 minutes

Serves 6

METRIC/IMPERIAL
1 kg/2lb courgettes
salt and pepper
150g/5oz smoked bacon
100ml/4fl oz oil
3 onions
flour to coat
1 small bouquet garni
2 cloves garlic
300 ml/½ pint fresh tomato sauce
(see page 310)
75g/3oz cheese, grated

Peel the courgettes and cut into sections about 5 cm/2 inches long. Cut these sections into sticks. Sprinkle lightly with salt and leave for 20 minutes.

Meanwhile, cut the bacon into small pieces and brown in 2 tablespoons (US 3 tablespoons) oil. Remove from the pan and keep warm.

In the same oil brown the sliced onions. Remove from the pan and add to the bacon.

Rinse and wipe the courgettes on absorbent paper. Coat in flour. Cook in the frying pan in the rest of the hot oil. When golden, drain.

In an ovenproof dish mix the courgettes, onions and bacon. Add the bouquet garni, chopped garlic and heated tomato sauce. Season and sprinkle with grated cheese.

Brown under the grill and serve very hot.

Preparation time 25 minutes
Cooking time 30 minutes

Serves 6

AMERICAN
2lb zucchini
salt and pepper
7–8 bacon slices
½ cup oil
3 onions
flour to coat
1 small bouquet garni
2 cloves garlic
1¼ cups fresh tomato sauce (see page 310)
¾ cup grated cheese

Stuffed courgettes

(Courgettes soufflées)

Preparation time 20 minutes
Cooking time 30 minutes

Serves 6

METRIC/IMPERIAL
6 courgettes
3 eggs
175 g/6 oz cream cheese
100 g/4 oz Gruyère cheese, grated
1 tablespoon semolina flour
150 ml/¼ pint single cream
1 tablespoon chopped mixed herbs
(parsley, chives, tarragon,
chervil)
salt and pepper
5 tablespoons olive oil
breadcrumbs to sprinkle

Cut off the ends of the courgettes and divide in half length-wise. Gently scoop out a hollow in each.

Break the eggs and separate the yolks from the whites.

In a bowl mix the beaten cream cheese, the grated Gruyère, semolina flour, cream, egg yolks, chopped herbs and seasoning.

Preheat the oven to moderately hot (200°C, 400°F, Gas Mark 6).

Grease a baking sheet with oil.

Whisk the egg whites until stiff and gently fold into the cheese mixture. Fill the courgettes with this mixture and place on the baking sheet. Sprinkle with breadcrumbs and oil and cook for 30 minutes in the moderately hot oven.

Serve the courgettes either hot from the oven or chilled and sprinkled with a herb vinaigrette sauce.

Preparation time 20 minutes
Cooking time 30 minutes

Serves 6

AMERICAN
6 zucchini
3 eggs
¾ cup full-fat cream cheese
1 cup grated Gruyère cheese
1 tablespoon semolina flour
⅔ cup light cream
1 tablespoon chopped mixed herbs
(parsley, chives, tarragon,
chervil)
salt and pepper
6 tablespoons olive oil
bread crumbs to sprinkle

Stuffed peppers

(Poivrons farcis)

Preparation time 30 minutes
Cooking time 1 hour

Serves 8

METRIC/IMPERIAL
75 g/3 oz raisins
225 g/8 oz long-grain rice
salt and pepper
pinch of saffron
2 onions
100 ml/4 fl oz oil
350 g/12 oz minced lamb
2 cloves garlic
2 tablespoons chopped parsley
8 green or red peppers

Soak the raisins in warm water.

Wash the rice then cook for 12 minutes in boiling salted water with the saffron. When cooked, drain thoroughly.

Lightly sauté the finely chopped onions in half the oil. When they are soft but not coloured, add the minced lamb. Cook until it changes colour then add the rice, the drained raisins, chopped garlic and parsley. Season well and mix all together over a gentle heat.

Slice the tops off the peppers, remove the core and seeds and fill with the rice mixture. Set the oven to moderately hot (200°C, 400°F, Gas Mark 6). Place the peppers in a greased ovenproof dish and sprinkle with the rest of the oil. Cook for 35–40 minutes and serve hot.

Preparation time 30 minutes
Cooking time 1 hour

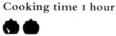

Serves 8

AMERICAN
6 tablespoons seeded raisins
1 cup long-grain rice
salt and pepper
dash of saffron
2 onions
½ cup oil
1½ cups ground lamb
2 cloves garlic
3 tablespoons chopped parsley
8 green or red peppers

Ratatouille

(La ratatouille)

Preparation time 30 minutes
Cooking time 1½ hours

Serves 6-8

METRIC/IMPERIAL
0.5 kg/1 lb onions
1 kg/2 lb aubergines
0.75 kg/1½ lb courgettes
salt and freshly ground pepper
0.75 kg/1½ lb tomatoes
0.5 kg/1 lb peppers
200 ml/7 fl oz olive oil
4 cloves garlic
1 small bouquet garni
2 bay leaves

Peel and finely slice the onions. Peel the aubergines and the courgettes, cut them into dice, sprinkle lightly with salt and leave for 20 minutes. Peel the tomatoes, cut into dice after having removed the seeds. Wash the peppers, deseed and cut into thin strips.

In a frying pan, soften the onions in half the hot oil, do not let them brown, remove from the pan.

In the same oil, sauté one after another the peppers, aubergines and finally the courgettes (having drained and wiped these last two vegetables).

Heat the rest of the oil in a heavy-bottomed flameproof casserole and fill with the vegetables in layers: onions, aubergines, tomatoes, courgettes and peppers, until used up. Season, add 3 crushed cloves of garlic and 1 whole, the bouquet garni and bay leaves. Cover and cook for 1 hour over a gentle heat, being careful that the vegetables do not catch. Serve hot or cold.

Preparation time 30 minutes
Cooking time 1½ hours

Serves 6-8

AMERICAN
1 lb onions
2 lb eggplant
1½ lb zucchini
salt and freshly ground pepper
1½ lb tomatoes
1 lb peppers
¾ cup olive oil
4 cloves garlic
1 small bouquet garni
2 bay leaves

Stuffed tomatoes

(Tomates farcies)

Preparation time 25 minutes
Cooking time 35-40 minutes

Serves 4

METRIC/IMPERIAL
8 round tomatoes
salt and pepper
50g/2oz dried breadcrumbs
40g/1½oz butter
300ml/½ pint fresh tomato sauce
(see page 310)
Stuffing
4 medium onions
40g/1½oz butter
225g/8oz sausagemeat
175g/6oz minced veal (or leftover cooked meat)
2 cloves garlic
1 tablespoon chopped parsley
75g/3oz dried breadcrumbs, soaked in milk and squeezed
1 egg (optional)

Slice the top off each tomato and scoop out the pulp with a teaspoon. Sprinkle the insides lightly with salt and leave upside down to drain.

Prepare the stuffing. Fry the finely chopped onions in the hot butter until golden. Add the sausagemeat and minced veal and brown well, crumbling with a fork and mixing with the onions. Remove from the heat and add the chopped garlic, parsley, breadcrumbs and beaten egg. If necessary, season with salt and pepper and mix well to obtain an even stuffing. Fill the drained tomatoes with this mixture and sprinkle with dried breadcrumbs. Place in a generously buttered ovenproof dish and top with the rest of the butter, melted. Pour in the tomato sauce.

Cook in a moderate oven (180°C, 350°F, Gas Mark 4) for about 30 minutes. Serve hot from the cooking dish.

Preparation time 25 minutes
Cooking time 35-40 minutes

Serves 4

AMERICAN
8 round tomatoes
salt and pepper
½ cup dry bread crumbs
3 tablespoons butter
1¼ cups fresh tomato sauce (see page 310)
Stuffing
4 medium onions
3 tablespoons butter
½ lb sausage meat
¾ cup ground veal (or leftover cooked meat)
2 cloves garlic
1 tablespoon chopped parsley
¾ cup dry bread crumbs, soaked in milk and squeezed
1 egg (optional)

Lebanese-style tomatoes

(Tomates Libanaises)

Preparation time 30 minutes plus 1 hour standing time

Serves 6

METRIC/IMPERIAL
6 large and 4 small tomatoes
salt and pepper
100g/4oz cornmeal (available from healthfood shops)
6 large spring onions
1 bunch parsley
2 small sprigs of mint
3 tablespoons olive oil
juice of 1 lemon
Garnish
sprigs of watercress

Wash and dry the 6 large tomatoes. Cut a slice off the top, scoop out the pulp with a teaspoon, sprinkle inside with salt and leave upside down to drain.

Leave the cornmeal to swell for 1 hour in cold water.

Finely chop the spring onions, parsley and mint.

Peel the small tomatoes, remove seeds and dice the pulp. Add this to the chopped herb mixture together with the well drained cornmeal.

Mix the oil and lemon juice, add salt and pepper to taste. Sprinkle over the herb mixture and stir gently.

Fill the drained tomatoes with this salad. Arrange on a serving platter and garnish with watercress sprigs. Serve chilled.

Preparation time 30 minutes plus 1 hour standing time

Serves 6

AMERICAN
6 large and 4 small tomatoes
salt and pepper
$\frac{2}{3}$ cup corn meal (available from healthfood stores)
6 large scallions
1 bunch parsley
2 small sprigs of mint
$\frac{1}{4}$ cup olive oil
juice of 1 lemon
Garnish
sprigs of watercress

Stuffed artichokes

(Artichauts à la Barigoule)

Preparation time 35 minutes
Cooking time 1¼ hours

Serves 6

METRIC/IMPERIAL
3 large onions
4 tablespoons oil
350g/12oz sausagemeat
2 cloves garlic
1 tablespoon chopped parsley
**50g/2oz fresh breadcrumbs,
moistened with milk**
1 egg
salt and pepper
6 globe artichokes
150g/5oz smoked streaky bacon

Prepare the stuffing. Brown the chopped onions in 2 table-spoons (US 3 tablespoons) oil. Add the sausagemeat, crumbling it with a fork, and brown all over. Into this mix the crushed garlic, chopped parsley, breadcrumbs and beaten egg. Season. The stuffing should be uniform and well bound together.

Wash the artichokes and cut the tips off the leaves, leaving only the edible parts. Blanch for 7–8 minutes in boiling salted water. Drain upside down. Carefully separate the leaves and scoop out the hairy choke with a small spoon. Fill with the stuffing.

Dice the bacon and cook until lightly browned in the rest of the hot oil. Transfer to an ovenproof dish and add the artichokes. Cover and cook in a moderate oven (180°C, 350°F, Gas Mark 4) for 45–50 minutes.

Serve hot.

Preparation time 35 minutes
Cooking time 1¼ hours

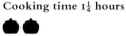

Serves 6

AMERICAN
3 large onions
⅓ cup oil
¾ lb sausage meat
2 cloves garlic
1 tablespoon chopped parsley
**1 cup fresh soft bread crumbs,
moistened with milk**
1 egg
salt and pepper
6 globe artichokes
7–8 bacon slices

Mushroom and sausage terrine

(Terrine de cèpes)

Preparation time 30 minutes
Cooking time 45 minutes

Serves 6

METRIC/IMPERIAL
2 onions
2 cloves garlic
1kg/2lb very firm cèpes or large
flat mushrooms
5 tablespoons olive oil
350g/12oz sausagemeat
2 tablespoons chopped parsley
½ teaspoon powdered thyme
50g/2oz fresh breadcrumbs, soaked
in milk and squeezed
salt and pepper
4 thin slices ham

Peel and finely chop the onions and garlic.

Trim the stalks of the mushrooms, clean them carefully without washing them. Separate the stalks from the caps; leave the caps whole and chop the stalks.

Lightly brown the onions in half the hot oil. When they are coloured, add the chopped mushroom stalks. Stir with a wooden spoon until soft, then add the sausagemeat, garlic, parsley and thyme. Brown well, crumbling and mixing these ingredients together. Mix in the breadcrumbs and season to taste.

Line the bottom of an ovenproof earthenware dish with a slice of ham, cover with a layer of the sausagemeat mixture then a layer of mushroom caps. Continue in this way until all the ingredients are used up, ending with the mushrooms. Sprinkle over the rest of the oil, cover with a lid or foil and cook in a hot oven (220°C, 425°F, Gas Mark 7) for 30 minutes.

Serve hot.

Preparation time 30 minutes
Cooking time 45 minutes

Serves 6

AMERICAN
2 onions
2 cloves garlic
2lb very firm cèpes or large flat
mushrooms
6 tablespoons olive oil
¾lb sausage meat
3 tablespoons chopped parsley
½ teaspoon powdered thyme
1 cup fresh soft bread crumbs,
soaked in milk and squeezed
salt and pepper
4 thin slices cooked ham

Cos lettuce salad

(Romaine aux oeufs mollets)

Preparation time 12 minutes
Cooking time 10 minutes

Serves 4–6

METRIC/IMPERIAL
1 cos lettuce
3 eggs
2 spring onions
1 tablespoon wine vinegar
salt and freshly ground pepper
3 tablespoons oil
Garnish
chopped chives

Clean the lettuce, tear the leaves into 4 or 5 pieces, wash and wipe them carefully.

Place the eggs in a saucepan of cold water, bring to the boil and simmer for 10 minutes. Plunge into cold water. Shell them carefully.

Trim and chop the spring onions.

Pour the vinegar into a bowl, add a pinch of salt and stir to dissolve it. Mix in the oil, beating or whisking to combine thoroughly. Season to taste with freshly ground pepper.

Arrange the lettuce in a salad bowl, add the chopped spring onions and sprinkle with the oil and vinegar dressing. Toss together gently, add the halved or quartered eggs and finally garnish with chopped chives.

Preparation time 12 minutes
Cooking time 10 minutes

Serves 4–6

AMERICAN
1 head Romaine lettuce
3 eggs
2 scallions
1 tablespoon wine vinegar
salt and freshly ground pepper
¼ cup oil
Garnish
chopped chives

Fennel and rice salad

(Salade Chita)

Preparation time 15 minutes
Cooking time 18 minutes

Serves 6

METRIC/IMPERIAL
225g/8oz long-grain rice
1 bulb fennel
3 tomatoes
2 peppers
1 mild onion
3 shallots
4 tablespoons olive oil
3 tablespoons wine vinegar
salt and pepper
100g/4oz black olives

Wash the rice carefully, toss it into a large quantity of boiling salted water. Cover and cook for 15–18 minutes, until just cooked but still firm to the bite. Drain and rinse in cold water then dry in a clean tea towel.

Wash the fennel, slice finely. Wash then dry the tomatoes and peppers. Remove the seeds and cut the flesh into small dice.

Peel and finely chop the onion and shallots. Place in a bowl with the oil, vinegar and seasoning. Mix well. Arrange the rice, fennel, tomatoes, peppers and olives in a wooden salad bowl, pour over the dressing and toss well together.

Serve chilled.

Preparation time 15 minutes
Cooking time 18 minutes

Serves 6

AMERICAN
1 cup long-grain rice
1 bulb fennel
3 tomatoes
2 peppers
1 mild onion
3 shallots
⅓ cup olive oil
¼ cup wine vinegar
salt and pepper
¼lb ripe olives

Springtime salad

(Salade de printemps)

Preparation time 15 minutes
Cooking time 10 minutes

Serves 6

METRIC/IMPERIAL
8 anchovy fillets
4 eggs
225 g/8 oz young spinach leaves
1 small endive
1 large bunch chervil
3 small onions (optional)
100 ml/4 fl oz olive oil
2 tablespoons vinegar
freshly ground pepper

Wash the anchovy fillets and soak in cold water.

Hard-boil the eggs for 10 minutes in simmering water.

Wash the spinach and endive and dry carefully. Tear the endive into small pieces. Strip the chervil leaves from the stalks. Peel the onions, slice finely and separate into rings.

Pound 3 anchovy fillets with 2 tablespoons (US 3 tablespoons) oil to obtain a smooth paste. Blend in the rest of the oil and the vinegar. Add pepper to taste.

Mix the spinach, endive and chervil in a salad bowl. Pour over the dressing, stir gently together. Arrange over the salad the remaining anchovy fillets, onion rings and the quartered hard-boiled eggs. Serve at once.

Preparation time 15 minutes
Cooking time 10 minutes

Serves 6

AMERICAN
8 anchovy fillets
4 eggs
½ lb young spinach leaves
1 small head chicory
1 large bunch chervil
3 small onions (optional)
½ cup olive oil
3 tablespoons vinegar
freshly ground pepper

Provence salad

(Salade Provençale)

Preparation time 20 minutes
Cooking time 10 minutes

Serves 6

METRIC/IMPERIAL
12 anchovy fillets
3 eggs
5 tomatoes
2 cloves garlic
salt and pepper
4 tablespoons olive oil
juice of 1 lemon
1 tablespoon wine vinegar
2 red peppers
1 small endive
1 cucumber
2 mild onions
100 g/4 oz French beans, cooked
100 g/4 oz small black olives

Wash the anchovy fillets and soak in cold water.

Hard-boil the eggs. Peel 1 tomato, remove seeds and crush it to a purée.

Peel the cloves of garlic, then pound them with a pinch of salt in a mortar, gradually incorporating the oil. Combine this very smooth mixture with the lemon juice, vinegar and crushed tomato. Season with pepper, then beat this dressing for a moment with a wire whisk.

Cut the rest of the tomatoes into slices and the peppers into strips. Wash, dry and shred the endive. Thinly slice the cucumber. Cut the hard-boiled eggs into quarters. Peel the onions, cut into rounds and separate into rings.

In a large salad bowl arrange the tomatoes, peppers, cucumber, French beans, endive, onion rings, olives, drained anchovy fillets and quartered hard-boiled eggs. Pour over the dressing and stir gently. Serve immediately.

Preparation time 20 minutes
Cooking time 10 minutes

Serves 6

AMERICAN
12 anchovy fillets
3 eggs
5 tomatoes
2 cloves garlic
salt and pepper
⅓ cup olive oil
juice of 1 lemon
1 tablespoon wine vinegar
2 red peppers
1 small head chicory
1 cucumber
2 mild onions
¼ lb green beans, cooked
¼ lb small ripe olives

Chef's salad

(Salade du chef)

Preparation time 15 minutes

Serves 6

METRIC/IMPERIAL
1 grapefruit
1 lettuce
½ cucumber
2 tomatoes
½ celery heart
225 g/8 oz peeled prawns
Sauce
150 ml/¼ pint mayonnaise (see page 314)
1 tablespoon lemon juice
1 tablespoon tomato ketchup
pinch of paprika
salt
pinch of cayenne
Garnish
chopped chervil

Cut the grapefruit in half and scoop out the flesh with a grapefruit knife. Wash and wipe the lettuce. Set aside 5 large green leaves and shred the rest finely.

Wash and dry the cucumber and tomatoes. Cut into slices. Finely chop the celery.

Prepare the sauce. Place the mayonnaise in a bowl with the lemon juice, tomato ketchup, paprika, salt and cayenne; mix well together.

Line a salad bowl with the whole lettuce leaves. Arrange over the bottom the shredded lettuce, finely chopped celery and grapefruit segments. Scatter with the prawns and surround with the tomato and cucumber slices. Spoon over the sauce and sprinkle the whole with chopped chervil.

Serve well chilled.

Preparation time 15 minutes

Serves 6

AMERICAN
1 grapefruit
1 head lettuce
½ cucumber
2 tomatoes
½ celery heart
½ lb shelled shrimp
Sauce
⅔ cup mayonnaise (see page 314)
1 tablespoon lemon juice
1 tablespoon tomato ketchup
dash of paprika pepper
salt
dash of cayenne pepper
Garnish
chopped chervil

Niçoise salad

(Salade Niçoise)

Preparation time 15 minutes
Cooking time 10 minutes

Serves 6

METRIC/IMPERIAL
3 eggs
1 endive or lettuce
6 tomatoes
3 sprigs of basil
2 cloves garlic
2 spring onions
1 (198-g/7-oz) can tuna
75 g/3 oz black olives
12 anchovy fillets
100 g/4 oz French beans, cooked
2 tablespoons lemon juice (or wine vinegar)
100 ml/4 fl oz olive oil
salt and pepper

Hard-boil the eggs for 10 minutes, dip into cold water then shell them. Leave to cool before cutting into quarters.

Wash the endive or lettuce, dry and shred the leaves. Wash and dry the tomatoes, cut into quarters. Chop the basil, garlic and spring onions. Drain and flake the tuna, reserving the oil. Place in a wooden salad bowl with the shredded endive, olives, anchovy fillets, French beans, basil, garlic and spring onions.

Mix the lemon juice with a tablespoon of the tuna oil, add the olive oil, season and mix well together. Pour over the salad, stir gently and top with the quartered hard-boiled eggs.

Preparation time 15 minutes
Cooking time 10 minutes

Serves 6

AMERICAN
3 eggs
1 head chicory or lettuce
6 tomatoes
3 sprigs of basil
2 cloves garlic
2 scallions
1 (7-oz) can tuna
½ cup ripe olives
12 anchovy fillets
¼ lb green beans, cooked
3 tablespoons lemon juice (or wine vinegar)
½ cup olive oil
salt and pepper

Italian-style salad

(Salade Italienne)

Preparation time 20 minutes
Cooking time 15 minutes

Serves 6

METRIC/IMPERIAL
100g/4oz long-grain rice
salt
3 eggs
4 tomatoes
2 green or red peppers
1 (200-g/7-oz) can artichoke hearts
1 (283-g/10-oz) can asparagus tips
75g/3oz small black olives
Dressing
small pinch of sea salt
2 cloves garlic
3 sprigs of basil
4 tablespoons olive oil
juice of 1 lemon
pepper

Wash the rice until the water becomes clear. Then toss into a large pan of boiling salted water and cook for about 15 minutes.

Hard-boil the eggs then dip into cold water, shell and cut into quarters.

When the rice is just cooked, drain it, rinse in cold water and leave to cool. Peel, deseed and quarter the tomatoes. Wash the peppers, discard core and seeds then cut the flesh into thin strips.

In a large salad bowl mix together the rice, tomatoes, peppers, hard-boiled eggs, drained and halved artichoke hearts and asparagus tips and the black olives.

Prepare the dressing. Place in a mortar the sea salt, peeled garlic and basil leaves. Pound all together well, gradually blending in the oil. Add the lemon juice and season to taste. Pour this dressing over the salad and mix gently.

Preparation time 20 minutes
Cooking time 15 minutes

Serves 6

AMERICAN
½ cup long-grain rice
salt
3 eggs
4 tomatoes
2 green or red peppers
1 (7-oz) can artichoke hearts
1 (10-oz) can asparagus tips
½ cup small ripe olives
Dressing
small dash of coarse salt
2 cloves garlic
3 sprigs of basil
⅓ cup olive oil
juice of 1 lemon
pepper

Gourmet salad

(Salade du gourmet)

Preparation time 30 minutes
Cooking time 20 minutes

Serves 6

METRIC/IMPERIAL
0.5kg/1lb potatoes
2 tablespoons dry white wine
2 crisp green dessert apples
3 medium tomatoes
little lemon juice
½ small green chilli pepper
50g/2oz stuffed green olives
2 slices processed cheese
100g/4oz ham
2 shallots
few chives
French dressing
½ teaspoon French mustard
2 tablespoons vinegar
salt and pepper
100ml/4fl oz oil

Cook potatoes in their jackets in boiling salted water. Drain as soon as they are cooked, peel and cut them into thin slices. Arrange in a salad bowl and sprinkle with the white wine.

Peel and core the apples, peel and deseed the tomatoes. Cut the apples into cubes and toss in a little lemon juice. Cut the tomatoes into quarters. Cut the pepper and olives into rings. Cut the cheese and ham into small strips. Chop the shallots and chives.

Arrange all these prepared ingredients over the potatoes, reserving a few chives for garnish.

Prepare the French dressing. Mix the mustard with the vinegar, add salt and pepper to taste and gradually beat in the oil with a whisk until combined thoroughly.

Pour this dressing over the salad and toss to mix. Sprinkle with the chopped chives and serve immediately.

Preparation time 30 minutes
Cooking time 20 minutes

Serves 6

AMERICAN
1lb potatoes
3 tablespoons dry white wine
2 crisp green dessert apples
3 medium tomatoes
little lemon juice
½ small green chili pepper
⅓ cup stuffed green olives
2 slices processed cheese
¼lb cooked ham
2 shallots
few chives
French dressing
½ teaspoon French mustard
3 tablespoons vinegar
salt and pepper
½ cup oil

Moroccan salad

(Salade Marocaine)

Preparation time 15 minutes

Serves 6

METRIC/IMPERIAL
1 crisp lettuce (Cos or Webb's)
4 small firm tomatoes
2 green or red peppers
2 oranges
1 large mild onion (optional)
100 g/4 oz black olives
Dressing
juice of 1 lemon
4 tablespoons olive oil
salt and pepper
Garnish
chopped chervil

Wash and dry the lettuce and tear the leaves into pieces. Wash and dry the tomatoes, cut into segments. Wash the peppers, remove seeds and cut into rings. Wash and slice the oranges, halve the slices. Peel and finely slice the onion, separate into rings.

Place all these ingredients in a salad bowl. Mix the lemon juice with the olive oil, season to taste and pour over the salad. Add the olives, stir gently and sprinkle with chopped chervil before serving.

Preparation time 15 minutes

Serves 6

AMERICAN
1 head crisp lettuce (Romaine or Bibb)
4 small firm tomatoes
2 green or red peppers
2 oranges
1 large mild onion (optional)
$\frac{1}{4}$ lb ripe olives
Dressing
juice of 1 lemon
$\frac{1}{3}$ cup olive oil
salt and pepper
Garnish
chopped chervil

Mexican salad

(Salade Mexicaine)

Preparation time 20 minutes
Cooking time 15 minutes

Serves 6

METRIC/IMPERIAL
150g/5oz **long-grain rice**
1 **green pepper**
1 **red pepper**
3 **bananas**
2 **tomatoes**
1 (312-g/11-oz) **can sweetcorn**
juice of 1 **lemon**
4 tablespoons **olive oil**
salt and pepper
50g/2oz **unsalted peanuts**
100g/4oz **shelled shrimps**
2 sprigs of **parsley**

Cook the carefully washed rice in one and a half times its volume of boiling salted water.

Halve the peppers, remove cores and seeds and cut the flesh into small dice. Peel and slice the bananas. Peel and chop the tomatoes. Drain the sweetcorn.

Mix the lemon juice and oil, season and beat this dressing for a moment. Grind the peanuts to reduce them to fine crumbs.

Tip into a salad bowl the rice, diced peppers, pieces of tomato, banana slices, sweetcorn and shrimps. Moisten all with the dressing, stir gently and sprinkle with the ground nuts. Scatter with parsley leaves and serve chilled.

Preparation time 20 minutes
Cooking time 15 minutes

Serves 6

AMERICAN
⅔ cup **long-grain rice**
1 **green pepper**
1 **red pepper**
3 **bananas**
2 **tomatoes**
1 (11-oz) **can corn**
juice of 1 **lemon**
⅓ cup **olive oil**
salt and pepper
½ cup **unsalted peanuts**
¼ lb **shelled shrimp**
2 sprigs of **parsley**

227

Celery and mussel salad

(Céleri aux moules)

Preparation time 20 minutes
Cooking time 7 minutes

Serves 6

METRIC/IMPERIAL
2 litres/3½ pints mussels
1 tender head celery
1 Spanish onion
2–3 crisp dessert apples
1 tablespoon lemon juice
Mayonnaise
1 teaspoon French mustard
2 egg yolks
200 ml/7 fl oz oil
salt and pepper
Garnish
lettuce leaves
chopped parsley

Scrape and wash the mussels, discarding any which do not close when given a sharp tap. Place in a heavy-bottomed pan, cover with 150 ml/¼ pint water and cook over a high heat until the shells open. Drain and remove from shells.

Cut off the celery leaves. Wash the stalks, dry and slice thinly. Peel the onion, cut into rounds and separate into rings. Peel, core and dice the apples. Sprinkle with lemon juice to prevent them discolouring.

Prepare a mayonnaise by blending together the mustard and egg yolks, adding the oil a little at a time. When thick, season. Gently mix in the celery, mussels and apples.

Line a salad bowl with lettuce leaves. Spoon the mayonnaise mixture into it and cover with onion rings. Garnish with chopped parsley and serve very cold.

Preparation time 20 minutes
Cooking time 7 minutes

Serves 6

AMERICAN
4 pints mussels
1 tender bunch celery
1 Spanish onion
2–3 crisp dessert apples
1 tablespoon lemon juice
Mayonnaise
1 teaspoon French mustard
2 egg yolks
¾ cup oil
salt and pepper
Garnish
lettuce leaves
chopped parsley

Fisherman's salad

(Salade du pecheur)

Preparation time 20 minutes
Cooking time 30 minutes

Serves 6

METRIC/IMPERIAL
0.5kg/1lb potatoes
salt
1 litre/1¾ pints mussels
1.4 litres/2½ pints cockles
3 shallots
5 tablespoons oil
4 tablespoons wine vinegar
freshly ground pepper
Garnish
chopped parsley

Cook the potatoes in their jackets in boiling salted water for 30 minutes.

Clean and sort the mussels and cockles, discarding any which do not close when given a sharp tap. Open them in separate saucepans in a little water over the heat. Drain and then remove them from their shells. Strain the liquid in which they were cooked and set it aside.

Peel and finely chop the shallots.

Pour the liquid from the mussels and cockles into a small saucepan. Add the oil and half the vinegar, the chopped shallots and the freshly ground pepper. Do not add salt, as the liquid from the shellfish is already salty. Bring to the boil and leave to simmer.

Peel the potatoes while very hot and cut into slices. Arrange in a fairly deep dish, add the mussels and cockles. Sprinkle the whole with the hot dressing then with the rest of the vinegar. Toss gently together.

Serve this warm salad generously sprinkled with finely chopped parsley.

Preparation time 20 minutes
Cooking time 30 minutes

Serves 6

AMERICAN
1lb potatoes
salt
2 pints mussels
3 pints cockles
3 shallots
6 tablespoons oil
⅓ cup wine vinegar
freshly ground pepper
Garnish
chopped parsley

Eggs en cocotte

(Oeufs en cocotte)

Preparation time 6 minutes
Cooking time 10-15 minutes

Serves 6

METRIC/IMPERIAL
1 bunch chives
25g/1oz butter
200ml/7fl oz double cream
salt and pepper
6 eggs

Wash, dry and chop the chives.

Preheat the oven to moderately hot (190°C, 375°F, Gas Mark 5).

Generously butter six individual cocotte dishes or ramekins.

Mix two-thirds of the chopped chives with half the cream, add salt and pepper. Put 1 tablespoon of this mixture into each cocotte dish and break an egg over it, taking care not to burst the yolk. Spoon over the rest of the cream and sprinkle with the remaining chives.

Place the cocotte dishes in a large, fairly deep baking tin or dish. Pour in hot water to come halfway up the cocottes and cook in the oven for 10–15 minutes. Serve at once.

 a Meursault (dry white)

Preparation time 6 minutes
Cooking time 10-15 minutes

Serves 6

AMERICAN
1 bunch chives
2 tablespoons butter
¾ cup heavy cream
salt and pepper
6 eggs

Eggs in red wine sauce

(Oeufs en meurette)

Preparation time 20 minutes
Cooking time 1 hour

Serves 5

METRIC/IMPERIAL
100 g/4 oz smoked streaky bacon
50 g/2 oz butter
1 large onion
1 carrot
1 bouquet garni
2 tablespoons flour
200 ml/7 fl oz stock
450 ml/¾ pint good red wine
1 clove garlic
salt and pepper
5 eggs

Cut the bacon into small dice. Fry in the hot butter until well coloured then remove.

Peel and finely chop the onion, cut the carrot into small dice. Soften these vegetables in the bacon fat with the bouquet garni. When golden, sprinkle with the flour and stir with a wooden spoon until coloured. Thin this roux with the stock and red wine and heat through, stirring. Add the crushed clove of garlic, season with salt and pepper and simmer without boiling for 45–50 minutes, over the lowest possible heat.

When the sauce is ready, strain it through a conical sieve. Divide the sauce and bacon between five ramekin or cocotte dishes. Carefully break an egg over each.

Place the ramekins in a baking tin containing hot water to come halfway up. Cook in a hot oven (220°C, 425°F, Gas Mark 7) for 5 minutes. Serve as soon as they come out of the oven.

Note You can also poach the eggs one by one in the sauce and then place them in the ramekins. In this case, serve without cooking in the oven.

 the same red wine as used for cooking

Preparation time 20 minutes
Cooking time 1 hour

Serves 5

AMERICAN
6 bacon slices
¼ cup butter
1 large onion
1 carrot
1 bouquet garni
3 tablespoons all-purpose flour
¾ cup stock
2 cups good red wine
1 clove garlic
salt and pepper
5 eggs

Dijon-style eggs

(Oeufs à la Dijonnaise)

Preparation time 10 minutes
Cooking time 10 minutes

Serves 4

METRIC/IMPERIAL
8 eggs
200 ml/7 fl oz double cream
2 tablespoons French mustard
2 teaspoons potato flour or
1 teaspoon cornflour
salt and pepper
Garnish
chopped parsley

Place the eggs in a saucepan of cold water and bring to the boil. Simmer for 10 minutes over a low heat, then dip into cold water. Shell and cut into quarters.

Meanwhile, pour the cream into a small saucepan and bring up to boiling point.

Mix the mustard with the flour, add to the cream and thicken over a low heat, stirring with a wooden spoon. Adjust seasoning and pour over the quartered eggs in a serving dish. Sprinkle with chopped parsley and serve hot.

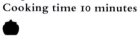 a Meursault (dry white)

Preparation time 10 minutes
Cooking time 10 minutes

Serves 4

AMERICAN
8 eggs
¾ cup heavy cream
3 tablespoons French mustard
2 teaspoons potato flour or
1 teaspoon cornstarch
salt and pepper
Garnish
chopped parsley

Salmon-stuffed eggs (Oeufs farcis au saumon)

Preparation time 20 minutes
Cooking time 20–30 minutes

Serves 5

METRIC/IMPERIAL
5 eggs
3 petits suisses (small cream cheeses)
1 (212-g/7½-oz) can salmon, drained
1 tablespoon chopped parsley
1 tablespoon chopped chives
Sauce
50g/2oz butter
50g/2oz flour
600ml/1 pint hot milk
salt and pepper
1 tablespoon tomato purée

Put the eggs to boil in a saucepan of cold water. Simmer for 10 minutes then dip into cold water. Shell and cut in half lengthwise.

Prepare the sauce. Melt the butter, mix in the flour and when this roux begins to bubble, add the hot milk. Simmer for 2–3 minutes, stirring all the time with a wooden spoon. Season and add the tomato purée.

Remove the yolks from the eggs and place in a bowl. Add the petits suisses, half the salmon, the chopped parsley and chives and 2 tablespoons (US 3 tablespoons) of the sauce. Mix these ingredients well together with a fork, to produce a smooth paste.

Fill the egg whites with this stuffing, mounding it into a dome. Place in an oval gratin dish.

Flake the rest of the salmon and mix into the sauce together with any remaining stuffing. Pour around the stuffed eggs. Brown the top slightly in a moderate oven (180°C, 350°F, Gas Mark 4) for 10–15 minutes. Serve hot in the gratin dish.

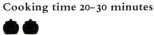 a Sauvignon (white)

Preparation time 20 minutes
Cooking time 20–30 minutes

Serves 5

AMERICAN
5 eggs
1 (3-oz) package full-fat cream cheese
1 (7½-oz) can salmon, drained
1 tablespoon chopped parsley
1 tablespoon chopped chives
Sauce
¼ cup butter
½ cup all-purpose flour
2½ cups hot milk
salt and pepper
1 tablespoon tomato paste

Farmer's wife's eggs

(Oeufs fermière)

Preparation time 20 minutes
Cooking time 20 minutes

Serves 6

METRIC/IMPERIAL
9 eggs
50g/2oz butter
50g/2oz flour
600ml/1 pint milk
salt and pepper
3 petits suisses (small cream cheeses)
1 small bunch chives
2 sprigs of parsley
2 spring onions

Put the eggs in a saucepan of cold water, bring to the boil and simmer for 10 minutes. Dip into cold water, shell and halve lengthwise.

Prepare the white sauce. Melt the butter over a gentle heat and stir in the flour. When the roux begins to bubble, stir in the hot milk. Simmer for 2–3 minutes, stirring constantly with a wooden spoon. Add salt and pepper to taste.

Place the egg yolks in a bowl, add the petits suisses, the very finely chopped herbs and spring onions, 2 tablespoons (US 3 tablespoons) of white sauce and seasoning to taste. Mix all together to give a smooth stuffing.

Take 2 tablespoons (US 3 tablespoons) of this stuffing and mix into the remaining white sauce. Use the rest of the stuffing to fill each egg white, mounding it into a dome. Arrange in an ovenproof dish, pour over the sauce and heat through for 7–8 minutes in a moderate oven (180°C, 350°F, Gas Mark 4). Serve very hot.

a Chablis (dry white)

Preparation time 20 minutes
Cooking time 20 minutes

Serves 6

AMERICAN
9 eggs
¼ cup butter
½ cup all-purpose flour
2½ cups milk
salt and pepper
1 (3-oz) package full-fat cream cheese
1 small bunch chives
2 sprigs of parsley
2 scallions

Herb-stuffed eggs

(Oeufs aux herbes)

Preparation time 25 minutes
Cooking time 15–20 minutes

Serves 6

METRIC/IMPERIAL
6 eggs
3 large cloves garlic
salt and pepper
225g/8oz sorrel or spinach
3 spring onions
25g/1oz butter
1 bunch chives
3 small sprigs of tarragon
1 bunch chervil
1 small sprig of parsley
Mayonnaise
1 teaspoon French mustard
2 egg yolks
200ml/7fl oz oil

Place the eggs in a saucepan of cold water; bring to the boil and simmer for 10 minutes. Dip into cold water, shell and leave to cool. Cook the cloves of garlic in boiling salted water for 5 minutes then peel. Clean the sorrel or spinach carefully and chop.

Peel and chop the spring onions. Soften over a gentle heat in the hot butter, then add the chopped sorrel and let that also soften. Dry out this mixture by stirring over a gentle heat then leave to cool.

Prepare the mayonnaise by blending together the mustard and egg yolks, adding the oil a little at a time.

Chop the chives, tarragon, chervil and parsley.

Cut the eggs in two lengthwise and remove the yolks. Place in an earthenware bowl and beat in the softened sorrel mixture, 2 tablespoons (US 3 tablespoons) mayonnaise, the chopped herbs and the chopped garlic. Season and mix well together. Pile this mixture into the egg whites, mounding it up.

Arrange the eggs in a serving dish, top with the rest of the mayonnaise and serve cold.

a Chablis (dry white)

Preparation time 25 minutes
Cooking time 15–20 minutes

Serves 6

AMERICAN
6 eggs
3 large cloves garlic
salt and pepper
½lb sorrel or spinach
3 scallions
2 tablespoons butter
1 bunch chives
3 small sprigs of tarragon
1 bunch chervil
1 small sprig of parsley
Mayonnaise
1 teaspoon French mustard
2 egg yolks
¾ cup oil

Eggs with sorrel sauce (Oeufs durs à l'oseille)

Preparation time 20 minutes
Cooking time 20 minutes

Serves 4

METRIC/IMPERIAL
1.5 kg/3 lb sorrel or spinach
4 eggs plus 1 egg yolk
50 g/2 oz butter
1 tablespoon flour
200 ml/7 fl oz hot milk
300 ml/½ pint double cream
salt and pepper

Clean the sorrel, cutting off the stalks. Wash in plenty of water and pat dry. Place the whole eggs in a saucepan of cold water, bring to the boil and simmer for 10 minutes.

Soften the sorrel over a gentle heat in a tablespoon of hot butter. Blend in a liquidiser or chop very finely. Prepare a white sauce by melting the remaining butter over a gentle heat. Add the flour, stirring constantly, and when this roux begins to bubble, stir in the hot milk. Cook for 5–10 minutes, stirring continuously with a wooden spoon. Blend this mixture with the sorrel, add half the cream and the egg yolk. Season and keep warm over a very gentle heat. Do not boil.

Gently heat the rest of the cream and season with salt and pepper. Dip the hard-boiled eggs into cold water then shell them. Carefully cut into quarters from the top almost to the base.

Pour the sorrel sauce into a heated serving dish. Arrange over it the eggs and spoon a little hot cream into each. Serve at once.

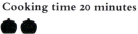 a Sancerre (dry white)

Preparation time 20 minutes
Cooking time 20 minutes

Serves 4

AMERICAN
3 lb sorrel or spinach
4 eggs plus 1 egg yolk
¼ cup butter
1 tablespoon all-purpose flour
¾ cup hot milk
1¼ cups heavy cream
salt and pepper

Basque-style eggs

(Oeufs durs à la Basquaise)

Preparation time 25 minutes
Cooking time 30-35 minutes

Serves 6

METRIC/IMPERIAL
6 rashers smoked streaky bacon
(about 8mm/⅜ inch thick)
2 large onions
4 peppers
1 kg/2lb ripe tomatoes
2 cloves garlic
9 eggs
4 tablespoons olive oil
salt and pepper

Cut the rashers of bacon into small strips, $5\,\text{mm}/\frac{1}{4}$ inch wide. Peel and coarsely chop the onions. Wash and wipe the peppers, remove core and seeds and cut into thin strips. Peel the tomatoes, quarter and remove seeds, peel and chop the garlic.

Hard-boil the eggs: place in a saucepan of cold water, bring to the boil and simmer gently for 10 minutes. Dip into cold water, shell and cut in half lengthwise.

Meanwhile, heat the oil in a frying pan and use to brown the bacon. When well cooked, drain and keep hot. In the same oil, cook the onions; leave them to soften over a moderate heat without browning. Remove them as soon as they are cooked and keep hot with the bacon pieces. Then fry the peppers and, when they are half cooked, add the tomatoes and leave to simmer for 10–15 minutes.

When the tomatoes and peppers are cooked, add the chopped garlic and seasoning. Return the bacon and onions to the pan with the hard-boiled eggs, heat through for a few moments and season to taste. Pour into a serving dish and serve at once, very hot.

 a rosé

Preparation time 25 minutes
Cooking time 30-35 minutes

Serves 6

AMERICAN
6 bacon slices (about ⅜ inch thick)
2 large onions
4 peppers
2lb ripe tomatoes
2 cloves garlic
9 eggs
⅓ cup olive oil
salt and pepper

Mushroom cream omelette

(Omelette forestière)

Preparation time 20 minutes
Cooking time 18 minutes

Serves 4

METRIC/IMPERIAL
350 g/12 oz dark flat mushrooms
2 shallots
75 g/3 oz butter
salt and pepper
8 eggs
150 ml/¼ pint double cream

Clean and very finely chop the mushrooms. Peel and chop the shallots and soften over a gentle heat in 40 g/1½ oz (US 3 tablespoons) butter, without browning. Add the mushrooms and season. Leave to cook for 8–10 minutes.

Break the eggs into a bowl, add salt and pepper and beat with a fork; stop beating as soon as they begin to foam. When the mushrooms are cooked, add the cream and thicken for a few moments over a low heat, stirring.

Lightly brown the rest of the butter in a frying pan then pour in the eggs and cook the omelette, taking care that it remains creamy.

Fill with half the creamed mushrooms, turn over and slide on to a serving plate. Surround with the rest of the mushrooms and serve at once.

a Touraine rosé

Preparation time 20 minutes
Cooking time 18 minutes

Serves 4

AMERICAN
¾ lb dark flat mushrooms
2 shallots
6 tablespoons butter
salt and pepper
8 eggs
⅔ cup heavy cream

Green herb omelette

(Omelette froide aux herbes)

Preparation time 15 minutes
Cooking time 15 minutes

Serves 4

METRIC/IMPERIAL
1 bunch watercress
225g/8oz sorrel or spinach
4 spring onions
1 small bunch chives
50g/2oz butter
8 eggs
salt and pepper

Discard the stalks from the watercress and sorrel. Wash and dry, then chop the watercress and sorrel leaves.

Chop the spring onions and the chives.

Heat 15g/½oz (US 1 tablespoon) of the butter in a pan. Add the watercress and sorrel and mix over a gentle heat with a wooden spoon. Leave to soften before adding the spring onions. Continue to cook for a further 5 minutes, stirring all the time.

Break the eggs into a bowl, add the sorrel mixture and the chives. Season with salt and pepper, beat lightly with a fork.

Slightly brown the rest of the butter in a large frying pan, pour in the beaten egg mixture and cook the omelette like a large pancake. Turn out flat on to the serving dish and leave to cool.

Serve this omelette cold, cut in wedges, with a green salad.

 a Listel (dry white)

Preparation time 15 minutes
Cooking time 15 minutes

Serves 4

AMERICAN
1 bunch watercress
½ lb sorrel or spinach
4 scallions
1 small bunch chives
¼ cup butter
8 eggs
salt and pepper

Aubergine and tomato omelette (Omelette Varoise)

Preparation time 25 minutes
Cooking time 15 minutes

Serves 4

METRIC/IMPERIAL
1 large aubergine
salt and pepper
100 g/4 oz smoked streaky bacon
100 ml/4 fl oz olive oil
flour to coat
2 tomatoes
1 tablespoon tomato purée
8 eggs
Garnish
chopped parsley

Peel the aubergine, cut into small dice. Sprinkle lightly with salt and leave for about 20 minutes.

Lightly brown the diced bacon in a frying pan in 2 tablespoons hot oil. Drain and keep hot, reserving the cooking oil.

Also drain then dry the diced aubergine. Toss in flour. Add 2 more tablespoons oil to the frying pan and lightly brown the diced aubergine. Drain on absorbent paper and keep hot.

Peel and slice the tomatoes, reserve 3 slices and lightly flour the remainder. Fry very quickly, still in the same cooking oil, then mix in the tomato purée.

Heat the remaining oil in a large frying pan. Break the eggs, season them, beat lightly with a fork and pour into the hot oil. Cook the omelette, keeping it soft and creamy inside.

Just before folding the omelette, fill with half the diced aubergine and bacon and the cooked tomato mixture. Slide on to a serving dish. Garnish the top of the omelette with the reserved tomato slices, surround with the remaining ingredients and sprinkle with chopped parsley. Serve immediately.

🍇 a Provence rosé

Preparation time 25 minutes
Cooking time 15 minutes

Serves 4

AMERICAN
1 large eggplant
salt and pepper
6 bacon slices
½ cup olive oil
flour to coat
2 tomatoes
1 tablespoon tomato paste
8 eggs
Garnish
chopped parsley

Tortilla

(La tortilla)

Preparation time 20 minutes
Cooking time 20 minutes

Serves 4

METRIC/IMPERIAL
4 potatoes
4 tablespoons oil
salt and pepper
8 eggs

Peel, rinse and dry the potatoes. Cut them into even dice about 1 cm/½ inch square.

Heat the oil in a large frying pan and toss in the diced potatoes. Leave to cook and turn golden brown, stirring often. Strain off any excess oil, leaving enough to cook the omelette. Season the potatoes and keep them hot in the frying pan.

Break the eggs and beat together with a fork. Season. As soon as they begin to foam, pour them into the frying pan over the potatoes. Cook like a large pancake (the under part must be well browned and the top still creamy).

With a single movement turn the tortilla over on to a serving dish, being careful not to fold it.

 a Beaujolais (light fruity red)

Preparation time 20 minutes
Cooking time 20 minutes

Serves 4

AMERICAN
4 potatoes
⅓ cup oil
salt and pepper
8 eggs

Creamy leek quiche

(Quiche aux poireaux)

**Preparation time 35 minutes
plus 2 hours chilling time
Cooking time 45–55 minutes**

Serves 6

METRIC/IMPERIAL
Pastry
**225g/8oz plain flour
pinch of salt
100g/4oz butter
2–3 tablespoons water**
Filling
**1kg/2lb leeks
salt and pepper
25g/1oz butter
1 tablespoon flour
250ml/8fl oz milk
100ml/4fl oz double cream
100g/4oz cheese, grated
freshly grated nutmeg**

Prepare the pastry. Sift the flour into a large bowl and make a well in the centre. Add a pinch of salt and the butter, cut into small pieces. Mix these ingredients quickly together with the fingertips. Mix in the water and when the pastry is smooth, roll it into a ball and chill in the refrigerator for 2 hours.

Trim the leeks and cut the white parts into 3.5-cm/1½-inch lengths. Wash and blanch them for 5 minutes in boiling salted water then drain carefully and dry well.

Roll out the pastry into a round 3 mm/⅛ inch thick and use to line a 25-cm/10-inch flan tin. Prick the pastry so that it does not swell. Bake 'blind' in a moderately hot oven (200°C, 400°F, Gas Mark 6) for 15 minutes.

Melt the butter and gently fry the leeks; sprinkle them with the tablespoon of flour and mix for 2 minutes over a gentle heat. Moisten with the boiling milk and cream and cook for 2–3 minutes, stirring continuously with a wooden spoon. Add 75g/3oz (US ¾ cup) grated cheese and season with salt, pepper and nutmeg.

Fill the flan case with this mixture and sprinkle over the rest of the cheese. Reduce the oven temperature to moderate (180°C, 350°F, Gas Mark 4) and cook for 30–40 minutes, until golden brown on top. Serve hot.

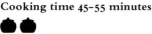 a red Côtes-de-Provence

**Preparation time 35 minutes
plus 2 hours chilling time
Cooking time 45–55 minutes**

Serves 6

AMERICAN
Dough
**2 cups all-purpose flour
dash of salt
½ cup butter
about ¼ cup water**
Filling
**2lb leeks
salt and pepper
2 tablespoons butter
1 tablespoon all-purpose flour
1 cup milk
½ cup heavy cream
1 cup grated cheese
freshly grated nutmeg**

Cheese flan

(Tarte au fromage)

**Preparation time 25 minutes plus 1 hour chilling time
Cooking time 45 minutes**

Serves 6

METRIC/IMPERIAL
Pastry
250g/9oz plain flour
125g/4½oz butter
1 egg
2 tablespoons water
½ teaspoon salt
Filling
3 eggs
350ml/12fl oz single cream
salt and pepper
freshly grated nutmeg
275g/10oz Emmenthal cheese, grated

Prepare the pastry. Make a well in the centre of the flour and add the butter cut into small pieces, the egg, water and salt. Mix these ingredients together with a fork, gradually blending in the flour.

When the pastry is smooth, roll it out. Butter and flour a 25-cm/10-inch flan dish or ring, line it with the pastry. Cool in the refrigerator for 1 hour to avoid the pastry shrinking when cooked. Bake 'blind' in a moderately hot oven (200°C, 400°F, Gas Mark 6) for 15 minutes.

Beat the eggs with the cream and season with salt, pepper and nutmeg. Sprinkle the grated cheese in the baked flan case and pour the egg mixture on top. Cook in a hot oven (230°C, 450°F, Gas Mark 8) for 30 minutes and serve immediately.

 a Riesling (fruity white)

**Preparation time 25 minutes plus 1 hour chilling time
Cooking time 45 minutes**

Serves 6

AMERICAN
Dough
2¼ cups all-purpose flour
½ cup plus 1 tablespoon butter
1 egg
3 tablespoons water
½ teaspoon salt
Filling
3 eggs
1½ cups light cream
salt and pepper
freshly grated nutmeg
2½ cups grated Emmenthal cheese

Mushroom and sorrel quiche (Tarte aux champignons)

**Preparation time 30 minutes
plus 2 hours chilling time
Cooking time 45-55 minutes**

Serves 6

METRIC/IMPERIAL
Pastry
225g/8oz plain flour
100g/4oz butter
1 egg
2 tablespoons water
pinch of salt
Filling
6 spring onions
75g/3oz butter
50g/2oz leaf beet or spinach
100g/4oz mushrooms
100g/4oz sorrel
5 eggs
300ml/½ pint milk
100ml/4fl oz single cream
salt and pepper

Prepare the pastry. Make a well in the centre of the flour and place in it the butter cut into small pieces. Rub in with the fingertips, then add the egg, water and salt. Mix these ingredients together quickly, roll the pastry into a ball and leave to chill for 2 hours.

Trim the spring onions, wash them and slice finely. Cook over a gentle heat in 15g/½oz (US 1 tablespoon) butter, moistening from time to time with a little hot water so they do not turn brown.

Remove the stalks from the leaf beet or spinach, wipe and chop the leaves. Clean and finely slice the mushrooms. Wash, dry and chop the sorrel. Then brown, in a little butter each time, the leaf beet, mushrooms and sorrel.

Roll the pastry out thinly to line a 25-cm/10-inch flan tin. Prick the base and bake 'blind' in a moderately hot oven (200°C, 400°F, Gas Mark 6) for 15 minutes. Beat the eggs with the milk and cream. Season, mix in all the vegetables and pour the whole into the flan case. Reduce the oven heat to 190°C, 375°F, Gas Mark 5, and cook for 30–40 minutes. Serve hot, as soon as it comes out of the oven.

a Meursault (dry white)

**Preparation time 30 minutes
plus 2 hours chilling time
Cooking time 45-55 minutes**

Serves 6

AMERICAN
Dough
2 cups all-purpose flour
½ cup butter
1 egg
3 tablespoons water
dash of salt
Filling
6 scallions
6 tablespoons butter
2oz leaf beet or spinach
¼lb mushrooms
¼lb sorrel
5 eggs
1¼ cups milk
½ cup light cream
salt and pepper

Spring onion quiche

(Tarte aux oignons nouveaux)

**Preparation time 25 minutes
plus 2 hours chilling time
Cooking time 40-50 minutes**

Serves 6

METRIC/IMPERIAL
Pastry
1 egg
2 tablespoons water
225g/8oz plain flour
100g/4oz butter
pinch of salt
Filling
0.5kg/1lb large spring onions
40g/1½oz butter
small pinch of castor sugar
salt and pepper
1 slice ham
4 eggs
300ml/½ pint milk
150ml/¼ pint double cream
freshly grated nutmeg

Prepare the pastry. Break the egg and beat it with the water. Pour into the centre of the flour, along with the butter cut into small pieces and the salt. Quickly work these ingredients together with a fork, gradually blending in the flour. As soon as the pastry is smooth, roll into a ball and chill in the refrigerator for 2 hours.

Trim the spring onions, keeping the tender part of the stem. Set aside 3 onions for garnish, finely slice the rest. Soften them in the hot butter over a very gentle heat, do not let them colour. Add the castor sugar, season and mix well. Continue cooking for 5 minutes before adding the finely chopped ham.

Roll out the pastry to a thickness of 3 mm/⅛ inch, and use to line a 25-cm/10-inch flan tin. Prick the base and bake 'blind' in a moderately hot oven (200°C, 400°F, Gas Mark 6) for about 10 minutes.

Beat the eggs with the milk and cream, season with salt, pepper and a little grated nutmeg. Add the onion and ham mixture and pour into the flan case. Garnish the top with the reserved onions, sliced and separated into rings.

Reduce the oven temperature to 190°C, 375°F, Gas Mark 5, and cook the quiche for about 30-40 minutes. Serve as soon as it comes out of the oven.

a Roussette de Savoie (light white)

**Preparation time 25 minutes
plus 2 hours chilling time
Cooking time 40-50 minutes**

Serves 6

AMERICAN
Dough
1 egg
3 tablespoons water
2 cups all-purpose flour
½ cup butter
dash of salt
Filling
1lb large scallions
3 tablespoons butter
small dash of sugar
salt and pepper
1 slice cooked ham
4 eggs
1¼ cups milk
⅔ cup heavy cream
freshly grated nutmeg

Brioche with baked eggs

(Turban d'oeufs à la crème)

Preparation time 15 minutes
Cooking time 15-20 minutes

Serves 6

METRIC/IMPERIAL
1 brioche ring (available from the delicatessen)
50g/2oz butter
6 eggs
150ml/¼ pint double cream
salt and pepper

Cut a thin slice from the top of the brioche. Hollow out six holes in this brioche, at regular intervals and without cutting through the bottom crust.

Melt the butter over a gentle heat. Sprinkle the whole brioche with it, moistening the hollows well. Heat through in a moderate oven (160°C, 325°F, Gas Mark 3) for 5 minutes.

Take the brioche out of the oven. Break an egg into each hollow and season well. Return to the oven for 5-10 minutes.

Take the brioche out again. Pour the cream carefully over the top, surrounding each egg with it. Return to the oven for 5 minutes then serve immediately. The eggs should still be soft inside.

Note If you cannot buy a brioche, substitute a small milk loaf.

 a new Beaujolais (light fruity red)

Preparation time 15 minutes
Cooking time 15-20 minutes

Serves 6

AMERICAN
1 brioche ring (available from the delicatessen)
¼ cup butter
6 eggs
⅔ cup heavy cream
salt and pepper

Piperade rolls

(Pains mollets à la piperade)

Preparation time 25 minutes
Cooking time 20 minutes

Serves 4

METRIC/IMPERIAL
4 finger rolls
50 g/2 oz butter
2 green peppers
2 onions
2 cloves garlic
3 tomatoes
3 tablespoons oil
1 tablespoon chopped parsley
salt and pepper
6 eggs
4 rashers smoked streaky bacon
Garnish
chopped parsley

Cut the top off each of the rolls then hollow them out. Butter lightly inside and brown slightly in a moderate oven (160°C, 325°F, Gas Mark 3) for 5–10 minutes.

Grill the peppers. When their skins begin to blacken, dip into cold water and then peel them; cut into dice. Chop the onions and garlic. Peel and deseed the tomatoes and crush the flesh.

Lightly brown the onions in the hot oil, add the peppers, leave to cook for 5–6 minutes, then add the tomato flesh, garlic and parsley. Cook for a further 7–8 minutes, season.

Break the eggs over the vegetables, add the rest of the butter and stir over a gentle heat with a wooden spoon until the eggs are creamy.

Brown the rashers of bacon in a frying pan. Fill the hollowed bread rolls with the pepper and tomato mixture, place a bacon rasher over each, garnish with parsley and serve immediately.

 an Irouléguy (Basque dry white)

Preparation time 25 minutes
Cooking time 20 minutes

Serves 4

AMERICAN
4 finger rolls
¼ cup butter
2 green peppers
2 onions
2 cloves garlic
3 tomatoes
¼ cup oil
1 tablespoon chopped parsley
salt and pepper
6 eggs
4 bacon slices
Garnish
chopped parsley

Ham and cheese croquettes

(Croquettes délices)

**Preparation time 35 minutes
plus overnight setting and
30 minutes chilling time
Cooking time 30 minutes**

Serves 6

METRIC/IMPERIAL
**100 g/4 oz butter
100 g/4 oz plain flour
450 ml/¾ pint milk
150 g/5 oz cheese, grated
2 slices ham
3 egg yolks
salt, pepper and freshly grated
nutmeg
oil for deep frying**
To coat the croquettes
**2 eggs
2 tablespoons water
1 tablespoon oil
salt and pepper
flour
dried breadcrumbs**

The day before required melt the butter in a saucepan. Add the flour and cook this white roux until it bubbles. Add the boiling milk all at once. Continue cooking, stirring with a wooden spoon to give a very thick béchamel sauce. Add the grated cheese and remove from the heat.

Chop the ham and add to the sauce with the egg yolks. Season with salt, pepper and a little grated nutmeg. Mix well.

Grease a baking sheet or a large rectangular dish and pour on the mixture in a thick layer. Leave until completely cold and set.

The following day break the eggs into a shallow dish and add the water and oil. Season and beat well together.

Cut the croquette mixture into small even rectangles and form into sausage shapes. Dip in flour then in the beaten egg mixture and finally in breadcrumbs. Chill in the refrigerator for 30 minutes.

Heat the oil to 180°C/360°F or until hot enough to turn a small piece of bread golden in under 1 minute. Fry the croquettes a few at a time and brown well all over.

Drain the croquettes on absorbent paper and place on a heated serving dish. Serve very hot.

 a Roussette de Savoie (light white)

**Preparation time 35 minutes
plus overnight setting and
30 minutes chilling time
Cooking time 30 minutes**

Serves 6

AMERICAN
**½ cup butter
1 cup all-purpose flour
2 cups milk
1¼ cups grated cheese
2 slices cooked ham
3 egg yolks
salt, pepper and freshly grated
nutmeg
oil for deep frying**
To coat the croquettes
**2 eggs
3 tablespoons water
1 tablespoon oil
salt and pepper
flour
dry bread crumbs**

Savoy cheese fondue

(La fondue Savoyarde)

Preparation time 15 minutes
Cooking time 25 minutes

Serves 6

METRIC/IMPERIAL
450 g/1 lb Comté or Caerphilly cheese
350 g/12 oz Beaufort or Gruyère cheese
350 g/12 oz Emmenthal cheese
2 cloves garlic
1 litre/1¾ pints dry white wine
pinch of pepper
2 teaspoons cornflour
2 tablespoons Kirsch
To serve
cubes of French bread

Cut the various cheeses into slices as finely as possible, or grate coarsely.

Rub the inside of the fondue pot with one of the cloves of garlic. Grate the other clove into the pot.

Pour in the white wine and heat. Add the pepper. Toss in a handful of the cheese and cook, stirring constantly with a wooden spoon until the cheese is melted and creamy. Continue until all the cheese has been incorporated into the wine.

Mix the cornflour with the Kirsch, stir into the fondue and thicken over a low heat.

Place the pot over the lighted burner on the dining table. Each guest in turn picks up a cube of bread on his fork and dips it into the mixture, stirring as he does so.

The fondue should stay thick. If it becomes too thick stir slowly with a wooden spoon while you add a little warmed white wine or Kirsch. If too runny, add more cheese and a little cornflour mixed with white wine.

🍇 a Roussette de Savoie (light white)

Preparation time 15 minutes
Cooking time 25 minutes

Serves 6

AMERICAN
1 lb Comté or Caerphilly cheese
¾ lb Beaufort or Gruyère cheese
¾ lb Emmenthal cheese
2 cloves garlic
4¼ cups dry white wine
dash of pepper
2 teaspoons cornstarch
3 tablespoons Kirsch
To serve
cubes of French bread

Chicory and ham au gratin

(Endives roulées au jambon)

Preparation time 30 minutes
Cooking time 1 hour

Serves 6

METRIC/IMPERIAL
6 heads chicory
50g/2oz butter
1 tablespoon oil
salt and pepper
1 sugar lump
6 slices ham
Sauce
50g/2oz butter
50g/2oz flour
600ml/1 pint milk
150g/5oz cheese, grated
salt and pepper
freshly grated nutmeg

Clean the chicory without washing and remove any withered leaves. Blanch in boiling water for 3 minutes. Heat 40g/1½oz (US 3 tablespoons) butter and the oil in a frying pan, add the chicory, seasoning and sugar lump. Cover and cook over a low heat for 45 minutes. Only add a little hot water if the chicory seem liable to catch.

Prepare the béchamel sauce. Melt the butter and mix in the flour with a wooden spoon. When this roux begins to bubble, gradually add the hot milk. Cook for 15 minutes, stirring continually.

Mix 100g/4oz (US 1 cup) grated cheese into the sauce and season to taste with salt, pepper and nutmeg.

Spread each slice of ham thinly with sauce. Place a head of chicory in the centre and roll the ham around it. Place the ham rolls in a greased ovenproof dish and pour over the rest of the sauce.

Melt the remaining butter and sprinkle over the dish with the rest of the cheese. Place under a preheated grill until golden brown on top.

a red Mâcon

Preparation time 30 minutes
Cooking time 1 hour

Serves 6

AMERICAN
6 heads Belgian endive
¼ cup butter
1 tablespoon oil
salt and pepper
1 sugar cube
6 slices cooked ham
Sauce
¼ cup butter
¼ cup all-purpose flour
2½ cups milk
1¼ cups grated cheese
salt and pepper
freshly grated nutmeg

Neapolitan pizza

(Pizza Napolitaine)

Preparation time 25 minutes
Cooking time 15-25 minutes

Serves 4

METRIC/IMPERIAL
4 onions
100 ml/4 fl oz olive oil
1 (56-g/2-oz) can anchovy fillets
0.5 kg/1 lb risen bread dough
100 g/4 oz Mozzarella or Gruyère cheese
3 tomatoes
1 teaspoon dried oregano
salt and freshly ground pepper
50 g/2 oz black olives

Peel and coarsely chop the onions. Soften in half of the olive oil over a moderate heat, but do not let them brown.

Drain the anchovy fillets and soak in water to remove excess saltiness.

Knead the risen dough well by hand, incorporating 1 tablespoon oil. Roll out in the shape of a circle, 5 mm/$\frac{1}{4}$ inch thick. Raise the edges slightly, pinching them, and place on a lightly oiled baking sheet. Brush the surface of the dough with a little of the remaining oil. Cover this dough with a layer of onions, then the cheese, cut into fine strips, and finally the sliced tomatoes. Sprinkle with oregano, pepper generously and salt very slightly.

Drain the anchovy fillets and split each in half lengthwise. Arrange in a lattice over the pizza; place a black olive in the centre of each square. Sprinkle the rest of the oil over all.

Cook for 15–25 minutes in a hot oven (230°C, 450°F, Gas Mark 8). Serve the pizza as soon as it comes out of the oven.

a Chianti (Italian red)

Preparation time 25 minutes
Cooking time 15-25 minutes

Serves 4

AMERICAN
4 onions
$\frac{1}{2}$ cup olive oil
1 (2-oz) can anchovy fillets
1 lb risen bread dough
$\frac{1}{4}$ lb Mozzarella or Gruyère cheese
3 tomatoes
1 teaspoon dried oregano
salt and freshly ground pepper
2 oz ripe olives

Oriental rice

(Riz à l'Orientale)

Preparation time 15 minutes
Cooking time 20 minutes

Serves 6

METRIC/IMPERIAL
100g/4oz seedless raisins
350g/12oz long-grain rice
salt and pepper
generous pinch of saffron
1 clove
12 black peppercorns
**small piece of fresh root ginger
(or a generous pinch of ground
ginger)**
pinch of sea salt
pinch of dried mint
pinch of cinnamon
1 tablespoon clear honey
juice of 1 lemon
100g/4oz blanched almonds
50g/2oz butter
pinch of cayenne

Wash the raisins and soak in warm water.

Boil 900ml/1½ pints (US 3¾ cups) water. Wash the rice then pour it into the boiling water; salt lightly, add the saffron and cover tightly. Cook over a very low heat for 15 minutes; do not stir during cooking.

In a mortar crush the clove, peppercorns, freshly grated ginger, sea salt, mint and cinnamon, to obtain a smooth even mixture. Mix in the honey, diluted with the lemon juice.

Lightly brown the almonds in a frying pan in a little of the butter. Add to the cooked rice with the drained raisins, the honey spice mixture and the rest of the butter cut into small pieces. Mix well together, adjust for seasoning, add a pinch of cayenne and heat through. Transfer to a serving dish and serve very hot.

 a Riesling (fruity white)

Preparation time 15 minutes
Cooking time 20 minutes

Serves 6

AMERICAN
¾ cup seeded raisins
1½ cups long-grain rice
salt and pepper
generous dash of saffron
1 clove
12 black peppercorns
**small piece of fresh ginger root
(or a generous dash of ground
ginger)**
dash of coarse salt
dash of dried mint
dash of cinnamon
1 tablespoon clear honey
juice of 1 lemon
1 cup blanched almonds
¼ cup butter
dash of cayenne pepper

Mediterranean rice

(Riz Méditerranée)

Preparation time 30 minutes
Cooking time 25 minutes

Serves 6

METRIC/IMPERIAL
2 aubergines
3 small courgettes
salt and pepper
2 peppers
4 onions
2 cloves garlic
0.5kg/1lb small tomatoes
225g/8oz long-grain rice
200ml/7fl oz olive oil
600ml/1 pint stock
pinch of saffron
flour to coat

Clean the aubergines and courgettes and peel if preferred. Cut into small sticks, sprinkle lightly with salt and leave to sweat for 30 minutes.

Wash the peppers, remove cores and seeds and cut into thin strips. Peel and finely slice the onions, crush the garlic. Peel the tomatoes, halve and remove seeds.

Sauté the rice in 2 tablespoons (US 3 tablespoons) hot oil. Just before it changes colour pour on the hot stock. Add the saffron, cover and cook over a low heat for about 15–20 minutes.

Drain and wipe the courgettes. Toss in flour and brown lightly in a frying pan in 3 tablespoons (US $\frac{1}{4}$ cup) hot oil. Drain and keep hot. In the same oil sauté the sticks of aubergine, also wiped and floured. When cooked, keep hot with the courgettes.

Pour a little more oil into the frying pan and lightly brown the onions. Add the peppers, tomatoes and finally the garlic. When they are all cooked, take out and keep hot with the other vegetables.

Heat the remaining oil in the frying pan. Tip in the cooked rice and all the other ingredients. Season and cook over a low heat until everything is heated through. Transfer to a serving dish and serve very hot.

a Var rosé

Preparation time 30 minutes
Cooking time 25 minutes

Serves 6

AMERICAN
2 eggplant
3 small zucchini
salt and pepper
2 peppers
4 onions
2 cloves garlic
1lb small tomatoes
1 cup long-grain rice
$\frac{3}{4}$ cup olive oil
$2\frac{1}{2}$ cups stock
dash of saffron
flour to coat

Rice and seafood ring

(Couronne de riz Hélène)

Serves 6

METRIC/IMPERIAL
100 ml/4 fl oz oil
250 g/9 oz long-grain rice
2 litres/3½ pints mussels
2 litres/3½ pints cockles
3 shallots
3 spring onions
1 small bunch parsley
4 tablespoons white wine vinegar
salt and pepper

Heat half the oil in a frying pan. Add the rice and cook until transparent. Place in an ovenproof dish and pour over twice its volume of boiling water. Cover and cook in a moderately hot oven (200°C, 400°F, Gas Mark 6) for 20–25 minutes, stirring occasionally with a fork.

Wash the mussels and cockles, discarding any which do not close when given a sharp tap. Place in two separate pans, add a little water and open over a high heat. Drain and reserve the cooking juices.

Remove the mussels and cockles from their shells. Peel the shallots and chop very finely with the spring onions. Chop the parsley. Into a bowl pour the vinegar, the rest of the oil, 5 tablespoons (US 6 tablespoons) mussel juice and 5 tablespoons (US 6 tablespoons) cockle juice. Season with pepper.

Beat this dressing with a fork or wire whisk then add the chopped shallots, spring onions and most of the parsley.

Take the rice out of the oven. Add half the dressing and mix carefully. Transfer to a 20-cm/8-inch oiled ring mould, press down well, chill then turn out on to a serving dish.

Mix the mussels and cockles with the rest of the dressing. Arrange in the centre of the rice and sprinkle all over with chopped parsley. Serve cold.

 a Muscadet (dry white)

Serves 6

AMERICAN
½ cup oil
1 cup plus 2 tablespoons long-grain rice
4½ pints mussels
4½ pints cockles
3 shallots
3 scallions
1 small bunch parsley
⅓ cup white wine vinegar
salt and pepper

Italian-style risotto

(Risotto à l'Italienne)

Preparation time 25 minutes
Cooking time 25 minutes

Serves 4-6

METRIC/IMPERIAL
2 slices ham (about 2.5cm/1 inch
thick)
3 onions
175 ml/6 fl oz olive oil
3 tomatoes
350 g/12 oz long-grain rice
900 ml/1½ pints stock
150 ml/¼ pint dry white wine
175 g/6 oz cooked green peas
2 tablespoons chopped parsley
salt and freshly ground pepper
100 g/4 oz Parmesan cheese, grated
Garnish
chopped parsley

Cut the ham into dice. Lightly brown the finely sliced onions in 3 tablespoons (US ¼ cup) oil. Peel the tomatoes, remove seeds and cut the flesh into small dice.

Heat the rest of the oil in a shallow frying pan, toss in the unwashed and dry rice. Stir continually with a wooden spoon until the rice begins to change colour. Pour on the hot stock and wine. Add the onions, diced ham, tomatoes, peas and chopped parsley. Season. Bring to the boil, cover and cook without stirring for about 15 minutes over a very low heat.

Remove from the heat, toss in half the grated Parmesan. Transfer to a heated serving dish and sprinkle with chopped parsley. Serve at once, accompanied by the rest of the Parmesan.

 a Savoy rosé

Preparation time 25 minutes
Cooking time 25 minutes

Serves 4-6

AMERICAN
2 slices cooked ham (about 1 inch
thick)
3 onions
¾ cup olive oil
3 tomatoes
1½ cups long-grain rice
3¾ cups stock
⅔ cup dry white wine
1¼ cups cooked green peas
3 tablespoons chopped parsley
salt and freshly ground pepper
1 cup grated Parmesan cheese
Garnish
chopped parsley

Seafood noodles

(Nouilles aux fruits de mer)

Preparation time 30 minutes
Cooking time 25 minutes

Serves 6

METRIC/IMPERIAL
1.4 litres/2 pints cockles
1.4 litres/2 pints mussels
100 ml/4 fl oz dry white wine
2 sprigs of parsley
salt and freshly ground pepper
1 shallot
1 clove garlic
350 g/12 oz noodles
50 g/2 oz butter
50 g/2 oz flour
100 ml/4 fl oz double cream
100 g/4 oz cheese, grated
Garnish
chopped parsley

Clean the cockles and mussels; discard those which do not close when given a sharp tap, wash the others.

Cook the mussels until open with the white wine, parsley, freshly ground pepper, the chopped shallot and garlic. In another saucepan, cook the cockles with a little water. Shell the cockles and mussels, keep hot and strain their cooking juices through a fine cloth or muslin.

Cook the noodles in plenty of boiling salted water, until firm to the bite.

Prepare a white sauce. Melt the butter then stir in the flour and cook for 1 minute. Thin this roux with the liquid from both the shells, made up to about 450ml/¾ pint (US 2 cups) with water, if necessary. Cook for 8 minutes, stirring constantly, then add the cream and continue cooking for 2–3 minutes. Do not boil.

Drain the noodles. Turn into a deep dish, cover with some of the seafood and sprinkle with chopped parsley.

Mix the rest of the mussels and cockles into the sauce. Serve very hot in a sauceboat to accompany the pasta. Hand the grated cheese separately.

a Sancerre (dry white)

Preparation time 30 minutes
Cooking time 25 minutes

Serves 6

AMERICAN
2½ pints cockles
2½ pints mussels
½ cup dry white wine
2 sprigs of parsley
salt and freshly ground pepper
1 shallot
1 clove garlic
3 cups noodles
¼ cup butter
½ cup all-purpose flour
½ cup heavy cream
1 cup grated cheese
Garnish
chopped parsley

Noodles with chicken livers (Nouilles aux foies de volailles)

Preparation time 25 minutes
Cooking time 25 minutes

Serves 4-6

METRIC/IMPERIAL
0.5 kg/1 lb chicken livers
75 g/3 oz butter
3 shallots
1 tablespoon flour
3 tablespoons dry white wine
250 ml/8 fl oz stock
salt and pepper
0.5 kg/1 lb noodles
100 ml/4 fl oz Madeira
100 g/4 oz cheese, grated
Garnish
chopped parsley

Wash and trim the livers. Separate the two lobes of each liver. Fry in half the hot butter until firm then remove.

In the same butter, brown the finely chopped shallots. Sprinkle with the flour and stir in. Moisten this roux with the white wine and stock. Season and cook for 5 minutes, stirring continuously.

Boil a large quantity of water, salt it and toss in the noodles. Cook according to the instructions on the packet. At the end of the cooking time they must remain firm when bitten (Italian 'al dente').

Place the chicken livers in the sauce, add the Madeira and heat through without boiling.

Drain the noodles. Mix with the grated cheese and the rest of the butter cut into small pieces. Arrange in a ring on a serving dish. Place the chicken livers and sauce in the centre and sprinkle with chopped parsley. Serve at once.

a red Côtes-de-Provence

Preparation time 25 minutes
Cooking time 25 minutes

Serves 4-6

AMERICAN
1 lb chicken livers
6 tablespoons butter
3 shallots
1 tablespoon all-purpose flour
¼ cup dry white wine
1 cup stock
salt and pepper
4 cups noodles
½ cup Madeira
1 cup grated cheese
Garnish
chopped parsley

Ravioli Milanese

(Ravioli Milanaise)

**Preparation time 1 hour
plus 2 hours standing time
Cooking time 50 minutes**

Serves 6

METRIC/IMPERIAL
Pasta
**500g/1lb 2oz plain flour
½ teaspoon salt
5 eggs**
Stuffing
**225g/8oz leftover braised beef or
minced beef
1 onion
2 tablespoons oil
175g/6oz fresh or frozen spinach
50g/2oz Parmesan cheese, grated
1 tablespoon tomato purée
1 egg
salt and pepper**
Sauce
**2 onions
100g/4oz minced beef
2 tablespoons olive oil
100g/4oz Parmesan cheese, grated
3 tablespoons tomato purée
250ml/8fl oz stock**

Prepare the pasta. Sift the flour and salt into a large bowl and make a well in the centre. Break in the eggs and mix, adding just enough water to obtain a paste which does not stick to the fingers. Roll into a ball, cover and leave to stand for 2 hours.

Prepare the stuffing. Mince the braised beef, if used. Soften the finely chopped onion in the oil, add the minced beef and spinach (blanched for 5 minutes in boiling salted water, well drained and chopped; or defrosted if using frozen). Mix over a fairly brisk heat, add the grated Parmesan. Bind this stuffing with the tomato purée and beaten egg to obtain a thick even mixture. Add seasoning to taste.

Prepare the sauce. Brown the chopped onions and minced beef in the oil. Add 50g/2oz (US ½ cup) cheese and the tomato purée. Stir in the stock, season and cook for 15 minutes.

Roll out the paste into two equal-sized rectangles, to a thickness of 1.5 mm/$\frac{1}{16}$ inch. Over one of them place small spoonfuls of the stuffing at 2.5-cm/1-inch intervals. Moisten the paste in between with water. Cover with the second layer of paste. Press with the fingers between the stuffing to seal the paste. Cut the ravioli into small squares with a pastry wheel.

Poach the ravioli for 15 minutes in boiling salted water. Drain on absorbent paper and arrange in layers in a gratin dish. Coat each layer with sauce and sprinkle with the remaining Parmesan. Brown in a hot oven.

Accompany with more grated Parmesan and tomato sauce, if liked.

 a Chianti (Italian red)

**Preparation time 1 hour
plus 2 hours standing time
Cooking time 50 minutes**

Serves 6

AMERICAN
Pasta
**4½ cups all-purpose flour
½ teaspoon salt
5 eggs**
Stuffing
**1 cup ground cooked beef
1 onion
3 tablespoons oil
6oz fresh or frozen spinach
½ cup grated Parmesan cheese
1 tablespoon tomato paste
1 egg
salt and pepper**
Sauce
**2 onions
½ cup ground beef
3 tablespoons olive oil
1 cup grated Parmesan cheese
¼ cup tomato paste
1 cup stock**

Venetian pasta

(Coquillettes Vénitiennes)

Preparation time 10 minutes
Cooking time 30 minutes

Serves 4

METRIC/IMPERIAL
175 g/6 oz shelled peas
salt and pepper
1 slice ham (1 cm/½ inch thick)
75 g/3 oz butter
225 g/8 oz pasta shells or short-cut
macaroni
100 g/4 oz Parmesan cheese, grated
200 ml/7 fl oz fresh tomato sauce
(see page 310), heated

Cook the peas in boiling salted water for 15–20 minutes and drain. Dice the ham. Heat a little of the butter in a covered casserole and gently sauté the peas and ham over a low heat.

Meanwhile, cook the pasta in plenty of boiling salted water for about 15 minutes (the cooking time varies according to brand and quality). When cooked the pasta should be firm when bitten.

Drain and place in a heated serving dish. Add the remaining butter, cut into small pieces, the Parmesan, peas and diced ham. Mix gently together. Serve very hot with the tomato sauce.

 a Tavel (rosé)

Preparation time 10 minutes
Cooking time 30 minutes

Serves 4

AMERICAN
1¼ cups shelled peas
salt and pepper
1 slice cooked ham (½ inch thick)
6 tablespoons butter
2 cups shell or other macaroni
1 cup grated Parmesan cheese
¾ cup fresh tomato sauce (see
page 310), heated

Apricot tart

(Tarte aux abricots)

**Preparation time 25 minutes
plus 2 hours chilling time
Cooking time 30-35 minutes**

Serves 6

METRIC/IMPERIAL
Pastry
**225 g/8 oz plain flour
100 g/4 oz butter
50 g/2 oz castor sugar
1 egg
pinch of salt**
Filling
**50 g/2 oz castor sugar
0.75 kg/1½ lb apricots
1 (227-g/8-oz) jar apricot jam
1 tablespoon Kirsch**

Prepare the pastry. Sift the flour into a large bowl and make a well in the centre. Add the butter cut into small pieces. Work these ingredients together with the finger-tips then add the sugar, egg and salt. As soon as the pastry becomes smooth, roll it into a ball, cover, then leave to chill in the refrigerator for 2 hours.

Preheat the oven to moderately hot (200°C, 400°F, Gas Mark 6).

Dust the working surface with flour, then roll out the pastry to a thickness of 3 mm/⅛ inch. Use to line a 25-cm/10-inch buttered flan tin or ring. Prick the bottom and bake 'blind' for 10–15 minutes, remove from the oven then sprinkle with the sugar. Reduce oven temperature to moderate (180°C, 350°F, Gas Mark 4).

Fill the tart with the peeled and stoned apricot halves, cut side up. Cook for 25 minutes in the oven.

Warm the jam over a gentle heat with 2 tablespoons (US 3 tablespoons) hot water and the Kirsch. Strain through a conical sieve and pour over the apricots as soon as the tart comes out of the oven. Serve warm with cream.

 a sweet Vouvray (white)

**Preparation time 25 minutes
plus 2 hours chilling time
Cooking time 30-35 minutes**

Serves 6

AMERICAN
Dough
**2 cups all-purpose flour
½ cup butter
¼ cup sugar
1 egg
dash of salt**
Filling
**¼ cup sugar
1½ lb apricots
1 (8-oz) jar apricot jam
1 tablespoon Kirsch**

Fresh orange flan

(Tarte à l'orange)

Preparation time 30 minutes
plus 2 hours chilling time
Cooking time 40 minutes

Serves 6

METRIC/IMPERIAL
Pastry
225 g/8 oz plain flour
100 g/4 oz butter
1 egg
50 g/2 oz castor sugar
pinch of salt
Filling
5 large oranges
275 g/10 oz castor sugar
4 tablespoons water
7 tablespoons orange marmalade
1 tablespoon lemon juice
1 tablespoon orange liqueur
(optional)

Prepare the pastry. Sift the flour into a bowl and make a well in the centre. Place in the well the butter cut into small pieces. Work quickly together with the fingertips then add the lightly beaten egg, sugar and salt. As soon as the pastry is smooth, roll into a ball and chill for 2 hours.

Meanwhile, wash and dry the oranges. Mark the rind into ridges with a cannelling knife, if liked. Cut into slices. Place the sugar and water in a saucepan and boil until still clear and the consistency of thick syrup (about 5 minutes). Toss the orange slices into this syrup and poach them for 8–10 minutes. Then turn into a sieve over a bowl. Return the syrup to the saucepan, add half the marmalade and the lemon juice and reduce by half by boiling over a moderate heat. Add the liqueur, if used.

Lightly flour the work surface and rolling pin, and roll out the pastry to a thickness of 3 mm/⅛ inch. Use to line a 25-cm/10-inch buttered flan tin or ring. Prick the base with a fork and bake 'blind' in a moderately hot oven (200°C, 400°F, Gas Mark 6) for 15 minutes. Reduce oven temperature to moderate (180°C, 350°F, Gas Mark 4) and bake for a further 10–15 minutes.

When the pastry is golden brown, spread the rest of the marmalade into the flan case. Over this arrange the orange slices, in overlapping circles, and finally glaze them with the reduced syrup.

 a Sainte Croix-du-Mont (sweet white)

Preparation time 30 minutes
plus 2 hours chilling time
Cooking time 40 minutes

Serves 6

AMERICAN
Dough
2 cups all-purpose flour
½ cup butter
1 egg
¼ cup sugar
dash of salt
Filling
5 large oranges
1¼ cups sugar
⅓ cup water
generous ½ cup orange marmalade
1 tablespoon lemon juice
1 tablespoon orange liqueur
(optional)

Pear cream flan

(Tarte aux poires)

**Preparation time 30 minutes
plus 2 hours chilling time
Cooking time 35 minutes**

Serves 6

METRIC/IMPERIAL
Pastry
**225 g/8 oz plain flour
100 g/4 oz butter
50 g/2 oz castor sugar
pinch of salt
1 egg**
Filling
**225 g/8 oz cream cheese
150 ml/¼ pint double cream
50 g/2 oz castor sugar
6 juicy dessert pears**
Glaze
**1 (227-g/8-oz) jar raspberry or
redcurrant jelly
50 g/2 oz castor sugar
2 tablespoons Kirsch
25 g/1 oz flaked almonds**

Prepare the pastry. Sift the flour into a bowl, make a well in the centre and add the butter cut into small pieces, the sugar and salt. Mix the ingredients, and rub the fat in with the fingertips until the consistency of fine breadcrumbs, then add the egg. As soon as the pastry is smooth, form it into a ball. Cover and chill in the refrigerator for 2 hours. Roll out to line a 25-cm/10-inch buttered flan tin or ring. Prick the base with a fork and bake 'blind' in a moderately hot oven (200°C, 400°F, Gas Mark 6) for 15 minutes. Reduce oven temperature to moderate (180°C, 350°F, Gas Mark 4) for a further 15 minutes. Leave to cool.

Beat the cream cheese with the cream and the sugar. Peel the pears, halve and remove cores and pips.

Heat the raspberry or redcurrant jelly for 5 minutes with 2 tablespoons (US 3 tablespoons) water, the sugar and Kirsch, until runny.

Toast the flaked almonds.

Fill the flan case with the cream cheese mixture and arrange over the pears, cut side down. Glaze with the raspberry or redcurrant jelly and sprinkle with the flaked almonds.

 an Anjou white

**Preparation time 30 minutes
plus 2 hours chilling time
Cooking time 35 minutes**

Serves 6

AMERICAN
Dough
**2 cups all-purpose flour
½ cup butter
¼ cup sugar
dash of salt
1 egg**
Filling
**1 cup full-fat cream cheese
⅔ cup heavy cream
¼ cup sugar
6 juicy dessert pears**
Glaze
**1 (8-oz) jar raspberry or red
currant jelly
¼ cup sugar
3 tablespoons Kirsch
¼ cup flaked almonds**

French grape tart

(Tarte aux raisins)

Preparation time 30 minutes
plus 2 hours chilling time
Cooking time 30 minutes

Serves 6

METRIC/IMPERIAL
Pastry
225g/8oz plain flour
pinch of salt
75g/3oz castor sugar
100g/4oz butter
1 egg
Filling
0.75kg/1½lb green grapes
150g/5oz castor sugar
3 tablespoons brandy
2 eggs plus 1 egg yolk
5 tablespoons milk
150ml/¼ pint double cream
50g/2oz ground almonds

Prepare the pastry. Sift the flour into a bowl and make a well in the centre. Add the salt, castor sugar and butter, cut into small pieces. Mix these ingredients quickly together with the fingertips then blend in the egg beaten with 1 tablespoon water. As soon as the pastry is smooth, roll into a ball and chill for 2 hours.

Wash the grapes, peel if liked and remove the pips. Place these grapes in an earthenware dish, sprinkle with 75g/3oz (US 6 tablespoons) sugar and the brandy and leave to steep for 1 hour.

Preheat the oven to hot (220°C, 425°F, Gas Mark 7). Butter a 25-cm/10-inch flan tin or ring.

Flour the work surface and rolling pin. Roll out the pastry to a thickness of 3mm/⅛ inch and use to line the flan tin. Prick the base and bake 'blind' in the oven for 10 minutes; the flan pastry must dry without colouring.

Mix well together the 2 eggs and egg yolk, the milk, cream and remaining sugar. Add the ground almonds and the drained grape liquor.

Remove the flan case from the oven. Fill with the cream mixture and arrange the grapes over it. Reduce the oven temperature to moderately hot (200°C, 400°F, Gas Mark 6) and cook for 20 minutes. Serve this tart preferably warm.

 a Muscat (sweet white)

Preparation time 30 minutes
plus 2 hours chilling time
Cooking time 30 minutes

Serves 6

AMERICAN
Dough
2 cups all-purpose flour
dash of salt
6 tablespoons sugar
½ cup butter
1 egg
Filling
1½lb white grapes
½ cup plus 2 tablespoons sugar
¼ cup brandy
2 eggs plus 1 egg yolk
6 tablespoons milk
⅔ cup heavy cream
½ cup ground almonds

Banana cups with custard   (Coupes de bananes à la crème)

Preparation time 30 minutes
Cooking time 25-30 minutes

Serves 6

METRIC/IMPERIAL
8 bananas
1 (227-g/8-oz) jar redcurrant jelly
Custard
600ml/1 pint milk
4 egg yolks
50g/2oz castor sugar
2 tablespoons rum

Prepare the custard. Bring the milk up to boiling point. Beat the egg yolks with the sugar until pale. Stir in the hot milk then strain back into the saucepan. Cook over the lowest possible heat, stirring continuously with a wooden spoon. Do not allow to boil. When the custard coats the back of the spoon remove from the heat. Flavour with rum and pour into a bowl to cool. Place in the refrigerator.

Cut the bananas into small cubes. Melt the redcurrant jelly over a low heat then use to coat the bananas. Cool.

Just before serving divide the cooled custard between six individual dishes. Add the banana cubes very carefully, so the jelly does not mix with the custard. Serve immediately.

 a Sainte Croix-du-Mont (sweet white)

Preparation time 30 minutes
Cooking time 25-30 minutes

Serves 6

AMERICAN
8 bananas
1 (8-oz) jar red currant jelly
Custard
2½ cups milk
4 egg yolks
¼ cup sugar
3 tablespoons rum

Apricot ring
(Couronne aux abricots)

Preparation time 20 minutes
Cooking time 35 minutes

Serves 6

METRIC/IMPERIAL
750 ml/1¼ pints milk
75 g/3 oz sugar
125 g/4½ oz semolina
50 g/2 oz butter
2 eggs
1 tablespoon Kirsch
Filling
0.75 kg/1½ lb apricots
100 g/4 oz sugar
4 tablespoons apricot jam
2 tablespoons Kirsch

Prepare the semolina ring. Heat the milk with the sugar. Sprinkle in the semolina and bring to the boil, stirring. Cook for 5 minutes over a gentle heat, stirring continuously. Remove from the heat, add the butter and cool until lukewarm. Beat in the egg yolks and Kirsch, then fold in the stiffly whisked egg whites. Pour into a greased 20-cm/8-inch ring mould, stand in a bain marie and cook in a moderate oven (180°C, 350°F, Gas Mark 4) for 25–30 minutes. Cool in the mould.

Halve the apricots, remove the stones and peel.

Make a syrup with the sugar and 175 ml/6 fl oz (US ¾ cup) water. Plunge the apricots into the boiling syrup. Cook for 10 minutes and drain the fruit. Reduce the syrup by half by open boiling. Melt the jam in the reduced syrup and stir in the Kirsch.

Remove the semolina ring from the mould. Place the apricots in the centre and pour over the syrup. Serve very cold.

 a sweet Vouvray (white)

Preparation time 20 minutes
Cooking time 35 minutes

Serves 6

AMERICAN
3 cups milk
6 tablespoons sugar
¾ cup semolina flour
¼ cup butter
2 eggs
1 tablespoon Kirsch
Filling
1½ lb apricots
½ cup sugar
⅓ cup apricot jam
3 tablespoons Kirsch

Caramel cream

(Oeufs au lait)

Preparation time 10 minutes
Cooking time 1-1¼ hours

Serves 6

METRIC/IMPERIAL
150g/5oz castor sugar
1 litre/1¾ pints milk
1 vanilla pod
6 eggs
Caramel
100g/4oz lump or granulated sugar
3 tablespoons water

Prepare the caramel. Heat the sugar and water slowly in a small saucepan, stirring to dissolve the sugar. Boil the mixture until it turns a light brown caramel colour. Pour immediately into an ovenproof cooking dish and tilt so that the caramel coats the dish completely. Leave to cool.

Dissolve the sugar in the milk, heating gently, then add the vanilla pod split in two. Bring to the boil, remove immediately from the heat. Leave to infuse for 5 minutes in a warm place. Remove the vanilla pod, wash and dry.

Break the eggs, mix lightly with a fork and gradually add the milk. Strain into the caramelised dish. Stand in a bain-marie, and cook in a moderate oven (160°C, 325°F, Gas Mark 3) for 1-1¼ hours.

Leave to cool completely and serve in the dish in which it has been cooked.

 a Muscat (sweet white)

Preparation time 10 minutes
Cooking time 1-1¼ hours

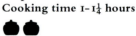

Serves 6

AMERICAN
½ cup plus 2 tablespoons sugar
4¼ cups milk
1 vanilla bean
6 eggs
Caramel
¼lb cube sugar
¼ cup water

Snow eggs

(Oeufs à la neige)

Preparation time 25 minutes
Cooking time 35 minutes

Serves 6

METRIC/IMPERIAL
1 vanilla pod
1 litre/1¾ pints milk
6 eggs
pinch of salt
225g/8oz castor sugar
crushed praline to sprinkle
(optional)

Split the vanilla pod in two. Boil the milk with the vanilla in a large saucepan. As soon as it starts to boil, remove from the heat and leave to infuse. Break the eggs, separating the whites from the yolks. Whisk the whites to a stiff peak, adding a pinch of salt. Gradually whisk in 75g/3oz (US 6 tablespoons) of the castor sugar.

Remove the vanilla pod from the milk. Return the milk to the heat but do not let it boil. Reduce the heat.

Place spoonfuls of the egg white mixture into the hot milk. Leave to swell for 2 minutes then turn over. Wait a further 2 minutes before draining carefully and placing on absorbent paper or a clean tea towel. You can repeat this process several times in order to avoid crowding in the saucepan.

Strain the milk to remove any small scraps of egg white. Beat the egg yolks with the remaining sugar until pale and frothy. Pour the hot milk little by little over this mixture, stirring well. Return to the saucepan and thicken the custard over a very gentle heat, stirring all the time and carefully avoiding boiling.

As soon as the custard coats the back of a wooden spoon and the froth has disappeared, remove the saucepan from the heat and pour into individual dishes. Float the egg whites on the custard and sprinkle with crushed praline, if liked. Serve very cold.

🍇 a Blanquette de Limoux (dry white sparkling)

Preparation time 25 minutes
Cooking time 35 minutes

Serves 6

AMERICAN
1 vanilla bean
4¼ cups milk
6 eggs
dash of salt
1 cup sugar
crushed praline to sprinkle
(optional)

Peach pancakes

(Crêpes aux pêches)

**Preparation time 45 minutes
plus 2 hours standing time
Cooking time 40 minutes**

Serves 4

METRIC/IMPERIAL
12 peaches
275g/10oz sugar
1 teaspoon vanilla essence
100g/4oz plain flour
300ml/½ pint milk
25g/1oz butter, melted
40g/1½oz castor sugar
pinch of salt
2 eggs
40g/1½oz butter
Sauce
1 egg plus 2 egg yolks
75g/3oz sugar
50g/2oz plain flour
450ml/¾ pint milk
40g/1½oz butter
6 macaroons
few drops of almond essence

Peel the peaches, halve and remove stones. Make a syrup with the 275g/10oz (US 1¼ cups) sugar, 150ml/¼ pint (US ⅔ cup) water and the vanilla. Cook for 4–5 minutes. Add the peach halves to the syrup and cook for about 10 minutes, or until tender. Drain the fruit carefully and discard any remaining syrup.

Prepare the pancake batter. Sift the flour into a large bowl and make a well in the centre. With a wooden spoon, beat in two-thirds of the milk, the melted butter, sugar and salt. Add the beaten eggs and leave to stand for 2 hours.

Prepare the sauce. Beat the whole egg and the yolks with the sugar, then beat in the sifted flour. Add the hot milk, pour into a saucepan and then thicken over a low heat, stirring continuously. Remove from the heat, add the butter, finely crumbled macaroons and almond essence. Leave to cool.

Add the rest of the milk to the pancake batter if necessary and cook 8 pancakes, using the 40g/1½oz (US 3 tablespoons) butter to fry.

Finely dice 8 of the peach halves. Add to the sauce and spread the pancakes with it. Roll up, arrange on a serving dish and place 2 peach halves on each. Serve warm or cold.

 a Sainte Croix-du-Mont (sweet white)

**Preparation time 45 minutes
plus 2 hours standing time
Cooking time 40 minutes**

Serves 4

AMERICAN
12 peaches
1¼ cups sugar
1 teaspoon vanilla extract
1 cup all-purpose flour
1¼ cups milk
2 tablespoons melted butter
3 tablespoons sugar
dash of salt
2 eggs
3 tablespoons butter
Sauce
1 egg plus 2 egg yolks
6 tablespoons sugar
½ cup all-purpose flour
2 cups milk
3 tablespoons butter
6 macaroons
few drops of almond extract

Duchess pancakes

(Crêpes duchesse)

**Preparation time 40 minutes
plus 2 hours standing time
Cooking time 45 minutes**

Serves 6

METRIC/IMPERIAL
200g/7oz plain flour
50g/2oz castor sugar
pinch of salt
1 teaspoon vanilla essence
75g/3oz butter
450ml/¾ pint milk
2 eggs
6 macaroons, crushed
100ml/4fl oz Kirsch
Sauce
75g/3oz butter
75g/3oz plain flour
450ml/¾ pint milk
40g/1½oz castor sugar
juice and rind of ½ lemon
1 egg
6 macaroons, crushed

Prepare the pancake batter. Sift the flour into a bowl and form a well in the centre. Into the well put the sugar, salt, vanilla essence and 25g/1oz (US 2 tablespoons) melted butter. Mix these ingredients with a wooden spoon, diluting gradually with two-thirds of the milk to make a smooth creamy batter. Add the beaten eggs and leave to stand for 2 hours.

Prepare the sauce. Place the butter, flour and milk in a saucepan and whisk together. Heat to boiling point, stirring all the time. Simmer gently for 2–3 minutes, stirring. Add the castor sugar, lemon juice and rind and the egg. Beat well then stir in the crushed macaroons.

Cook the pancakes in the rest of the butter, thinning the batter if necessary with all or part of the remaining milk. Keep the cooked pancakes hot in a warm oven, covered with foil. (This batter will make about 12 pancakes.)

Spread each pancake with sauce and roll up. Arrange side by side on a heated serving dish. Sprinkle with the 6 remaining crushed macaroons. Spoon over the Kirsch and flame at the table.

 a Sainte Croix-du-Mont (sweet white)

**Preparation time 40 minutes
plus 2 hours standing time
Cooking time 45 minutes**

Serves 6

AMERICAN
1¾ cups all-purpose flour
¼ cup sugar
dash of salt
1 teaspoon vanilla extract
6 tablespoons butter
2 cups milk
2 eggs
6 macaroons, crushed
½ cup Kirsch
Sauce
6 tablespoons butter
¾ cup all-purpose flour
2 cups milk
3 tablespoons sugar
juice and rind of ½ lemon
1 egg
6 macaroons, crushed

Coffee creams

(Crème au café)

Preparation time 15-20 minutes
Cooking time 35 minutes

Serves 4

METRIC/IMPERIAL
600 ml/1 pint milk
4 tablespoons strong black coffee
(or 1-2 tablespoons coffee
essence)
4 egg yolks
125 g/4½ oz castor sugar
2 tablespoons potato flour or
4 teaspoons cornflour
1 tablespoon brandy

Heat the milk to boiling and add the coffee.

Place the egg yolks and castor sugar in a large bowl. Whisk until creamy then pour in the hot milk, mixing well.

Turn into a heavy-bottomed saucepan and stir with a wooden spoon until the cream coats the back of the spoon. Take care the mixture does not boil. When the cream is cooked remove the pan from the heat and continue stirring for 1 minute.

Mix the potato flour or cornflour with the brandy and pour into the cream. Continue to stir over a low heat until the cream thickens to setting point. Pour into individual glass dishes and leave to cool before putting in the refrigerator.

Serve very cold with chocolate or wafer biscuits.

an Anjou white

Preparation time 15-20 minutes
Cooking time 35 minutes

Serves 4

AMERICAN
2½ cups milk
⅓ cup strong black coffee
4 egg yolks
½ cup plus 1 tablespoon sugar
3 tablespoons potato flour or
4 teaspoons cornstarch
1 tablespoon brandy

Chocolate mousse

(Mousse au chocolat)

Preparation time 30 minutes
Cooking time 6 minutes

Serves 6

METRIC/IMPERIAL
250 g/9 oz plain chocolate
3 tablespoons strong black coffee
6 eggs
200 g/7 oz castor sugar
1 tablespoon rum

Break the chocolate into small pieces, place in an ovenproof dish with the coffee and melt in the oven until creamy. Or melt in a bowl over a pan of hot water.

Break the eggs, separating the yolks from the whites. Beat the yolks with half the sugar until pale and creamy. Add the rum and combine with the melted chocolate.

Whisk the egg whites until they form stiff peaks, sprinkling them gradually with the rest of the sugar. Fold carefully into the chocolate cream mixture. Chill in the refrigerator until ready to serve.

 a sparkling Vouvray (dry white)

Preparation time 30 minutes
Cooking time 6 minutes

Serves 6

AMERICAN
9 squares semi-sweet chocolate
¼ cup strong black coffee
6 eggs
¾ cup plus 2 tablespoons sugar
1 tablespoon rum

Lemon soufflé

(Mousse au citron)

**Preparation time 15 minutes
plus 3 hours chilling time
Cooking time 25 minutes**

Serves 6

METRIC/IMPERIAL
**8 lemons
4 eggs
225g/8oz castor sugar
25g/1oz plain flour**

Wash and dry the lemons. Carefully grate the zest of one of them, being careful not to include any white pith. Squeeze all the lemons to give 250ml/8fl oz (US 1 cup) juice.

Break the eggs, separating the yolks from the whites. Place the egg yolks in an earthenware bowl with the sugar and mix well with a wooden spoon. Then add the sifted flour, lemon juice and grated zest. Mix all well together and place in a bowl over a pan of simmering water. Stir continuously until the mixture coats the back of the spoon. Leave to cool.

Whisk the egg whites until stiff. Fold into the cooled mixture with a fork, lifting the mixture so as not to break the whites.

Pour into a large glass bowl and chill in the refrigerator for 3 hours.

Serve immediately with wafer biscuits.

 a Blanquette de Limoux (dry white sparkling)

**Preparation time 15 minutes
plus 3 hours chilling time
Cooking time 25 minutes**

Serves 6

AMERICAN
**8 lemons
4 eggs
1 cup sugar
¼ cup all-purpose flour**

Frosted orange sorbets

(Oranges givrées)

**Preparation time 20 minutes
plus 6 hours freezing time
Cooking time 5–6 minutes**

Serves 6

METRIC/IMPERIAL
**6 oranges
4 sugar lumps
3 tablespoons water
250g/9oz castor sugar
1 teaspoon lemon juice
2 egg whites
2–3 drops of orange food colouring**

Two hours before use, turn the refrigerator to its coldest setting.

Wash and dry the oranges. Rub 2 of the oranges with the sugar lumps to absorb the zest. Put the water in a small saucepan with 150g/5oz (US ½ cup plus 2 tablespoons) castor sugar and the sugar lumps and dissolve over a low heat to obtain a syrup. Allow to cool.

Cut off the tops of the oranges, scoop out the insides carefully without damaging the shells. Strain the pulp through a fine sieve. Mix 150ml/¼ pint (US ⅔ cup) of the juice obtained with the sugar syrup and the lemon juice. Leave to set in the freezing compartment of the refrigerator for 2 hours. When it reaches the 'slushy' stage, whisk the mixture or use an ice cream machine to break down the ice crystals.

Whisk the egg whites into stiff peaks, sprinkling gradually with the rest of the castor sugar. Fold carefully into the semi-frozen mixture and add the food colouring. Fill the orange shells with this sorbet and replace lids. Leave to freeze for 3–4 hours in the freezing compartment of the refrigerator or in the freezer.

**Preparation time 20 minutes
plus 6 hours freezing time
Cooking time 5–6 minutes**

Serves 6

AMERICAN
**6 oranges
4 sugar cubes
¼ cup water
1 cup plus 2 tablespoons sugar
1 teaspoon lemon juice
2 egg whites
2–3 drops of orange food coloring**

Strawberry ice cream

(Glace aux fraises)

**Preparation time 30 minutes
plus 6 hours freezing time**

Serves 6

METRIC/IMPERIAL
**1 kg/2 lb strawberries
1 tablespoon lemon juice
100 g/4 oz castor sugar
200 ml/7 fl oz double cream
2 tablespoons cold milk**
Italian meringue
**1 egg white
50 g/2 oz castor sugar
2 tablespoons water**

Two hours before making the ice cream turn the refrigerator to the coldest setting.

Gently wipe the strawberries but do not wash. Remove the stalks. Reduce half the fruit to a purée with a wooden spoon through a nylon sieve. Do not use metal. Quickly mix the obtained purée with the lemon juice and castor sugar.

Whip the cream with the cold milk until thick. Fold into the strawberry purée.

Prepare the Italian meringue. Whisk the egg white until very stiff. Dissolve the sugar and water over a low heat. Boil to give a syrup which will form threads: 110°C/230°F on a sugar thermometer (it becomes a very pale yellow and bubbles form on the surface). Pour it at once in a thin trickle on to the egg white, whisking continuously for 4 minutes.

Gently fold this meringue into the strawberry mixture. Pour into a freezer proof container or ice cream mould. Leave to set in the freezer or freezing compartment of the refrigerator for at least 6 hours.

Chill the serving plate in the refrigerator. Turn the ice cream out on to it just before serving and decorate with the rest of the strawberries.

**Preparation time 30 minutes
plus 6 hours freezing time**

Serves 6

AMERICAN
**2 lb strawberries
1 tablespoon lemon juice
½ cup superfine sugar
¾ cup heavy cream
3 tablespoons cold milk**
Italian meringue
**1 egg white
¼ cup sugar
3 tablespoons water**

Coffee ice cream

(Glace moka)

**Preparation time 25 minutes
plus 5-6 hours freezing time**

Serves 8

METRIC/IMPERIAL
250 ml/8 fl oz evaporated milk
6 egg yolks
200 g/7 oz castor sugar
200 ml/7 fl oz double cream
2 tablespoons cold milk
2 tablespoons coffee essence
I tablespoon rum (optional)
50 g/2 oz flaked almonds

This ice cream is prepared the day before required.

Turn the refrigerator to its coldest setting. Place the evaporated milk in the freezing compartment to chill thoroughly.

In a large bowl whisk the egg yolks and sugar together until a smooth light cream. Use an egg whisk or preferably an electric mixer.

Whip the cream with the cold milk until thick. Also whip the chilled evaporated milk until thick.

Add the coffee essence and rum to the egg yolk mixture. Mix in the whipped cream then the evaporated milk and whisk for a few moments. Pour into a metal mould that has been rinsed out with cold water and place in the freezer or freezing compartment of the refrigerator. Leave the ice cream to set for 5–6 hours.

Turn out of the mould on to a serving dish and sprinkle with toasted flaked almonds. Serve with langues de chats biscuits.

**Preparation time 25 minutes
plus 5-6 hours freezing time**

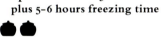

Serves 8

AMERICAN
1 cup evaporated milk
6 egg yolks
¾ cup plus 2 tablespoons sugar
¾ cup heavy cream
3 tablespoons cold milk
3 tablespoons strong black coffee
I tablespoon rum (optional)
½ cup flaked almonds

Exotic fruit salad

(Coupes exotiques)

Preparation time 10–15 minutes plus 30 minutes chilling time

Serves 4

METRIC/IMPERIAL
2 small lemons or limes
castor sugar to frost
4 slices pineapple
2 oranges
½ (312-g/11-oz) can lychees
½ (425-g/15-oz) can kumquats or mangoes
5 tablespoons sugar syrup (made with 5 tablespoons sugar and 3 tablespoons water)
3 tablespoons white rum
2 tablespoons pineapple juice

Begin by frosting four individual glasses. Cut a groove 1 cm/½ inch deep in one of the lemons and rub the rim of the glasses in this groove, pressing well. Dip the rim of the glass at once into castor sugar, to achieve a frosted effect. Cut 4 slices from the lemon or lime and place over the rim of each glass. Keep cool in the refrigerator.

Cut the pineapple slices into pieces. Peel the oranges and dice the flesh. Drain the lychees and kumquats, reserving 2 tablespoons (US 3 tablespoons) of lychee juice. If using mangoes, drain and cut into small segments. Squeeze the juice from the second lemon.

Put the pineapple, oranges, lychees and kumquats into a large bowl.

Mix the sugar syrup with the rum, pineapple juice, lychee juice and lemon juice.

Pour over the fruit and mix gently together. Spoon into the frosted glasses. Place in the refrigerator and serve very cold.

a fruit punch

Preparation time 10–15 minutes plus 30 minutes chilling time

Serves 4

AMERICAN
2 small lemons or limes
sugar to frost
4 slices pineapple
2 oranges
½ (11-oz) can lychees
½ (15-oz) can kumquats or mangoes
6 tablespoons sugar syrup (made with 6 tablespoons sugar and ¼ cup water)
¼ cup white rum
3 tablespoons pineapple juice

Melon cups

(Coupes Montaigu)

**Preparation time 20 minutes
plus 30 minutes chilling time**

Serves 4

METRIC/IMPERIAL
2 Ogen or Charentais melons
1 (227-g/8-oz) can pineapple slices
3 bananas, not over-ripe
1 small dessert apple
16 blanched almonds
50g/2oz castor sugar
300ml/½ pint sweet white wine

Cut the melons in half and remove the seeds. Spoon out the flesh. Chill the four melon skin cups in the refrigerator.

Cut the pineapple slices into small pieces and slice the bananas. Cut the melon flesh and apple into small cubes. Coarsely chop the almonds.

Mix all the fruits and the nuts with the castor sugar. Fill the melon cups with this mixture. Sprinkle each one with the wine and chill in the refrigerator for 30 minutes.

Serve very cold on crushed ice.

🍇 a Frontignan muscatel (sweet golden)

**Preparation time 20 minutes
plus 30 minutes chilling time**

Serves 4

AMERICAN
2 cantaloupe melons
1 (8-oz) can pineapple slices
3 bananas, not over-ripe
1 small dessert apple
16 blanched almonds
¼ cup superfine sugar
1¼ cups sweet white wine

Pears belle Hélène

(Poires belle Hélène)

Preparation time 10 minutes
Cooking time 20-30 minutes

Serves 4

METRIC/IMPERIAL
4 firm dessert pears (or 8 canned pear halves)
200g/7oz castor sugar
500ml/17.6fl oz vanilla ice cream
Chocolate sauce
200g/7oz plain chocolate
40g/1½oz butter
¾ teaspoon vanilla essence
4 tablespoons double cream

Peel the pears, cut in half, remove the cores and pips. Poach over a gentle heat with the castor sugar in enough water to just cover them, for 15–20 minutes. When they are cooked but still firm (they must not break up), drain and leave to cool. If using canned pears drain these.

Prepare the chocolate sauce. Break the chocolate into small pieces in a heavy-bottomed saucepan. Add the butter and 2 tablespoons (US 3 tablespoons) hot water. Melt over a gentle heat, stirring with a wooden spoon until a smooth creamy consistency. Then stir in the vanilla essence and the cream and mix well.

Just before serving, divide the ice cream between four individual glass dishes, top with the pear halves and quickly pour over the hot chocolate sauce. Serve at once.

 a sweet Vouvray (white)

Preparation time 10 minutes
Cooking time 20-30 minutes

Serves 4

AMERICAN
4 firm dessert pears (or 8 canned pear halves)
¾ cup plus 2 tablespoons sugar
1 pint vanilla ice cream
Chocolate sauce
7 squares semi-sweet chocolate
3 tablespoons butter
¾ teaspoon vanilla extract
⅓ cup heavy cream

Ratafia peaches

(Pêches gastronome)

Preparation time 30 minutes
Cooking time 35 minutes

Serves 6

METRIC/IMPERIAL
12 peaches
100g/4oz castor sugar
1 vanilla pod
1 (227-g/8-oz) jar apricot jam
18 ratafias or small macaroons
Custard
2 whole eggs plus 4 egg yolks
150g/5oz sugar
50g/2oz plain flour
750ml/1¼ pints milk
2 tablespoons Kirsch

Peel the peaches. Poach them whole for 10 minutes in a saucepan with the castor sugar, vanilla pod and enough water to just cover them. (If wished, cut them in two and remove the stones.) Drain and leave to cool.

Prepare the custard. Mix the eggs, egg yolks, sugar and flour with the milk. Place in a bowl over a pan of simmering water and cook, stirring continuously with a wooden spoon, until the custard coats the spoon. Carefully avoid boiling. Add the Kirsch and leave to cool.

Heat the apricot jam with 1 tablespoon water. Finely crush 8 ratafias.

Pour half the cooled custard into a serving dish and cover with half the peaches. Pour over the rest of the custard, and top with the remaining peaches.

Spoon over the melted apricot jam, sprinkle with the crushed ratafias and decorate with the remainder.

Serve very cold.

🍇 a Sainte Croix-du-Mont (sweet white)

Preparation time 30 minutes
Cooking time 35 minutes

Serves 6

AMERICAN
12 peaches
½ cup sugar
1 vanilla bean
1 (8-oz) jar apricot jam
18 ratafias or small macaroons
Custard
2 whole eggs plus 4 egg yolks
½ cup plus 2 tablespoons sugar
½ cup all-purpose flour
3 cups milk
3 tablespoons Kirsch

Apples with rum

(Pommes au rhum)

Preparation time 10 minutes
Cooking time 10 minutes

Serves 6

METRIC/IMPERIAL
6 good-quality dessert apples
3 tablespoons rum
5 tablespoons castor sugar
pinch of cinnamon
strip of lemon peel
2 tablespoons redcurrant jelly
6 glacé cherries

Peel the apples, remove the cores and pips with an apple corer.

Place the apples over the bottom of a large saucepan. Pour in the rum and 300ml/½ pint (US 1¼ cups) water. Add the sugar, cinnamon and lemon peel. Cover and cook over a gentle heat for 10 minutes.

Remove the apples from the saucepan and arrange in a bowl. Reduce the cooking liquid to 150ml/¼ pint (US ⅔ cup) by open boiling. Add to it the redcurrant jelly, mix well and leave to cool.

Spoon the jelly over the apples and decorate each with a glacé cherry. Serve with macaroons or small sweet biscuits.

 a Sauternes (sweet white)

Preparation time 10 minutes
Cooking time 10 minutes

Serves 6

AMERICAN
6 good-quality dessert apples
¼ cup rum
6 tablespoons sugar
dash of cinnamon
strip of lemon peel
3 tablespoons red currant jelly
6 candied cherries

Pear and raspberry compote

(Poires framboisine)

**Preparation time 20 minutes
plus 2–3 hours chilling time
Cooking time 30 minutes**

Serves 6

METRIC/IMPERIAL
**1kg/2lb small pears
450ml/¾ pint rosé wine
175g/6oz sugar
1 small piece cinnamon stick
350g/12oz raspberries
3 tablespoons raspberry liqueur or
brandy**

Peel the pears, cut in half, remove the cores and pips.

Bring the rosé wine with the sugar and cinnamon stick to the boil. Plunge the pear halves into the boiling syrup and simmer for 15–20 minutes over a low heat, until tender.

Drain the pears and arrange in a compote dish.

Press half the raspberries through a nylon sieve and add this juice to the pear syrup. Remove the cinnamon stick and reduce by two-thirds by open boiling.

Remove from the heat, add the raspberry liqueur with the remaining whole raspberries and pour over the pears. Leave to cool then place in the refrigerator for 2–3 hours in order to serve well chilled.

 a rosé

**Preparation time 20 minutes
plus 2–3 hours chilling time
Cooking time 30 minutes**

Serves 6

AMERICAN
**2lb small pears
2 cups rosé wine
¾ cup sugar
1 small piece cinnamon stick
¾lb raspberries
¼ cup raspberry liqueur or brandy**

Twelfth-day tart

(Galette des rois)

Preparation time 30 minutes
Cooking time 30-40 minutes

Serves 6

METRIC/IMPERIAL
2 (212-g/7½-oz) packets frozen puff
pastry, thawed
1 egg, beaten
Filling
100g/4oz butter
100g/4oz castor sugar
2 small eggs
1½ tablespoons plain flour
3 tablespoons rum
125g/4½oz ground almonds

First make the filling. Cut the butter into small pieces and place in a bowl. Work with a wooden spoon until soft, then add the sugar and continue to cream. Stir in the beaten eggs, flour, rum and ground almonds. The mixture should be smooth and uniform.

Set the oven to hot (220°C, 425°F, Gas Mark 7).

Roll the pastry into two 25-cm/10-inch circles, 3mm/ ⅛ inch thick.

Place one circle on a damp baking sheet. Cover with the almond filling, leaving a border of about 2.5cm/1 inch around the edge. Moisten this slightly with water and cover with the second pastry circle.

Mark a pattern on top of the tart. Brush with beaten egg. Put in the oven and cook for 30–40 minutes. Serve the tart preferably warm.

Note This tart is so called because it is customarily eaten in France on the twelfth day after Christmas. The French often slip a small trinket into the tart before cooking.

a Sainte Croix-du-Mont (sweet white)

Preparation time 30 minutes
Cooking time 30-40 minutes

Serves 6

AMERICAN
2 (7½-oz) packages frozen puff
paste, thawed
1 egg, beaten
Filling
½ cup butter
½ cup sugar
2 small eggs
2 tablespoons all-purpose flour
¼ cup rum
1¼ cups ground almonds

Bilberry charlotte

(Charlotte aux myrtilles)

**Preparation time 20 minutes
plus overnight chilling**

Serves 8-10

METRIC/IMPERIAL
**200 g/7 oz castor sugar
5 tablespoons water
3 tablespoons bilberry liqueur
(or Maraschino or Kirsch)
48 sponge finger biscuits
1 (454-g/1-lb) jar bilberry jam
300 ml/½ pint double cream,
whipped**
To decorate
**lightly whipped cream (optional)
small silver balls**

This dessert should be prepared 12–24 hours in advance.

Place the sugar with the water in a small saucepan over low heat. When the sugar has dissolved, bring to the boil and simmer for 8 minutes. Leave this syrup to cool then add the liqueur.

Dip all the biscuits individually into the syrup to moisten them. Immediately place around the sides and over the base of a charlotte mould, 18–20 cm/7–8 inches in diameter, trimming to fit. Reserve 6 finger biscuits and crumble the remainder.

Cover the base with a layer of bilberry jam, then a layer of whipped cream and finally a layer of biscuit crumbs. Continue layering in this way until the ingredients are all used up. Finish off with the 6 reserved biscuits, trimming to fit.

Place a small plate on top to weigh down the charlotte and stand overnight in the refrigerator.

Just before serving turn the charlotte out of the mould on to a serving dish. Top with lightly whipped cream if liked, and decorate with silver balls.

Serve well chilled.

a sweet white Anjou

**Preparation time 20 minutes
plus overnight chilling**

Serves 8-10

AMERICAN
**¾ cup plus 2 tablespoons sugar
6 tablespoons water
¼ cup blueberry liqueur (or
Maraschino or Kirsch)
48 ladyfingers
1 (16-oz) jar blueberry jam
1¼ cups heavy cream, whipped**
To decorate
**lightly whipped cream (optional)
small silver balls**

Choux buns

(Choux à la crème)

Preparation time 40 minutes
Cooking time 45 minutes

Serves 6

METRIC/IMPERIAL
Choux pastry
150g/5oz plain flour
75g/3oz butter
pinch of salt
50g/2 oz castor sugar
250ml/8fl oz water
4 eggs
icing sugar to sprinkle
Confectioners' custard
250ml/8fl oz milk
3 whole eggs plus 2 egg whites
125g/4½oz castor sugar
1 tablespoon flour
1 tablespoon Kirsch or rum, or
1 teaspoon vanilla essence, to
flavour
7g/¼oz powdered gelatine

Set the oven to hot (220°C, 425°F, Gas Mark 7).

Prepare the choux pastry. Begin by sifting the flour (this is essential). In a saucepan melt the butter, salt and sugar with the water over a low heat. When dissolved bring to the boil quickly. As soon as the liquid begins to boil remove the pan from the heat and immediately add the flour all at once. Beat quickly and return to the heat. Dry out the mixture, beating with a wooden spoon, until it no longer sticks to the sides and bottom of the pan. Remove from the heat, allow to cool for 5 minutes then beat in the first egg. Mix well. When well incorporated, add the remaining eggs one at a time, beating well.

Grease a baking sheet and place on it small spoonfuls of the pastry, well apart. Bake in the hot oven for 10 minutes then reduce to moderately hot (190°C, 375°F, Gas Mark 5) for a further 20 minutes. Cool the buns on a wire tray.

Now prepare the custard. Warm the milk in a saucepan. Break the whole eggs, separating the yolks from the whites.

Mix together the egg yolks, sugar and flour. Add the hot milk and flavour as required. Thicken over a low heat, stirring continuously and without boiling. Meanwhile, soak the gelatine in 2 tablespoons (US 3 tablespoons) water for 2–3 minutes, then dissolve over a low heat. Remove the custard from the heat, add the dissolved gelatine and allow to cool slightly. Whisk the 5 egg whites until stiff, then fold into the custard.

Cut open the choux buns at the side and fill with the cooled custard. Sprinkle with icing sugar to serve.

 a Sainte Croix-du-Mont (sweet white)

Preparation time 40 minutes
Cooking time 45 minutes

Serves 6

AMERICAN
Choux paste
1¼ cups all-purpose flour
6 tablespoons butter
dash of salt
¼ cup sugar
1 cup water
4 eggs
confectioners' sugar to sprinkle
Pastry cream
1 cup milk
3 whole eggs plus 2 egg whites
½ cup plus 1 tablespoon sugar
1 tablespoon all-purpose flour
1 tablespoon Kirsch or rum, or
1 teaspoon vanilla extract, to
flavor
1 envelope gelatin

Cherry croûtes

(Croûtes aux cerises)

Preparation time 20 minutes
Cooking time 30 minutes

Serves 4

METRIC/IMPERIAL
0.5kg/1lb cherries
100g/4oz castor sugar
200ml/7fl oz rosé wine
1 small piece cinnamon stick
2 eggs
200ml/7fl oz milk
1 tablespoon Kirsch
4 thick slices bread
75g/3oz butter
icing sugar to sprinkle

Remove the stalks and stones from the cherries and place in a saucepan with 65g/2½oz (US 5 tablespoons) sugar, the rosé wine and cinnamon stick. Cook for 15–20 minutes. Remove from the heat.

Break the eggs into a shallow bowl, add the milk, Kirsch and remaining sugar. Beat well together.

Dip the slices of bread into the egg mixture, turning so that they absorb the liquid well.

Heat the butter in a frying pan and add the bread. Brown on both sides. Arrange on the serving dish and sprinkle with icing sugar.

Drain the cherries and place on the slices of bread, between them and in the centre of the dish.

Boil and reduce the cherry cooking liquor until syrupy. Pour over the cherries and serve preferably warm.

 a Frontignan (sweet golden)

Preparation time 20 minutes
Cooking time 30 minutes

Serves 4

AMERICAN
1lb cherries
½ cup sugar
¾ cup rosé wine
1 small piece cinnamon stick
2 eggs
¾ cup milk
1 tablespoon Kirsch
4 thick slices bread
6 tablespoons butter
confectioners' sugar to sprinkle

Baked fruit pudding

(Flan garde-chasse)

Preparation time 20 minutes
Cooking time 1½–1¾ hours

Serves 6–8

METRIC/IMPERIAL
1 apple
1 pear
2 bananas
25g/1oz butter
175g/6oz castor sugar
1 tablespoon water
50g/2oz currants
20g/¾oz candied orange peel
6 walnuts, chopped
12 cooked pancakes
750ml/1¼ pints milk
5 eggs
100ml/4fl oz rum
1 (227-g/8-oz) jar redcurrant or blackcurrant jelly

Remove the peel and pips from the apple and pear. Cut into thin slices with the bananas. Cook these fruits in a saucepan with 20g/¾oz (US 1½ tablespoons) butter, 25g/1oz (US 2 tablespoons) sugar and the water. Remove from the heat, strain off any juices, then add the currants, chopped peel and nuts to the fruit. Place all these ingredients in a large bowl and add the diced pancakes.

Boil the milk with the remaining sugar. Beat the eggs and gradually combine with the milk and sugar. Pour over the fruit mixture and flavour with half the rum. Mix well.

Grease a 20-cm/8-inch charlotte mould or 25-cm/10-inch deep cake tin with the remaining butter and pour the mixture into it. Stand in a bain marie and cook in a moderate oven (180°C, 350°F, Gas Mark 4) for 1½–1¾ hours. Leave to cool.

Just before serving turn the pudding out on to an ovenproof serving dish. Surround with the redcurrant jelly. Warm the rest of the rum and flame the pudding at the table.

 a medium dry champagne

Preparation time 20 minutes
Cooking time 1½–1¾ hours

Serves 6–8

AMERICAN
1 apple
1 pear
2 bananas
2 tablespoons butter
¾ cup sugar
1 tablespoon water
⅓ cup currants
¾oz candied orange peel
6 walnuts, chopped
12 cooked crêpes
3 cups milk
5 eggs
½ cup rum
1 (8-oz) jar red currant or black currant jelly

Festival fritters

(Beignets de carnaval)

**Preparation time 20 minutes
plus 2 hours standing time
Cooking time 3 minutes per fritter**

Serves 6

METRIC/IMPERIAL
**300g/11oz plain flour
pinch of salt
25g/1oz dried yeast
50g/2oz butter
75g/3oz castor sugar
grated lemon peel, orange-flower
water or rum, to flavour
3 eggs
flour to sprinkle
oil for deep frying
icing sugar to dust**

Sift the flour with the salt into a large bowl and make a well in the centre. Add the yeast, dissolved in 3 tablespoons (US ¼ cup) warm water.

Scald a bowl with boiling water, dry and place in it the butter, cut into small pieces. Work with a wooden spoon until it forms a cream. Place this cream in the well of the flour together with the sugar, flavouring and lightly beaten eggs. Knead the ingredients together with the fingertips until they form a smooth dough. Roll into a ball and leave for 2 hours.

Liberally flour the rolling pin and work surface and roll out the dough to 5mm/¼ inch thick. Cut into small squares, circles or any other shapes.

Heat the oil in a deep pan. When very hot add the fritters. If the oil is hot enough the fritters will immediately rise to the surface. Allow the fritters to turn golden then drain them on absorbent paper.

Remove the pan from the heat for a moment before cooking further fritters in order to reduce the temperature slightly.

Dust the fritters with icing sugar before serving.

**Preparation time 20 minutes
plus 2 hours standing time
Cooking time 3 minutes per fritter**

Serves 6

AMERICAN
**2¾ cups all-purpose flour
dash of salt
2 packages active dry yeast
¼ cup butter
6 tablespoons sugar
grated lemon peel, orange-flower
water or rum, to flavor
3 eggs
flour to sprinkle
oil for deep frying
confectioners' sugar to sprinkle**

Rum baba

(Baba au rhum)

Preparation time 5 minutes
plus 1½ hours rising time
Cooking time 1 hour 20 minutes

Serves 6

METRIC/IMPERIAL
25g/1oz fresh yeast or
15g/½oz dried yeast
300ml/½ pint warm milk
450g/1lb plain flour
grated rind and juice of ½ lemon
pinch of salt
200g/7oz butter
200g/7oz castor sugar
3 large or 4 small eggs
100g/4oz raisins
50g/2oz ground almonds
Syrup
100g/4oz castor sugar
3 tablespoons red jam
300ml/½ pint water
200ml/7fl oz rum
To decorate
glacé cherries
angelica
blanched almonds

Dissolve the fresh yeast in the milk in a large bowl. If using dried yeast, stir the yeast into the milk and set aside for 10 minutes. Mix in half the flour and the grated lemon rind, lemon juice and salt. Cover the bowl with a cloth and leave in a warm place for 20 minutes until frothy.

Cream the butter until soft and gradually beat in the sugar and eggs. Beat the remaining flour into the yeast mixture and combine with the butter mixture. Mix in the raisins and almonds and beat well (use an electric mixer if liked). Place in a well greased 23–25-cm/9–10-inch savarin tin (the tin should be only half-full). Smooth the mixture in the tin and leave covered in a warm place until the mixture has risen to the rim. Bake in a moderately hot oven (200°C, 400°F, Gas Mark 6) for 30 minutes. Reduce the heat to moderate (180°C, 350°F, Gas Mark 4) and cook for a further 50 minutes.

Just before removing the tin from the oven prepare the syrup. Dissolve the sugar and jam in the water, bring to the boil and boil for 10 minutes. Remove from the heat and add the rum.

Take the baba out of the oven and immediately pour the hot syrup over it. When cool, turn out and decorate with the cherries, angelica and blanched almonds.

 a sweet Vouvray (white)

Preparation time 5 minutes
plus 1½ hours rising time
Cooking time 1 hour 20 minutes

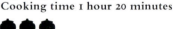

Serves 6

AMERICAN
1 cake compressed yeast or
  1 package active dry yeast
1¼ cups warm milk
4 cups all-purpose flour
grated rind and juice of ½ lemon
dash of salt
¾ cup plus 2 tablespoons butter
¾ cup plus 2 tablespoons sugar
3 large or 4 small eggs
⅔ cup seeded raisins
½ cup ground almonds
Syrup
½ cup sugar
¼ cup red jam
1¼ cups water
¾ cup rum
To decorate
candied cherries
angelica
blanched almonds

Cherry savarin

(Savarin aux cerises)

**Preparation time 25 minutes
plus 1–2 hours rising time
Cooking time 1 hour**

Serves 6

METRIC/IMPERIAL
20g/¾oz fresh yeast or
7g/¼oz dried yeast
3 tablespoons warm milk
300g/11oz plain flour
pinch of salt
125g/4½oz castor sugar
3 eggs
125g/4½oz butter plus 15g/½oz for
the mould
Filling
0.75kg/1½lb cherries
275g/10oz sugar
4 tablespoons water
3 tablespoons Kirsch
little whipped cream
Syrup
100g/4oz sugar
150ml/¼ pint water
3 tablespoons brandy
1 tablespoon Kirsch

Mix the yeast with the milk. Sift the flour into a large bowl and make a well in the centre; add the pinch of salt, sugar, lightly beaten eggs, the yeast mixture and the butter, cut into small pieces. Mix all these ingredients well with the fingertips and work the dough until it is elastic and no longer sticks to the fingers.

Place in a buttered 20-cm/8-inch savarin tin, filling only halfway up. Leave to rise in a warm place for about 1–2 hours until the dough doubles in volume. Then cook in a moderately hot oven (190°C, 375°F, Gas Mark 5) for 1 hour.

Meanwhile, prepare the filling. Wash and carefully drain the cherries, remove their stalks and stones. Place the cherries, sugar and water in a saucepan and cook for 20 minutes over a gentle heat. If they make too much juice, drain and reduce this juice before adding the Kirsch to it. Leave the cherries to cool in this juice.

When the savarin is almost cooked, prepare the syrup. Mix the sugar and water in a saucepan, bring to the boil and cook for 7–8 minutes without stirring. Remove from the heat then add the brandy and Kirsch. Sprinkle the savarin while hot, straight from the oven, with this boiling syrup. Leave to cool in the tin.

To serve, turn the savarin out on to a serving dish. Pile the cherries in the centre and decorate with blobs of whipped cream, topped with a cherry.

a Coteaux-du-Layon (sweet white)

**Preparation time 25 minutes
plus 1–2 hours rising time
Cooking time 1 hour**

Serves 6

AMERICAN
¾ cake compressed yeast or
½ package active dry yeast
¼ cup warm milk
2¾ cups all-purpose flour
dash of salt
½ cup plus 1 tablespoon sugar
3 eggs
½ cup plus 1 tablespoon butter
plus 1 tablespoon for the mold
Filling
1½lb cherries
1¼ cups sugar
⅓ cup water
¼ cup Kirsch
little whipped cream
Syrup
½ cup sugar
⅔ cup water
¼ cup brandy
1 tablespoon Kirsch

Apricot doughnuts

(Les Krapfen)

**Preparation time 50 minutes
plus 3 hours rising time
Cooking time 8 minutes per
doughnut**

Serves 6

METRIC/IMPERIAL
**225g/8oz plain flour
I teaspoon castor sugar
7g/¼oz fresh yeast or
I teaspoon dried yeast
100ml/4fl oz warm milk
½ teaspoon salt
25g/1oz butter
I egg
I (227-g/8-oz) jar apricot jam
oil for deep frying
icing sugar to dust**

Prepare the yeast batter: mix together 50g/2oz (US ½ cup) flour, the sugar, fresh or dried yeast and the warm milk in a large bowl. Cover and set aside until bubbly, about 20 minutes in a warm place, longer in a cool one.

Mix the remaining flour with the salt and rub in the butter. Beat the egg, add to the yeast batter with the dry ingredients, and mix well to give a soft dough, adding extra flour if the dough is too sticky to handle.

Turn the dough on to a lightly floured surface and knead until smooth and elastic. (It will take about 10 minutes by hand or 2–3 minutes with a mixer and dough hook.) Shape the dough into a ball, place inside a large oiled polythene bag and leave to rise until doubled in size.

Turn the risen dough on to a lightly floured board, knock back and knead until the dough is firm, about 2 minutes. Roll out the dough with a rolling pin until 5mm/¼ inch thick. Cut into circles, each 6cm/2½ inches in diameter. In the centre of every second circle place a generous teaspoon of apricot jam. Lightly moisten the edges of the dough around the jam, cover with a plain circle of dough and pinch the edges together. Leave to rise again in a warm place until doubled in size.

Heat the frying oil. Add the doughnuts and brown well, turning when half cooked. Drain on absorbent paper.

Sprinkle with icing sugar and serve at once.

**Preparation time 50 minutes
plus 3 hours rising time
Cooking time 8 minutes per
doughnut**

Serves 6

AMERICAN
**2 cups all-purpose flour
I teaspoon sugar
¼ cake compressed yeast or
¼ package active dry yeast
½ cup warm milk
½ teaspoon salt
2 tablespoons butter
I egg
I (8-oz) jar apricot jam
oil for deep frying
confectioners' sugar to sprinkle**

Orange almond cake

(Quatre-quarts à l'orange)

Preparation time 25 minutes
Cooking time 35 minutes

Serves 6

METRIC/IMPERIAL
3 eggs
175g/6oz castor sugar
175g/6oz butter
175g/6oz plain flour
4 tablespoons Cointreau or orange liqueur
100g/4oz ground almonds
225g/8oz icing sugar
1 tablespoon cold water
grated rind of 2 oranges

Beat the eggs and sugar in a large mixing bowl until pale. Work the butter with a wooden spoon until creamy, beat it into the egg mixture. Pour in, little by little, the sifted flour, then 2 tablespoons (US 3 tablespoons) Cointreau and 90g/3½oz (US generous ¾ cup) ground almonds. Mix all together well.

Butter and flour a 20-cm/8-inch square cake tin. Pour the cake mixture into it and cook for 35 minutes in a moderately hot oven (200°C, 400°F, Gas Mark 6). Turn out on to a wire rack and leave to cool.

Prepare the icing. Combine the icing sugar with the cold water, mix in the rest of the Cointreau and flavour with the grated orange rind.

Split the cake in half and sandwich together with a little of the icing and the rest of the ground almonds. Spread the remaining icing over the top and sides of the cake.

🍇 a Blanquette de Limoux (dry white sparkling)

Preparation time 25 minutes
Cooking time 35 minutes

Serves 6

AMERICAN
3 eggs
¾ cup sugar
¾ cup butter
1¾ cups all-purpose flour
⅓ cup Cointreau or orange liqueur
1 cup ground almonds
1¾ cups confectioners' sugar
1 tablespoon cold water
grated rind of 2 oranges

Christmas kugelhopf

(Kouglof de Noël)

**Preparation time 1 hour
plus 2 hours rising time
Cooking time 45 minutes**

Serves 6

METRIC/IMPERIAL
25g/1oz fresh yeast or 15g/½oz
dried yeast
3 tablespoons milk
400g/14oz plain flour
pinch of salt
75g/3oz castor sugar
3 large eggs
150g/5oz butter
100g/4oz raisins
50g/2oz ground almonds
icing sugar to dust

Dissolve the yeast in the milk which should be just warm. Work this mixture with 100g/4oz (US 1 cup) flour to obtain a soft dough. Roll into a ball, cut a cross on the top and leave to rise in a warm place.

When the dough has doubled in size, place the rest of the flour in a large bowl and make a well in the centre. In the well place the risen dough with the salt, sugar and eggs. Work this dough with the fingertips for a long time to incorporate a lot of air until it becomes elastic. Then work in the butter, which must be of a similar consistency to the dough, and the raisins.

Roll the dough into a ball, flour, cover with a cloth and leave to rise in a warm place.

Grease a 23-cm/9-inch fluted savarin tin and sprinkle with almonds before adding the dough to half-fill it. Cover and leave to rise until the dough reaches the top of the tin. Cook in a hot oven (225°C, 425°F, Gas Mark 7) for about 45 minutes.

Turn out of the tin and leave to cool. Serve the kugelhopf dusted with icing sugar and finally decorate with holly and candles.

**Preparation time 1 hour
plus 2 hours rising time
Cooking time 45 minutes**

Serves 6

AMERICAN
1 cake compressed yeast or
1 package active dry yeast
¼ cup milk
3½ cups all-purpose flour
dash of salt
6 tablespoons sugar
3 large eggs
½ cup plus 2 tablespoons butter
¾ cup raisins
½ cup ground almonds
confectioners' sugar to sprinkle

Pear dessert cake

(Gâteau aux poires)

Preparation time 15 minutes plus 30 minutes–1 hour rising time
Cooking time 45 minutes

Serves 6

METRIC/IMPERIAL
225g/8oz plain flour
7g/¼oz dried yeast
50g/2oz castor sugar
150ml/¼ pint water
50g/2oz cream cheese
50g/2oz butter
grated rind of ½ lemon
1 egg
3 pears
Topping
25g/1oz butter, melted
1 tablespoon demerara sugar

Place 2 tablespoons (US 3 tablespoons) flour, the yeast, half the sugar and half the water in a bowl and mix well together. Stand in a warm place until frothy.

Place the remaining flour and sugar in a mixing bowl. Cream the cheese, butter and lemon rind together and mix in the egg and yeast mixture. Add to the flour together with the remaining water, and beat until smooth and elastic, about 5–10 minutes. Place in a 20-cm/8-inch greased cake tin.

Peel, core and quarter the pears and place on top of the dough. Leave to rise in a warm place for 30 minutes–1 hour.

Bake in a moderately hot oven (200°C, 400°F, Gas Mark 6) for 30 minutes. Remove from the oven and brush the top of the cake with melted butter and sprinkle with demerara sugar. Return to the oven for a further 10–15 minutes, covering with foil if necessary. Serve hot with cream.

 a sparkling Vouvray (dry white)

Preparation time 15 minutes plus 30 minutes–1 hour rising time
Cooking time 45 minutes

Serves 6

AMERICAN
2 cups all-purpose flour
½ package active dry yeast
¼ cup sugar
⅔ cup water
¼ cup cream cheese
¼ cup butter
grated rind of ½ lemon
1 egg
3 pears
Topping
2 tablespoons melted butter
1 tablespoon brown sugar

Chocolate ring cake

(Gâteau Anglais au chocolat)

**Preparation time 15 minutes
plus 2 hours rising time
Cooking time 50 minutes**

Serves 6–8

METRIC/IMPERIAL
175g/6oz plain chocolate
350g/12oz plain flour
50g/2oz cocoa powder
175g/6oz castor sugar
25g/1oz fresh yeast or
15g/½oz dried yeast
150ml/¼ pint water
50g/2oz butter
75g/3oz cream cheese
3 eggs
2 teaspoons grated orange rind
Chocolate icing
200g/7oz plain chocolate
15g/½oz butter
3 tablespoons cream
2 tablespoons icing sugar

Grate the chocolate. Sift the flour and cocoa into a mixing bowl and make a well in the centre. Into the well put the sugar, grated chocolate, the yeast dissolved in the warmed water, softened butter, cream cheese, lightly beaten eggs and grated orange rind. Mix with a wooden spoon to give a smooth paste then beat for 4–5 minutes with a whisk or 3 minutes only with an electric mixer.

Preheat the oven to moderately hot (190–200°C, 375–400°F, Gas Mark 5–6).

Butter a 23-cm/9-inch ring mould and pour in the cake mixture, to come two-thirds of the way up. Leave to rise in a warm place for 2 hours. Place in the oven and cook for 45 minutes. Leave to cool before removing from the mould.

Prepare the chocolate icing. Break the chocolate into small pieces. Place in a saucepan with the butter, cream and sugar and melt over a low heat, stirring with a wooden spoon until smooth and creamy. Pour over the cake after removing from the mould.

This cake is best eaten within 2 days of cooking.

**Preparation time 15 minutes
plus 2 hours rising time
Cooking time 50 minutes**

Serves 6–8

AMERICAN
6 squares semi-sweet chocolate
3 cups all-purpose flour
½ cup unsweetened cocoa powder
¾ cup sugar
1 cake compressed yeast or
1 package active dry yeast
⅔ cup water
¼ cup butter
1 (3-oz) package cream cheese
3 eggs
2 teaspoons grated orange rind
Chocolate icing
7 squares semi-sweet chocolate
1 tablespoon butter
¼ cup light cream
3 tablespoons confectioners' sugar

Basque cake

(Gâteau Basque)

**Preparation time 20 minutes
plus 1 hour chilling time
Cooking time 40 minutes**

Serves 6

METRIC/IMPERIAL
**450g/1lb plain flour
200g/7oz butter, softened
pinch of salt
1 egg plus 3 egg yolks
200g/7oz castor sugar
grated rind of 1 lemon
1 (454-g/1-lb) jar black cherry jam**

Prepare the pastry. Sift the flour into a large bowl and form a well in the centre. Into this put the softened butter and a pinch of salt. Work these ingredients together then add the egg and 2 yolks, sugar and grated lemon rind. Work the whole well together by hand, then leave the pastry to stand in a cool place for 1 hour. Set the oven to moderately hot (200°C, 400°F, Gas Mark 6).

Grease and flour a shallow 25-cm/10-inch flan tin. Roll out half the pastry until about 1 cm/½ inch thick. Line the tin with the pastry, leaving a slight overlap around the edge. Fill with the black cherry jam.

Roll out the remaining pastry to cover the tin. Seal the edges together with a little water and mark a chequered pattern on top with a knife. Thin the last egg yolk with a teaspoon of water and brush the top of the tart so that it browns well. Place in the oven and cook for 40 minutes.

Leave the tart to cool before removing from the tin. Serve cold.

Variation Try apricot jam instead of black cherry.

 a Béarn rosé

**Preparation time 20 minutes
plus 1 hour chilling time
Cooking time 40 minutes**

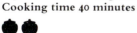

Serves 6

AMERICAN
**4 cups all-purpose flour
¾ cup plus 2 tablespoons softened
  butter
dash of salt
1 egg plus 3 egg yolks
¾ cup plus 2 tablespoons sugar
grated rind of 1 lemon
1 (16-oz) jar black cherry jam**

Marzipan fruits

(Fruits déguisés)

**Preparation time 30 minutes
plus overnight soaking**

Makes 36 fruits

METRIC/IMPERIAL
12 prunes, soaked overnight
12 large dates
24 walnut halves
Marzipan
150g/5oz ground almonds
150g/5oz icing sugar
1 tablespoon potato flour or
2 teaspoons cornflour
2 tablespoons warm water
2 tablespoons Kirsch
3 drops of green food colouring
3 drops of pink food colouring

First make the marzipan. In a bowl mix the ground almonds with the icing sugar, potato flour or cornflour, warm water and Kirsch. Knead these ingredients with the fingertips to give a smooth fine paste.

Divide the paste in half. Colour one half with green food colouring and the other with pink. Knead each half again.

Drain the prunes and dry thoroughly on absorbent paper. Cut open the prunes and dates and remove the stones. Fill each with a little marzipan in the shape of a large nut. Fill half the fruits with pink marzipan and half with green.

Form six small balls of green marzipan and six pink. Flatten out slightly. Place each between 2 walnut halves.

Put each marzipan fruit in a sweet paper case.

**Preparation time 30 minutes
plus overnight soaking**

Makes 36 fruits

AMERICAN
12 prunes, soaked overnight
12 large dates
24 walnut halves
Almond paste
1¼ cups ground almonds
generous cup confectioners' sugar
1 tablespoon potato flour or
2 teaspoons cornstarch
3 tablespoons warm water
3 tablespoons Kirsch
3 drops of green food coloring
3 drops of pink food coloring

Liqueur cherries

(Cerises à l'eau de vie)

Preparation time 20 minutes
Cooking time 10 minutes

Makes 4 (0.5-kg/1-lb) jars

METRIC/IMPERIAL
1.5kg/3lb cherries, preferably
Montmorency
450g/1lb sugar
750ml/1¼ pints gin

Make sure the cherries are sound. Wash and dry them and cut off the stems halfway along. With a large needle prick the flesh through to the stone several times.

Boil some water in a large saucepan. Add the cherries and simmer for 10 seconds. Drain and cool in cold water, then dry carefully.

Pour the sugar and 100ml/4fl oz (US ½ cup) water into a saucepan. Allow the sugar to dissolve over a low heat. Bring to the boil and boil until the mixture forms threads, that is until a drop of syrup will form a thin thread when stretched between a damp thumb and finger.

Place the cherries in warmed jars and cover with the hot but not boiling syrup. Leave to cool until the next day before adding the gin. Stir carefully and cover. Wait several months before eating these liqueur cherries.

Preparation time 20 minutes
Cooking time 10 minutes

Makes 4 (1-lb) jars

AMERICAN
3lb cherries
2 cups sugar
3 cups gin

Cherry jam

(Confiture de cerises)

Preparation time 40 minutes
Cooking time 30 minutes

Makes 8–10 (0.5-kg/1-lb) jars

METRIC/IMPERIAL
4kg/9lb cherries
1.5kg/3lb redcurrants
about 3kg/6½lb preserving sugar

Wash the cherries, drain and dry on absorbent paper. Repeat for the redcurrants.

Remove the cherry stalks and stones. Pick off the redcurrant stems.

Place the cherries in a preserving pan and heat gently to release the juices. Drain and weigh them. (The juice is not needed and can be used to make a syrup.)

Crush the redcurrants in a nylon sieve and weigh the juice.

Weigh out the exact quantity of sugar required, equal to the weight of the cherries plus the weight of the redcurrant juice. Pour this sugar into the preserving pan. Moisten with the redcurrant juice, mix and bring to the boil. Boil for 5 minutes. Pour in the cherries and cook until a drop of syrup sets on a cold plate without spreading.

Pour into warmed jars. Leave until the next day to cool before covering.

Preparation time 40 minutes
Cooking time 30 minutes

Makes 8–10 (1-lb) jars

AMERICAN
9lb cherries
3lb red currants
about 6½lb sugar

Strawberry jam

(Confiture de fraises)

Preparation time 35 minutes
Cooking time 40 minutes

Makes 8–10 (0.5-kg/1-lb) jars

METRIC/IMPERIAL
3kg/6½lb strawberries
about 2.75kg/6lb preserving sugar
175ml/6fl oz water

Wipe the strawberries carefully but do not wash them.

Place the sugar in a preserving pan and add the water. Bring to the boil and cook until it forms beads, that is until a little in a spoon forms bubbles when you blow over it.

Tip the strawberries into the boiling syrup and cook for 5 minutes. Remove and drain carefully.

Continue cooking the syrup until a drop sets immediately on a cold plate.

Remove the syrup from the heat, return the strawberries to it and immediately fill the warmed jars. Leave overnight to cool.

The following day cover and seal.

Preparation time 35 minutes
Cooking time 40 minutes

Makes 8–10 (1-lb) jars

AMERICAN
6½lb strawberries
about 6lb sugar
¾ cup water

Quince jelly

(Gelée de coings)

Preparation time 40 minutes
Cooking time 1 hour

Makes 10–12 (0.5-kg/1-lb) jars

METRIC/IMPERIAL
4kg/9lb ripe quinces
juice of 1 lemon
800g/1¾lb granulated or preserving
sugar for each 1 litre/1¾ pints
quince juice

Wipe the quinces. Cut into pieces without peeling or removing cores and pips. Sprinkle with the lemon juice.

Place in a preserving pan and cover with 3½ litres/6 pints (US 7½ pints) water. Cook until the quinces can be crushed with a fork.

Drain the quinces then squeeze in a sieve to extract the juice.

Measure the juice and add 800g/1¾lb (US 3½ cups) sugar for each 1 litre/1¾ pints (US 4¼ cups) of juice. Simmer. The jelly is cooked when a drop on a cold plate wrinkles and forms a skin when pushed with the forefinger.

Fill the warmed jars immediately but wait until the next day before covering.

Preparation time 40 minutes
Cooking time 1 hour

Makes 10–12 (1-lb) jars

AMERICAN
9lb ripe quinces
juice of 1 lemon
3½ cups sugar for each 4¼ cups
quince juice

Rhubarb jam

(Confiture de rhubarbe)

Preparation time 15 minutes
plus 24 hours standing time
Cooking time 35 minutes

Makes 3–4 (0.5-kg/1-lb) jars

METRIC/IMPERIAL
about 1.5kg/3lb rhubarb
1.25kg/2½lb castor sugar
1 lemon, quartered

Clean the rhubarb, trim and remove any stringy threads. Cut into pieces about 5cm/2 inches long. Place in the preserving pan, add the sugar and mix. Leave to stand for 24 hours. The rhubarb juice and sugar will form a syrup.

Remove the rhubarb from the pan and drain. Place the pan of syrup over a high heat. Boil for 5 minutes before returning the rhubarb to the pan together with the quartered lemon. Finish cooking, taking care that the rhubarb does not stick to the pan. The jam is ready when a drop of syrup sets immediately on a cold plate without spreading.

Pour at once into warmed jars. Wait until the following day before covering.

Preparation time 15 minutes
plus 24 hours standing time
Cooking time 35 minutes

Makes 3–4 (1-lb) jars

AMERICAN
about 3lb rhubarb
2½lb sugar
1 lemon, quartered

Pickled cucumbers

(Cornichons au vinaigre)

**Preparation time 1 hour
plus 6 hours steeping time**

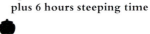

Makes 4 (0.5-kg/1-lb) jars

METRIC/IMPERIAL
**2kg/4½lb small pickling
cucumbers
0.5kg/1lb sea salt
450g/1lb pickling onions
1 bunch tarragon
peppercorns
1 litre/1¾ pints white vinegar**

Make sure the cucumbers are clean but do not wash them. Place in layers in a bowl and sprinkle each layer with a little salt. Leave to steep for 6 hours to rid them of any impurities.

Take the cucumbers out of the salt and wipe with absorbent paper to remove the small prickles which cover them.

Clean the onions without peeling.

Arrange the cucumbers in jars, adding a few small onions, a little tarragon and a sprinkling of peppercorns to each jar. Pour over the vinegar to completely cover the cucumbers. Seal the jars.

After 10 days you can (but it is not essential) drain the vinegar without disturbing the cucumbers. Boil the vinegar for 5 minutes. Leave until quite cool then pour back into the jars. Top up with enough vinegar to cover the cucumbers. Leave for 2 months before eating.

**Preparation time 1 hour
plus 6 hours steeping time**

Makes 4 (1-lb) jars

AMERICAN
**4½lb small sweet dill pickles
1lb coarse salt
1lb pickling onions
1 bunch tarragon
peppercorns
4¼ cups white vinegar**

Preserved mushrooms

(Cèpes à l'huile)

Preparation time 1 hour
Cooking time 5–10 minutes

Makes about 10 (0.5-kg/1-lb) jars

METRIC/IMPERIAL
3kg/6½lb small firm fresh mushrooms
3 litres/5 pints good-quality olive oil

Clean the mushrooms, trimming off the base of the stem. Do not wash but wipe carefully. Cut away any damaged parts then cut the mushrooms into pieces.

Heat half the oil and when very hot slowly add the mushrooms. Cook well for 5–10 minutes but do not allow to brown. Drain carefully.

When all the mushrooms are cooked leave to cool. Leave the cooking oil to cool, then strain.

Boil the jars and rubber rings in a large saucepan. Drain and dry the jars upturned on wire rungs of a hot oven for 20–30 minutes. Fill with the mushrooms and divide the cooking oil between them. Top up with the rest of the oil, to cover the mushrooms.

Check the seal on each jar before storing in a cool place.

Preparation time 1 hour
Cooking time 5–10 minutes

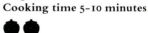

Makes about 10 (1-lb) jars

AMERICAN
6½lb small firm fresh mushrooms
6½ pints good-quality olive oil

Blackcurrant liqueur

(Liqueur de cassis)

Preparation time 30 minutes
Cooking time 10-15 minutes

Makes 2 litres/3½ pints liqueur

METRIC/IMPERIAL
1.25 kg/2½ lb blackcurrants
20 very small blackcurrant leaves
1 litre/1¾ pints spirit, e.g. gin or vodka
675 g/1½ lb granulated sugar
150 ml/¼ pint water

Wash and wipe the blackcurrants, discarding stalks. They must be absolutely dry. Put into a large glass jar and add the blackcurrant leaves. Pour over the spirit to completely cover. Leave to steep in this way for 4–5 months (or even longer, for the liqueur can only improve).

At the time of making the liqueur strain the spirit. Remove the leaves, crush the blackcurrants or blend in a liquidiser. Strain through muslin or leave to decant through filter paper. Mix with the spirit.

Prepare a thick syrup by dissolving the sugar and water over a low heat until the sugar has completely dissolved. Simmer gently for 5 minutes. Cool. Pour slowly into the blackcurrant mixture, stirring continuously, and adding only as much as seems necessary, according to taste. Pour into bottles, seal and store.

Preparation time 30 minutes
Cooking time 10-15 minutes

Makes 4½ pints liqueur

AMERICAN
2½ lb black currants
20 very small black currant leaves
4½ pints spirit, e.g. gin or vodka
3 cups sugar
⅔ cup water

White butter sauce

(Le beurre blanc)

Preparation time 7 minutes
Cooking time 9 minutes

Makes about 300 ml/½ pint

METRIC/IMPERIAL
225 g/8oz salted butter
3 shallots
100 ml/4 fl oz white wine vinegar
freshly ground pepper

Cut the butter into small pieces and beat with a wooden spoon until soft and creamy.

Chop the shallots very finely. Place in a heavy-bottomed saucepan with the vinegar and pepper. Boil and reduce over a high heat until a generous tablespoon of liquid remains.

Reduce the heat and gradually add the butter in small pieces, beating well with a wire whisk until creamy. Do not boil.

Remove from the heat immediately. Pour into a heated sauceboat and serve at once.

Serve white butter sauce with fish cooked in a court-bouillon.

Preparation time 7 minutes
Cooking time 9 minutes

Makes about 1¼ cups

AMERICAN
1 cup salted butter
3 shallots
½ cup white wine vinegar
freshly ground pepper

Béchamel sauce

(Sauce béchamel)

Preparation time 5 minutes
Cooking time 15 minutes

Makes 600ml/1 pint

METRIC/IMPERIAL
50g/2oz butter
50g/2oz flour
600ml/1 pint hot milk (or a
mixture of milk and cooking
stock)
salt and pepper
freshly grated nutmeg (optional)

Melt the butter in a saucepan over a fairly gentle heat without letting it brown. Add the flour and stir with a wooden spoon until the mixture begins to bubble. Pour on the hot milk all at once and beat rapidly with a wire whisk. Cook over a gentle heat without boiling for about 10 minutes, stirring continuously. Season with salt, pepper and a little nutmeg.

For a thin sauce, use half the quantities of butter and flour. For a thicker sauce, increase the amounts of butter and flour to 75g/3 oz (US 6 tablespoons and $\frac{3}{4}$ cup).

The béchamel sauce is a basic sauce, and many flavourings can be added to it. It is a good accompaniment to poached fish, white meats and most cooked vegetables.

Preparation time 5 minutes
Cooking time 15 minutes

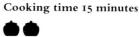

Makes 2½ cups

AMERICAN
¼ cup butter
½ cup all-purpose flour
2½ cups hot milk (or a mixture of
milk and cooking stock)
salt and pepper
freshly grated nutmeg (optional)

Cream sauce

(Sauce à la crème)

Preparation time 15 minutes
Cooking time 25 minutes

Makes 750ml/1¼ pints

METRIC/IMPERIAL
300ml/½ pint double cream
225g/8oz mushrooms (optional)
50g/2oz butter
salt and pepper
Béchamel sauce
50g/2oz butter
50g/2oz flour
450ml/¾ pint hot milk

Prepare the béchamel sauce. Melt the butter in a heavy-bottomed saucepan over a gentle heat, without allowing it to brown. Add the flour and mix with a wooden spoon to obtain a roux. Pour in the hot milk, beating rapidly with a wire whisk. Cook over a gentle heat for 10 minutes, stirring continuously. Do not allow to boil.

Add the cream to the béchamel, mix in well, stirring with a wooden spoon.

Trim and wash the mushrooms. Wipe them and slice thinly. Soften in 25g/1oz (US 2 tablespoons) butter for 10 minutes, then add to the sauce.

Remove the sauce from the heat. Stir in the remaining butter. Season to taste and heat through gently without boiling for 1–2 minutes.

Pour this sauce over the dish it accompanies and serve the remainder in a sauceboat.

Serve with ham, vegetables, eggs, fish and poultry.

Preparation time 15 minutes
Cooking time 25 minutes

Makes 3 cups

AMERICAN
1¼ cups heavy cream
½lb mushrooms (optional)
¼ cup butter
salt and pepper
Béchamel sauce
¼ cup butter
½ cup all-purpose flour
2 cups hot milk

Hunter's sauce

(Sauce chasseur)

Preparation time 10 minutes
Cooking time 35-40 minutes

Makes 450ml/¾ pint

METRIC/IMPERIAL
100g/4oz mushrooms
50g/2oz butter
3 shallots
25g/1oz flour
100ml/4fl oz dry white wine
450ml/¾ pint chicken stock
1 small bouquet garni
1 tablespoon tomato purée
chopped parsley (optional)
salt and pepper

Clean and trim the mushrooms and stalks. Wash quickly, wipe and slice finely. Sauté in the hot butter and leave to turn slightly golden.

Peel and finely chop the shallots.

When the mushrooms are slightly golden, take them out and in the same butter soften the shallots. When golden sprinkle them with the flour. Mix with a wooden spoon until the flour darkens. Then stir in the white wine and stock, add the bouquet garni and tomato purée.

Cook for 20–25 minutes over a very gentle heat, stirring all the time with a wooden spoon. The sauce must scarcely simmer while cooking.

Strain this sauce through a conical sieve, return to a low heat. Add the mushrooms and cook for a further 2–3 minutes. Sprinkle with chopped parsley, if liked, and adjust the seasoning.

Serve with red meats and poultry. It is particularly good with leftover chicken or turkey.

Preparation time 10 minutes
Cooking time 35-40 minutes

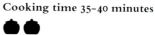

Makes 2 cups

AMERICAN
¼lb mushrooms
¼ cup butter
3 shallots
¼ cup all-purpose flour
½ cup dry white wine
2 cups chicken stock
1 small bouquet garni
1 tablespoon tomato paste
chopped parsley (optional)
salt and pepper

Madeira sauce

(La sauce Madère)

Preparation time 20 minutes
Cooking time 30 minutes

Makes 450ml/¾ pint

METRIC/IMPERIAL
1 carrot
2 medium onions
1 small stick celery
few sprigs of parsley
1 sprig of thyme
1 small bay leaf
75g/3oz bacon
50g/2oz butter
40g/1½oz flour
200ml/7fl oz brown stock
100ml/4fl oz dry white wine
250ml/8fl oz Madeira
salt and pepper

Peel the carrot and cut into very small dice. Peel and finely chop the onions. Finely chop the celery. Prepare the bouquet garni by tying together the parsley, thyme and bay leaf. Dice the bacon.

Heat the butter in a saucepan and brown the prepared carrot, onions, bacon, celery and bouquet garni, stirring with a wooden spoon. When these ingredients are well cooked, sprinkle with the flour and cook until golden.

Stir the stock into this roux, add the white wine and half the Madeira, season. Cook for 20 minutes over a gentle heat, stirring, then strain through a conical sieve. Return to a low heat, add the rest of the Madeira and cook for a further 3–4 minutes, without boiling. Pour into a heated sauceboat and serve very hot.

Serve with offal (kidneys, tongue), vegetables (braised spinach and lettuce), ham and cooked meats.

Preparation time 20 minutes
Cooking time 30 minutes

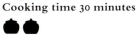

Makes 2 cups

AMERICAN
1 carrot
2 medium onions
1 small stalk celery
few sprigs of parsley
1 sprig of thyme
1 small bay leaf
4–5 bacon slices
¼ cup butter
6 tablespoons all-purpose flour
¾ cup brown stock
½ cup dry white wine
1 cup Madeira
salt and pepper

Tomato sauce

(Sauce Provençale)

Preparation time 20 minutes
Cooking time 30 minutes

Makes 300 ml/½ pint

METRIC/IMPERIAL
1 bunch spring onions
1 kg/2lb ripe tomatoes
2 small sticks celery
1 clove garlic
1 small sprig of basil
4 tablespoons olive oil
150 ml/¼ pint stock
salt and pepper

Trim and finely chop the onions. Peel the tomatoes, remove seeds and crush the flesh. Wash the celery and slice it very finely. Peel and crush the garlic. Chop the basil.

Heat the oil and brown the onions, celery and garlic, then reduce the heat; these ingredients must soften and turn golden without becoming too dark.

Add the tomatoes, stock and basil. Season and continue cooking over a gentle heat for 20 minutes, stirring with a wooden spoon.

Strain this sauce through a conical sieve or blend in a liquidiser, then return it to a gentle heat for a few minutes. Taste to adjust seasoning.

Serve with pasta, white meats, eggs, vegetables and fish.

Preparation time 20 minutes
Cooking time 30 minutes

Makes 1¼ cups

AMERICAN
1 bunch scallions
2lb ripe tomatoes
2 small stalks celery
1 clove garlic
1 small sprig of basil
⅓ cup olive oil
⅔ cup stock
salt and pepper

Nantua sauce

(Sauce Nantua)

Preparation time 30 minutes
Cooking time 30 minutes

Makes 600ml/1 pint

METRIC/IMPERIAL
3 dozen live crawfish with red claws
3 tablespoons oil
2 onions
1 carrot
1 bouquet garni
100ml/4fl oz brandy
300ml/½ pint strong fish stock or chicken stock
100ml/4fl oz white wine
salt and pepper
100g/4oz butter
50g/2oz flour
100ml/4fl oz double cream
pinch of cayenne

Wash the crawfish and gut them (to do this, twist off the middle tail fin, drawing away the small intestine with it). Wipe on absorbent paper.

Heat the oil in a shallow frying pan and add the chopped onions, finely diced carrot and bouquet garni. When these ingredients are well browned, add the crawfish. Sauté over a brisk heat and when they are red, flame with the brandy. Add the fish stock or chicken stock (according to the use of the sauce: whether for fish and shellfish or for poultry and egg dishes), the white wine and seasoning; cook gently for 10 minutes. Drain the crawfish. Remove the flesh from the tails and chop very finely. Keep hot.

In a mortar, crush the crawfish shells and claws with the cooked vegetables. Strain with the juices from the pan through a conical sieve; keep hot.

Prepare a white roux with 50g/2oz (US ¼ cup) butter and the flour. Moisten with the strained crawfish mixture, add the chopped flesh and cook for 15 minutes, stirring constantly. Then add the cream and the rest of the butter, cut into small pieces. Whisk over a gentle heat, adjust seasoning and add a small pinch of cayenne.

Serve with quenelles, fish and shellfish, fish pâtés and certain poultry and egg dishes.

Preparation time 30 minutes
Cooking time 30 minutes

Makes 2½ cups

AMERICAN
3 dozen live crayfish with red claws
¼ cup oil
2 onions
1 carrot
1 bouquet garni
½ cup brandy
1¼ cups strong fish stock or chicken stock
½ cup white wine
salt and pepper
½ cup butter
½ cup all-purpose flour
½ cup heavy cream
dash of cayenne pepper

Mousseline sauce

(La sauce mousseline)

Preparation time 10 minutes
Cooking time 12 minutes

Makes 300ml/½ pint

METRIC/IMPERIAL
3 tablespoons wine vinegar
½ teaspoon freshly ground pepper
3 egg yolks
125g/4½oz butter
½ teaspoon lemon juice
100ml/4fl oz double cream
salt and pepper

Put the vinegar and freshly ground pepper into a small saucepan. Evaporate over a moderate heat until only 1 tablespoon of liquid remains.

Meanwhile, thin the egg yolks with 1 tablespoon cold water.

Cut the butter into small pieces and melt in a saucepan.

Remove the reduced vinegar from the heat and pour on to the egg yolks, whisking well. Pour into a small basin and place over a saucepan of hot water, continuing to beat with a wire whisk until the eggs have a creamy appearance. Then gently pour in the melted butter, whisking all the time over the heat.

When the sauce is thickened, remove from the heat, add the lemon juice then fold in the lightly whipped cream. Season to taste and serve immediately.

Serve with fish and vegetables; it is especially good with asparagus.

Preparation time 10 minutes
Cooking time 12 minutes

Makes 1¼ cups

AMERICAN
¼ cup wine vinegar
½ teaspoon freshly ground pepper
3 egg yolks
½ cup plus 1 tablespoon butter
½ teaspoon lemon juice
½ cup heavy cream
salt and pepper

Béarnaise sauce

(Sauce Béarnaise)

Preparation time 10 minutes
Cooking time 20 minutes

Makes 150ml/¼ pint

METRIC/IMPERIAL
4 sprigs of tarragon
3 shallots
½ teaspoon freshly ground pepper
100ml/4fl oz white wine vinegar
125g/4½oz butter
2 egg yolks
2 sprigs of chervil
squeeze of lemon juice
salt

Wash and dry the tarragon. Peel and finely chop the shallots.

Place in a small saucepan half the tarragon, the shallots, pepper and vinegar. Reduce over a gentle heat until there remains only 1 tablespoon of vinegar. Cut the butter into small pieces.

Thin the egg yolks with 1 tablespoon cold water. Remove the tarragon from the saucepan.

Pour the eggs into the reduced vinegar and place over a very gentle heat, whisking continuously. When the mixture begins to become creamy, gradually add the butter, continuing to whisk all the time. When all the butter has been added, the sauce should have the consistency of a mayonnaise.

Finely chop the rest of the tarragon and the chervil. Add these herbs to the sauce together with a few drops of lemon juice and a little salt, to taste.

Serve immediately in a sauceboat, sprinkled with a little extra chervil if liked.

Serve with grilled fish and grilled or roast meats.

Preparation time 10 minutes
Cooking time 20 minutes

Makes ⅔ cup

AMERICAN
4 sprigs of tarragon
3 shallots
½ teaspoon freshly ground pepper
½ cup white wine vinegar
½ cup plus 1 tablespoon butter
2 egg yolks
2 sprigs of chervil
squeeze of lemon juice
salt

Mayonnaise

(Les mayonnaises)

Preparation time 8 minutes

Makes 300ml/½ pint

METRIC/IMPERIAL
1 teaspoon French mustard
250ml/8fl oz oil
2 egg yolks (at room temperature)
salt and pepper

Place the mustard in a bowl and combine with 1–2 tablespoons (US 2–3 tablespoons) oil, stirring until the mixture looks smooth and well thickened.

Then mix in the egg yolks. Continue to add the oil in a thin trickle, whisking all the time with a wire whisk; the mayonnaise must become very thick and firm. Season to taste. (If liked, add a tablespoon of boiling vinegar at the last minute; this helps the mayonnaise to keep better.)

Mayonnaise can accompany numerous cold meat, fish or vegetable dishes, hard-boiled eggs, salads, etc.

Variations
Green mayonnaise (for cold fish and shellfish). Add finely chopped herbs (parsley, chives, chervil, tarragon).
Indian-style mayonnaise (for fish and cold chicken). Season the mayonnaise with 1–2 teaspoons curry powder or paste.
Gelatine-strengthened mayonnaise (for aspics, salads and all coating or covering). Blend in 7g/¼oz (US 1 envelope) powdered gelatine, dissolved in 2 tablespoons (US 3 tablespoons) water. Use speedily, for it sets quickly.
Chantilly mayonnaise (for vegetables cooked in water and served cold, particularly asparagus). Fold 100ml/4fl oz (US ½ cup) lightly whipped double cream into the mayonnaise.

Preparation time 8 minutes

Makes 1¼ cups

AMERICAN
1 teaspoon French mustard
1 cup oil
2 egg yolks (at room temperature)
salt and pepper

Green herb sauce

(Sauce Vincent)

Preparation time 15 minutes

Makes 300ml/½ pint

METRIC/IMPERIAL
1 teaspoon French mustard
2 egg yolks
250ml/8fl oz oil
½ bunch watercress
1 bunch herbs (chervil, tarragon, parsley and chives)
2 tablespoons gherkins
1 tablespoon capers
salt and pepper

Prepare a thick mayonnaise by blending together the mustard and egg yolks, adding the oil a little at a time.

Clean and trim the stalks from the watercress. Finely chop or reduce to a purée in a blender or through a vegetable mill.

Wash and chop the herbs. Chop the gherkins. Mix the watercress purée, herbs, gherkins and capers into the mayonnaise. Taste to adjust seasoning and sprinkle with a few extra capers and chopped chives to serve.

Serve with grilled fish and meat, shellfish and vegetables.

Preparation time 15 minutes

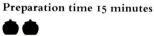

Makes 1¼ cups

AMERICAN
1 teaspoon French mustard
2 egg yolks
1 cup oil
½ bunch watercress
1 bunch herbs (chervil, tarragon, parsley and chives)
3 tablespoons sweet dill pickles
1 tablespoon capers
salt and pepper

Index